Rebel Rock

Rebel Rock
The Politics of Popular Music

John Street

Basil Blackwell

© John Street 1986

First published 1986

Basil Blackwell Ltd
108 Cowley Road, Oxford OX4 1JF, UK

Basil Blackwell Inc.
432 Park Avenue South, Suite 1503,
New York, NY 10016, USA

British Library Cataloguing in Publication Data
Street, John
    Rebel rock:the politics of popular
    music.
    1. Music, Popular (Songs, etc.)
    2. Music and society
    I. Title
    780'.42   ML3470

        ISBN 0–631–14344–0
        ISBN 0–631–14345–9 Pbk

Library of Congress Cataloging in Publication Data
Street, John, 1952–
    Rebel Rock

    Bibliography: p.
    Includes index.
    1. Music, Popular (Songs, etc.) – Political
    aspects. I. Title.
    ML3470.S8 1986   784.5'009   85–30807
    ISBN 0–631–14344–0
    ISBN 0–631–14345–9 (pbk.)

Typeset by Cambrian Typesetters, Frimley, Surrey
Printed in Great Britain by T. J. Press Ltd, Padstow

Contents

For
Alex, Claire and Vicky

Preface

If my house was on fire, I would probably save my record collection before my books. This book is an attempt to justify that decision. What I intend *Rebel Rock* to do is to give reasons for taking popular music seriously while trying to understand why it gives me and millions of others so much pleasure. My musical tastes will become clear, and some readers may wonder whether my records are worth saving. But while my taste may seem eccentric or erratic, I hope my arguments as to why and how pop works will at least provoke thoughts about the way political values, actions and experiences are filtered through and shaped by popular music.

Pop, rather like politics, is something everyone has an opinion on, and I am grateful to friends who have shared my obsessions, suffered my abuse, and helped in many ways: Steve Smith, Dave Sinclair, John Wulfsohn, Ian Forbes, Philip Williams, Steve Reilly and Angela Jameson. Others have got away less lightly; they have read tentative drafts, and I thank them for being tactfully rude and generously encouraging: Kim Pickin, Bernice Martin, Chris Kinrade, Mark Hustwitt, Parke Puterbaugh, Julia Mosse, Sue Miller, Pru Hone, Chris Cutler, Irena Pond, Robert Pring-Mill, Jumbo and Mary Vanrenen at Earthworks, Andy Linehan at the National Sound Archive, Dave Howling at *Melody Maker* and Terry Kendrick at the Norwich Reference Library have all helped in various ways. I owe a special debt to Simon Frith: not only was he once compelled to teach me sociology, but since then he has provided me with countless ideas, criticisms and suggestions; although he is not to blame for the results, he is responsible for a lot. My parents deserve a word of thanks, not least because it was their money that paid for my first single, 'Foot Tapper' by the Shadows, and it was their ears that heard it 50 times a day. Finally, I owe a great deal to Marian Brandon. She has read half-finished chapters, listened to incoherent arguments, and been unfailingly helpful and encouraging.

Introduction
One, Two, Three . . .

Well, it's One for the Money. . .

August 1985: Madonna has three records in the British top twenty. Nude photographs of her are in the latest editions of *Playboy* and *Penthouse*. Her marriage to the actor Sean Penn is reported in almost every national and local paper. Madonna is a star. Just like pop itself, she is everywhere. The previous month she had performed at Live Aid to raise money for the victims of starvation in Ethiopia.

August 1985: In Washington, USA, Mrs Susan Baker addresses a press conference called by the Parents' Music Resource Center. Mrs Baker recites the lyrics of songs by Sheena Easton and Prince. They are, she says, lewd and profane, and are liable to corrupt their teenage listeners. She advocates the introduction of a certificate scheme which labels records 'V' for violence, 'X' for 'profanity and lewdness'.

August 1985: The *New Musical Express*, one of Britain's leading pop papers, carries a two-page article on the link between politics and popular music. It is illustrated by a photograph which shows the leader of the Labour Party sharing a joke with Billy Bragg, whose song 'Between the Wars' had been a modest hit. Bragg was about to tour the country playing his music in support of 'Labour's Jobs and Industry Campaign'. *The Face*, the magazine that mixes fashion and music into a chic cocktail, interviews David Owen, leader of the Social Democratic Party.

August 1985 was just another month in pop's bizarre and contradictory history. Its particular combination of seriousness and superficiality captures the essence of pop and its politics. But it would be wrong to assume that the politics are to be found in what is apparently serious, and to be missing from what seems superficial.

Often when people speak of the link between politics and pop, they are referring to particular eras – sixties Flower Power or seventies punk – or particular performers – John Lennon, Bob Marley, the Clash, Paul Weller, Gil Scott-Heron. Here pop is seen as protest music. But politics also becomes involved when people try to use or control pop. Governments, political activists and musicians, all deliberately 'politicize' pop when they employ it to convey a particular message or elicit a certain response. Here pop is used as propaganda. The music is also political in other, less obvious, but more effective ways. Politics is introduced into the making, manufacturing and distribution of music, in the decisions about how music is to be marketed and sold. Here pop is made for profit. But although these are indeed examples of pop and politics being allied, they just scratch the surface of the relationship. The politics of punk, for instance, only make sense if we understand how popular music works and what kind of politics can be accommodated. Concentrating on punk's politics would be to miss its sound. To understand the political significance of the Sex Pistols' 'Anarchy in the UK', we also have to appreciate the magic of the Ronettes' 'I Saw Momma Kissing Santa Claus'. Here the politics is in the pleasure.

Pop's pleasures can be as politically important as its pomposities. Certainly, no attempt to speak of the politics of popular music can afford to concentrate exclusively on those moments when pop and politics seem inescapably intertwined: when the Specials sing 'Free Nelson Mandela', when governments imprison musicians and ban songs, when musicians join campaigns like 'Rock Against Racism', when political parties recruit rock musicians, when musicians support politicians, when record companies announce that 'the revolutionaries are on CBS'. All of these are important instances of the politics of popular music, but they mean little unless we also understand the pleasures of pop itself.

Madonna's success may be brief. The faded memory of countless faded stars suggests that the world's love is fickle. But while the glory lasts, Madonna's activities are reported on the front pages of newspapers; her songs are more easily recalled than Mrs Thatcher's manifesto; and her face is more familiar than that of any locally elected politician. And most important of all, people dance, shop, love and jog to the sound of Madonna's music. The images and sensations of pop are an inextricable part of everyday life. Pop can chronicle feelings; it can block out worries. It can polish the tarnished clichés through which we tend to live. Pop can make tired expressions and familiar experiences seem more dignified; it can make them seem important. Pop panders to our sense of individuality, and yet it addresses the crowd. What makes a pop song a hit is the fact that everyone hears it and shares its pleasures. While a pop song helps us feel special, it also reminds us that we are not alone. That, at least, is the idea.

Pop's better moments are always matched by moments of crass commercialism or sickly sentimentality. And if pop's successes matter, then so do its failures. The guardians of public morality see only a series of bad moments. But in this they share the view that pop matters, that it affects the way people act and think. Whether pop is banal or brilliant, it is political because it affects or reflects the way people behave. It may make little difference to the way they vote, but votes make little difference to the way politicians behave. What it affects or reinforces are the politics of the everyday. Its concerns are with our pleasures and our relationships, and the intuitions that inform both. These, as the women's movement has made clear, are profoundly political, being concerned with issues of power, equality and personal identity. Pop's delight in sexual confusion – from Little Richard to David Bowie to Boy George to Annie Lennox – makes pleasure out of the feelings that conventional assumptions seek to hide. Pop can give a voice to desires which would otherwise be unspoken.

But even if pop never changed a thing, even if it was neither brilliant nor banal, it would still warrant attention; it would still be politically important. Live Aid not only raised £50 million for the famine victims of Ethiopia, it also reminded people that pop is big business. The money raised by the singles 'Do they Know it's Christmas?' and 'We are the World', was the profit that record companies chose or were forced to forego.

But the cash raised by Live Aid looks like loose change when compared to the money made by the record industry. Pop is now an international commodity. Few countries have escaped its influence (and many have come to resent it as it has squeezed out local or traditional music). But though the market has grown, it has continued to be dominated by a few companies based in the USA and Britain. Yearly $10 billion is taken in record sales throughout the world. In Britain in 1983, 77 million singles, 56 million albums and 32 million cassettes were distributed to shops. They were worth £271.5 million. When Bruce Springsteen toured Britain in 1985, he was seen by nearly 500,000 people who together paid £6 million. It is figures like this that have inspired books such as *Rock'n'Roll is Here to Pay, One for the Money, Solid Gold*.[1] The cynicism implicit in such titles overlooks what also accompanies pop's profits: its populism.

Pop is one of the few cultural forms which is both popular and relatively democratic. It is not the exclusive preserve of a social or political elite. Compared to cinema, TV, the press and the literary world, pop remains more accessible, more susceptible to changes in popular fashion and taste, more responsive to new experiences. And yet compared to folk music, which also displays similar qualities, it does not pay for its accessibility in its popularity and its rejection of commercialism. Without the business, there would be no pop and yet despite pop's status as big business, the control exercised by those with the money is never as complete or as total as it is, say, in movies. Pop's pleasures are important because they can be shared by the many, even when they are being exploited by the few. But while pop's importance may not be in doubt, what the sales and sounds signify is much less clear.

Two for the Show . . .

One obvious source of confusion stems from what is meant by 'pop' itself. It is almost pointless to pretend that a single label fits Barry Manilow and Bruce Springsteen, Buck's Fizz and the Sex Pistols. Only sweeping generalizations can work. Most pop music is mass-produced for mass sales to the young. Most pop is some variant of the sound which emerged in the USA in the 1950s, although rock'n'roll had its origins in the sounds and styles which were borrowed and burgled from the popular music of Southern whites and city blacks, and many others besides. Throughout its post-war history it has remained culturally rooted in the USA and, to a lesser extent, Britain.

The pop industry which grew up in the 1950s to sell the new sounds directed its attention to the music's new customer: the teenager. Pop's subjects and images were tied to the pleasures and frustrations of youth: falling in love, having fun, and fighting authority. Pop's links with youth gave it an air of rebelliousness. It played host to ideas and activities which older generations could neither afford nor accept. Elvis Presley's gyrating crutch stirred them in the fifties just as Frankie Goes to Hollywood's exhortation 'Relax, if you want to come' offended others in the 1980s. Records have been burned and banned, and youth admonished, for fear of pop's effects.

Such responses have, of course, been fuelled by the rhetoric of pop's followers. Pop has been celebrated as the sound of the generations at war. Children have armed themselves with 'their music' to strike a blow for independence against the tyrannies of parental power. Pop is seen to belong to the world of Colin McInnes's novel of teenage life in the 1950s, *Absolute Beginners*, a world in which two competing ways of life struggle for control:

> youth has power, a kind of divine power straight from mother nature. All the old tax-payers know of this because, of course, for

one thing, the poor old sordids recollect their own glorious
teenage days, but yet they're so jealous of us . . . As for the boys
and girls, the dear absolute beginners, I sometimes feel that if they
only *knew* this fact, this very simple fact, namely how powerful
they really are, then they could rise up overnight and enslave the
old tax-payers, the whole damn lot of them – toupets and falsies
and rejuvenators and all – even though they number millions and
sit in the seats of strength.[2]

The talk was as exaggerated as were the fears of its polluting effect, but
what matters is the way pop's meaning is tied to more than the sounds
themselves. Images and gestures count too. And as pop has changed
and developed since the 1950s, it has acquired new forms and new
meanings.

As the styles have proliferated, plagiarism and cross-fertilization
have spread too, so that now types of pop cannot easily be
distinguished from each other. The categories fade confusingly into
each other. And yet understanding the music depends on appreciating
the 'rules' which accompany each style and which structure the way
the music is heard and appreciated. Chart-oriented pop can be
distinguished from rock, for example, by the emphasis on live
performance and by the character of its audience. Rock's following
tends to be male; pop fans tend to be younger and female. Pop's
essence is captured on record, rock's in concert.

These things matter, they affect the expectations that audiences
have of performers and their relationship with them. Pop musicians
are neither expected nor asked to make political statements; rock and
folk performers are not so constrained. Many may choose to stay silent
on politics, but the opportunity to speak out remains. In rock, there is
the ethos of self-expression which draws an intimate tie between the
personal and the performance. In pop, and in other musical forms like
soul, this connection does not weigh so heavily. Take the case of
personal wealth. Simon Le Bon of Duran Duran owns a million pound
yacht. No one thought to criticize him for this or to suggest that he
could have better spent the sum in a donation to Live Aid. Pop stars
may be the subject of gossip, but they are not the objects of political
scrutiny. No one is going to be interested in Le Bon's money except his
accountant. A rock star like Bruce Springsteen has to win approval for
his wealth – by giving generously to good causes, by adopting the
image and the concerns of the working man. Rock and pop stars play
to different rules.

But although rock's conventions can insist on a particular public
role, it can compensate for this by allowing musicians a wider range of
topics for their songs. Musical forms differ in what they allow

performers to speak about: country musicians are no more likely to sing Prince's 'Little Red Corvette', than Jagger would sing Tammy Wynette's 'D–I–V–O–R–C–E'. Conversely, rock, soul and folk musicians can talk about politics, and country singers about marriage and children, in ways that are denied to most pop musicians. As with all such rules, there are exceptions. Two bands with considerable chart success, Paul Weller's Style Council and Jerry Dammers' Specials Aka, have concerned themselves with conventional politics. However, it is clear that there are real difficulties in writing a song which is both politically correct and musically engaging. After all, it is not usually the politics that sells a record, it is the sound.

These stylistic conventions are not the only factors affecting the music and its politics. A record is not just the sum total of the notes which compose it. Because pop cannot be separated from the industry that produces it, understanding the sound entails understanding the system that creates and propagates it. Record executives, lawyers, accountants, producers, engineers, publicists, sales personnel, radio programmers, disc jockeys, music journalists and a host of others come between a song's composition and its first hearing. A single is not a piece of pure art; it is the result of countless choices and compromises, using criteria that mix the aesthetic, the political and the economic.

If the production of pop is complicated, then so is its consumption. No two people hear a pop song in the same way. It is heard in different settings and by different means – on the radio, in concert, on a Walkman, on record. And even then, nothing is certain. Hearing USA for Africa's song for the starving of Ethiopia, 'We are the World', sung at Live Aid is quite different from hearing it, as I did, at a disco to accompany a raffle for bottles of champagne. For the DJ at the disco, and for the dancers, 'We are the World' was just another pop song; to those watching Live Aid, it had a quite different, if confused message – smug self-satisfaction versus selfless generosity. At the time of the 1983 British General Election, Elvis Costello released a song, 'Pills and Soap': 'Give me the needle/Give me the rope/We're going to melt them down for pills and soap.' I was not sure then what the chorus actually meant; I'm still not. The verses scattered clues, but nothing more. However that song, with its simple, bleak sound, captured my particular despondency at Mrs Thatcher's victory. It hardly matters whether what 'Pills and Soap' meant to me was what Elvis Costello actually intended. The writer cannot control how a song is heard or where it's heard. He can tell his audience what he intended; but he cannot tell them how to listen.

The enjoyment of 'Pills and Soap' was a private one, it was also public in two important respects: it was tied to the world of politics;

and it was shared with other people. Others clearly found something in the song. They made it a hit. They too may have shared my incomprehension. What is intriguing, therefore, is what the song's popularity meant. The answer lies in the way the private feelings tapped by the song are linked to the public world which shapes the listener's experiences. Bringing together the public and the private, the individual and the collective, is precisely the way in which pop seems to work.

Such combinations are only possible because of the ambiguity in the words and the importance of the much less well-defined sounds. A song does not mean what it says. There is no definitive interpretation, not even of a 'poetic' writer like Bob Dylan. Literary critics may analyse the lyrics, but they cannot analyse the song and its sound by the same technique. Pop's meaning is inevitably confusing. What did Springsteen's British fans mean when they sang 'Born in the USA'? Because a song is heard differently and because it is heard in different settings, there is no agreed critical vantage point. This is further compounded by uncertainty as to what matters in any given song: the sound, the tune, the words, the rhythm. Not only is there no critical vantage point, there is no agreed critical language. The significance of all this for the music's involvement with politics varies according to what is understood by 'politics'.

It is often said that politics is about the use and distribution of power – who gets what, when and how. In pop, politics is involved, therefore, when governments control or promote music – when in the Soviet Union, the authorities register and licence groups; when in Britain, the Conservative Party decides whether to introduce a levy on blank tapes; and when in South Africa, the government calls for a ban on Stevie Wonder records because of his public opposition to apartheid. All of these acts are explicitly political, because of the power being used and its consequences. One interest is preferred over another.

Power is not exclusively the preserve of government. Governments rely on other agencies and institutions to give effect to their wishes. Decisions about what records to play are rarely made by government; that is what the broadcasting authorities are for, and even they are unlikely to deliberate long over any given record. The process of control and selection is buried in a whole series of conventions and rules – 'common sense' – about what makes 'good' broadcasting.

Power and politics take on the guise of common sense in the record industry too. The most obvious instance of this can be seen in the way the industry as a whole has accepted, or reinforces, the division between black and white music. Within companies, power is hidden in the custom and practice which guides the treatment of artists as contracted workers and their music as a product. Companies exercise power in the decisions they take about the resources made available to artists.

Other sorts of power and another sort of politics can be seen in the relationship of artists to their audience and in the audience's relationship to society. Sometimes, as in the case of their support for a cause (the Sandinistas, CND etc.), performers can use their audience to deliver a message. Alternatively, audiences can come to represent a political movement in its own right (Rock Against Racism). Here pop's politics emerge in the desire for power and influence, rather than in its possession.

Politics is not, however, just about power. Nor is popular music. They are both about how we should act and think. Power is pointless without a purpose, without a goal. Judging actions and goals is an essential part of politics – has power been used justly or to good purpose? These questions are raised in the context of public and private life. The women's movement has increased awareness that even the 'private' world involves a series of political questions about the distribution of power between men and women. In turn, this has focused attention on sexuality, on matters of how people identify themselves and their interests. Questions are raised about the nature of desire and why people have particular wants. Pleasure is bound up with politics. Even without the impact of feminism, the boundary between the 'private' and the 'public' has been eroded by the way doctrinaire national politics has exaggerated the tensions between public duty and private conscience. More particularly, the meaning of 'leisure' is no longer so simple in a world where unemployment dominates the political agenda.

Different conceptions of politics draw attention to different facets of popular music. Just as politics can take the form of a government decision, a party, a movement, or an ideology, so pop can be political because of the way it is used, the effect it has, the way it is produced or the values it propagates. Behind this relationship between pop and politics are a whole range of questions about why governments and politicians become involved with popular music, about how political movements come to use music, about how the record industry controls the music's politics, about why some musicians adopt politics and others ignore it, about how music shapes and reflects our pleasures, about what ideologies are embedded in different musics. These are some of the questions which *Rebel Rock* tries to answer.

Three to Get Ready . . .

Throughout the book, two basic themes predominate. One is the relationship between public life and private experience. All popular music works by mediating or reinterpreting this connection. The other theme is the link between political populism and musical popularity. A populist message is no guarantee of popularity, and vice versa. Whatever the form of the music or the style of its performance, these themes persist.

The book is divided into three parts. Part One is about the way states, political parties and movements have used (and abused) popular music in pursuit of their own interests and goals. While social scientists have, with notable exceptions, paid little attention to popular music (except to condemn it), governments have been less aloof. They have both censored and sponsored popular music in an attempt to manage dissent or create consensus. Similarly, politicians and political activists have employed popular music to advance their careers or their causes. State and individual involvement with pop has tended to reveal more about the politics of the government or the politician than about the music, but it raises interesting questions about how and when music can serve pre-conceived political goals. Sometimes it seems as if musicians represent audiences in the same way that politicians represent their constituents; often the relationship is more complex because the politics of populism work quite differently to the politics of musical popularity.

Part Two is about the creation and management of that 'popularity' by the industry, the broadcasters and the musicians. It examines the ways in which political choices are made and expressed in the production of popular music. Pop is occasionally misunderstood as a brand of folk music in which the people express themselves through their music. It is not clear that this was actually how folk music itself functioned, but certainly it is not true for pop music. But while pop may not be 'folk' music, it is not correct to leap, as some writers do, to the opposite conclusion: that pop is just a mass-produced commodity. To do this is to ignore the tensions and pressures which are lived out within the industry, and to overlook the part played both by musicians and audiences in the way the product takes on a meaning which goes beyond its apparent exchange value. A good pop record is not simply a profitable product; being 'popular' means satisfying more than market demands.

Part Three explores the way music acquires a meaning through and beyond its product status. My concern is with how the personal consumption of pop music relates to public experiences. By considering pop in terms of the ideas of liberalism, conservatism and socialism, and by distinguishing between the forms of popular music (reggae, soul, country, rock and pop), I try to show how certain political issues and ideas can be included or ignored. Rod Stewart's 'The Killing of Georgie' seems to work better – musically and politically – than Tom Robinson's 'Glad to be Gay'. Such an argument may strike some readers as wrongheaded or simply perverse. But no one should be surprised by a disagreement of this kind. These disputes are inevitable in pop. The point is to recognize the way that pop encourages divergent interpretations. Its openness allows it to shape and heighten pleasure, to bridge private and public experience, and to link an individual with a collective politics.

With pop musicians raising money for the starving of Africa, for the poor farmers of the USA ('Farm Aid'), and for the families of British miners, with records being released to protest against apartheid ('Sun City') and to support SWAPO ('The Wind of Change'), and with politicians both trying to court and censor the music business, the 'politics of popular music' seems to be an important and confusing subject. Together, these examples certainly provide a good excuse for this book.

Part One
Politics and Popular Music

1
Breaking Butterflies

In 1982, Ivan Jirous was sentenced by a Czech Court to three and a half years in a high security prison. The judge described him as a 'dangerous recidivist'. Jirous' previous stay in prison had been for the same offence: 'creating a public nuisance'. Jirous was artistic director of a Czech rock band, the Plastic People of the Universe.

In 1976, the Plastic People had been arrested for disturbing the peace by 'singing indecent songs'. One song in particular was cited in the charge:

What do you resemble in your greatness?
Are you the truth?
Are you God?
What do you resemble in your greatness?
A piece of shit, a piece of shit, a piece of shit . . .

Formally, the state prosecuted the performers for their use of the word 'shit'; informally, it was understood that the jail sentence of one and a half years was for mocking the state. Jirous' arrest in 1982 followed a public reading of a poem which criticized the authorities for their persecution of dissident opinion.

In 1967 in England, Keith Richards and Mick Jagger of the Rolling Stones were given prison sentences for drug offences. But these particular rock musicians were luckier than their Czech colleague. The establishment came to the rescue. The editor of *The Times*, William Rees-Mogg, asked, 'Who Breaks a Butterfly on a Wheel?'. The Stones, he said, were being punished for who they were, rather than for what they had done. The Court of Appeal agreed. Jagger received a conditional discharge and Richards's conviction was dismissed. The judges concurred with the editor of *The Times*: rock musicians were not very important. They were mere butterflies, whose bright existence was brief and insignificant. For the British establishment, rock musicians were of no great political interest; they were, if anything, minor irritants, albeit ones that continue to inflame the sensibilities of guardians of public morality. In 1985, George Gale cautioned readers of the *Daily Express* that: 'Minds indeed become mindless when stuffed with the trash poured out by the pop industry everyday, without restraint, without control, without decency, without discipline.'[1] For the Czech authorities, however, rock performers seem to pose a constant threat to the established order. Rock is a matter for the state; it is political. Czech rock musicians may, like those in the West, look like butterflies, but they could sting like bees.

Neither interpretation need necessarily be right. The Czechs – just like the judge in the original Stones' trial – may have over-reacted. Or William Rees-Mogg may have been too complacent. Either way, rock found itself subjected to the scrutiny of the political establishment, and what mattered, it seems, was not what the music actually sounded like, but what it and the musicians symbolized to those in power. The authorities' worries counted for more than the music's sounds. But why should those with so much political power be concerned about those with so little? How do states and their agents find themselves caught in the rhythm of rock'n'roll?

No two states are alike, indeed there is little common agreement as to what defines the state itself. Crude distinctions between Western and Eastern states, between communism and capitalism, between democracy and dictatorship, only just touch on the confusion. There is no simple generalization about how certain kinds of state 'typically' treat popular music. For example, two ideologically very different states, South Africa and the Soviet Union, both use popular music to reinforce the dominant values and to defuse political tension. The South African government uses rural African music to give credence to the idea that the blacks of the country actually belong in the artificially created tribal homelands, and not in the cities where they work (for the whites). Similarly, the Soviet government, while being critical of Western popular music elsewhere within its territories, has encouraged it in the Central Asian republics, in an attempt to offset the Islamic influences which threaten its control and which explain its war in Afghanistan.

In the West, politicians have found different, but equally cynical, uses for popular music. They have employed pop music to advance their immediate political interests. The British Prime Minister, Harold Wilson, awarded MBEs to the Beatles in 1965; more recently, Neil Kinnock, newly elected to leadership of the Labour Party, appeared in a Tracey Ullman video; and in the 1984 US Presidential campaign both Walter Mondale and Ronald Reagan presented themselves as fans of Bruce Springsteen. Musicians have also been used, in the UK and the

USA, to raise funds, to promote causes and to polish tarnished party images (see chapter 3). While the politicians have rubbed shoulders with musicians, the Western establishment, in contrast to the Soviet and South African authorities, has presented the appearance of indifference and aloofness. But this is not an altogether accurate impression.

No one should overlook the moral panic inspired by rock and pop. In the USA in the 1950s, Elvis Presley records were burnt in public. Church leaders spoke out against the new music, arguing that it came from the devil to subvert the youth of America. They demanded that the music be banned. In 1955, according to John Orman, 'the Juvenile Delinquency and Crime Commission of Houston, Texas, banned more than fifty songs in one week'.[2] A decade later, rock stars still retained some of their power to shock, as John Lennon showed when he announced that the Beatles were more popular than Jesus. 'Pastor Thurmond Babbs of Cleveland, Ohio,' writes Philip Norman, 'threatened to excommunicate any of his flock who attended a Beatles concert', and Beatles records were cremated in Tennessee and in several other Southern states.[3] Even in the 1960s, Southern racists printed posters which demanded,

> Help Save The Youth of America. Don't buy Negro records. The screaming idiotic words and savage music of these records are undermining the morals of our white youth in America.[4]

More recently, the racism has been replaced by a moral puritanism. The Washington-based organization, Parents Music Resource Center (PMRC), has set itself the task of monitoring the content of pop records and identifying instances of lewdness, violence and profanity. Their campaign brought them before the Senate Commerce Committee; taking the witness stand to oppose PMRC were Frank Zappa, John Denver and Dee Snider of Twisted Sister. The political pressure has been felt throughout the music business. These events recall an earlier era when record company bribery scandals ('payola' and 'drugola') were used as excuses to attack the music; or when the Federal Communications Commission asked radio stations to abstain from playing records which advocated the use of drugs. Then the pressure came from the White House. Vice-President Spiro T. Agnew believed that the 'drug culture' was propagated by pop. 'I may be accused of advocating "song censorship" for pointing this out, but have you really heard the words of some of these songs?', he said, and then went on to quote the lyrics of the Beatles' 'With a Little Help From My Friends' and Jefferson Airplane's 'White Rabbit'.[5] Under President Reagan, the White House has taken to wondering whether the Beach Boys were a fitting group to represent popular music at national celebrations. Such concerns have a more serious history.

In the early 1950s, the House Un-American Activities Committee (better known as the McCarthy Committee) summoned a number of folk singers to testify about their associations with, or membership of, left-wing organizations. As a result of their appearance (rather than what they actually said), a number of singers found themselves on the infamous 'blacklist'. One of McCarthy's victims was the popular folk singer Pete Seeger, who suddenly found that TV companies no longer wanted to book him, and that his group, The Weavers, were not asked to play in major venues any more.

McCarthy's fall from grace in the mid-fifties did not, however, put an end to establishment interest in popular music. In the guise of the Federal Bureau of Investigation, McCarthy was replaced by J. Edgar Hoover as the scourge of the popular musician. The protest singer Phil Ochs was a subject of intensive FBI surveillance. When John Lennon applied for US citizenship, he too found himself under constant scrutiny by the FBI. The FBI and the Immigration and Naturalization Service together accumulated 26 lbs of paper on Lennon. (This does not include those papers which were held back for reasons of 'national security'.) FBI agents attended Lennon's concerts, reporting to Hoover the songs that were sung and what announcements were made from the stage – one agent's report included the lyrics to the song 'John Sinclair'. Lennon's phone was tapped and his movements monitored.

There is a danger of seeing McCarthy's investigations and Hoover's surveillance operations as indications of the political power of popular music. It is much more reasonable to explain them in terms of the delusions and interests of the politicians and their servants. The FBI's curiosity owed more to the paranoia surrounding President Nixon's re-election campaign than it did to Lennon's ability to inspire revolutionary fervour. Once Nixon had been re-elected, Lennon was no longer considered a 'threat'. Besides, Lennon was an exception. Jon Wiener, who was responsible for publicizing the FBI files, observes that no other rock star worried the government in the same way.[6] Neither McCarthy's nor Hoover's efforts were part of a systematic attempt to control or suppress popular music; nor did rock'n'roll ever threaten to undermine religious belief or the state's foundations. What rock did manage to do, however, was to expose some of the insecurities and prejudices of those in positions of power.

If the US political establishment has shown only occasional interest in popular music, then its British equivalent has seemed a model of almost total indifference. Britain can offer no parallel to Senator McCarthy or Spiro T. Agnew, with the possible exception of Sir

Waldron Smithers, a Conservative MP. In 1949, he informed the Beveridge Committee on Broadcasting that 'one of the main weapons of Communism is to demoralize the people. "Morning Music" and "Bright and Early" [two BBC radio shows] are designed to this end. All crooning and much of the jazz and rhythm should be forbidden.'[7] Despite these warnings, parliament and government then, as now, continued to show little interest in the music industry, except as a source of revenue; although the BBC has banned records for their political content, rather than their subversive form (Paul McCartney's 'Give Ireland Back to the Irish', for example). Only occasionally have MPs felt driven to comment on the music itself. The Sex Pistols' 'God Save the Queen' and Crass's 'How Does It Feel (to be the Mother of 1000 Dead)?' have been among the exceptions. 'God Save the Queen' was considered in poor taste in Jubilee Year, and the BBC duly banned it. The Crass single, a splenetic attack on Mrs Thatcher's Falkland's campaign, was described by the Conservative MP Timothy Eggar as a 'vicious, scurrilous attack on the Prime Minister and the government'. He made a vain attempt to have the song prosecuted under the Obscene Publications Act. 'Authority', he argued, 'has to draw a limit somewhere.'[8] Another Crass record, 'Sheep Farming in the Falklands', was investigated by a Commons Select Committee for a possible breach of parliamentary privilege because of its use of radio broadcasts from Parliament. Not all politicians have looked so unsympathetically upon pop music; Harold Wilson said of the Beatles that they had 'a transforming effect on the minds of youth, mostly for the good'.[9] And the British equivalent of PMRC, Mary Whitehouse's National Viewers and Listeners Association, has paid little attention to pop, although it did complain about Chuck Berry's 'My Ding-a-Ling'.

The establishment's apparent indifference to popular music should not be taken to indicate a lack of state involvement. Both the record industry and the broadcasting organizations are subject to scrutiny. The business relationship has recently developed a new intimacy following an extensive campaign by record companies for a levy on blank tapes. Having initially opposed the proposal, the government appears to have been persuaded to introduce a levy, thereby siding with the business against the consumer. (There is little sign that the interests of performers and composers feature very prominently in the industry's wish for a levy.) Such decisions are political, not just because they are made by politicians, but because of the values and interests they sustain. They are, albeit indirectly, decisions about how leisure is to be controlled and enjoyed.

Interestingly though, the state has not always stood in opposition to the music fan. The pop festival, for all the rhetoric and moral panic associated with it, has met with relatively little resistance in the corridors of power. Local feelings may have run high, but nationally the government and the proponents of pop festivals have enjoyed quite a harmonious relationship. Though festival organizers and their opponents appeared to be involved in a clash of opposing life-styles and ideologies, the conflict has until recently taken a benign form in practice. This changed when police brutally resisted attempts to hold a Free Festival at Stonehenge in 1985. Before this, disagreements had been settled in such a way that the worst fears of MPs, concerned to protect the peace and quiet of their constituents, were not realized, just as the plans of the festival organizers for an alternative society were unfulfilled. Writing before events at Stonehenge, Michael Clarke concluded his study of the politics of pop festivals by observing that 'Britain stands out as the only country in which it is legal to hold a festival without the prior agreement of the local authority or the police'.[10] Such conclusions may no longer hold, but it probably is still true that pop festivals have posed little threat to the established order. Police behaviour at Stonehenge may owe little to the character of the proposed festival and more to the political climate and police tactics engendered by the miners' strike.

The music festival has started to take on a new political guise in recent years. The Greater London Council, defending itself against Government plans for its abolition, promoted various musical events with the intention of advancing its own cause and to provide opportunities for music of all kinds to be heard. The Labour Party has plans to follow the GLC's example, including in their festivals 'a sprinkling of politics'. The Party's new General Secretary explained:

> If we had three hours of music and a 30 minute harangue by the Minister of Culture it could all rebound. As long as you keep the politics to a small degree and keep out big business then you've got a political message which isn't too heavy and leads to an identity.[11]

Apart from such plans, the sponsorship of music and musical events has been left to local government, (although Henry Cow once received a grant of £7000 from the Arts Council). Beside the GLC's work, Liverpool City Council has helped to fund two compilation records of Merseyside musicians, and Sheffield's council has helped a local venue, The Leadmill.

In the UK and USA, the central political institutions (and their agents) have little to do with the political management of popular music. They have even less to do with the use of pop for their own purposes. Only during wartime has popular music been used for government propaganda. In the fight against the Nazis, the US Office of Strategic Services translated, and amended, popular American songs for broadcast to Germany. Emigrées like Marlene Dietrich and Lotte Lenya were recruited to sing them. Otherwise, popular music has been ignored. In the UK, for example, popular music is not recognized as part of the 'arts', and thereby not worthy of subsidy, support or serious study. The Arts Council ignores it; and there is no musical equivalent of the British Film Institute or the National Film Finance Corporation. It would seem that neither censorship nor sponsorship of popular music is typical of these governments; they prefer instead the politics of neglect. The same, however, cannot be said of certain other Western states.

The stars of USA for Africa may sing 'We are the World', but theirs is, in fact, a very particular world. Pop music may be sold all over the globe, but its production and character derive largely from the 'worlds' of the USA and Britain. Pop's appearance in other countries, with music and cultures of their own, can seem an unwarranted intrusion. For this reason, governments in Canada and Sweden, for example, have attempted to restrict such intervention and to protect indigenous music. In Canada, all AM and FM rock stations are required to include a certain amount (30 per cent) of Canadian music in their broadcasts. The definition of 'Canadian' is broad, allowing music produced, written or performed by Canadians to be included, and thus emigrés to the USA like Neil Young or Joni Mitchell qualify. In Finland, quotas operate specifically to encourage local talent and local industry. Where no such quotas apply (in the Philippines, for example), the swamping of national music by multinational products is a source of political conflict and struggle. Attempts to preserve or destroy a national or cultural identity through music inevitably, it seems, draw the state into the world of popular music, a fact that is most dramatically demonstrated in South Africa.

In South Africa, music is involved in the government's attempts to shore up apartheid. The censorship of pop is the most obvious part of the white establishment's strategy. Popular music is seen as a possible source of 'alien' or politically unacceptable ideas. Pink Floyd's '*The Wall*' was banned because of the line 'We don't want no education', a slogan used by schoolchildren in Soweto (and elsewhere) who boycotted their schools in protest against state-imposed changes to the educational system. Other banned records include Peter Gabriel's 'Biko', Peter Tosh's 'Equal Rights' and Sonny Okosun's 'Fire in Soweto'. Moral purity is almost as important as racial purity to the South African censor. Sexual explicitness is not tolerated, hence the banning of Donna Summers' 'Love to Love You, Baby' and Marianne

Faithfull's 'Broken English'. The musical *Hair*, with its highly commercial blend of free sex and liberal politics, never stood a chance. Religion too is a sensitive subject. While *Jesus Christ Superstar* was playing to packed houses in the USSR, it was banned in South Africa. The Government Gazette lists those literary or musical items to be censored. In banning a cassette tape by the South African singer Barry Gilder, the Gazette reported the opening words of each of 16 songs ('We may not live to change the world'; 'They call it the law' etc.) so as to identify the offending objects. Use of the word 'freedom' is regarded with suspicion wherever it appears.

The censor's concerns seem to be exclusively with the lyrics. The words are read as if they were some kind of political tract. It is, of course, much harder to censor sounds, because it is difficult to know what they mean; and pop's delight in metaphors and euphemism further adds to the authorities' problems. The censor reads songs literally (not musically), asking whether they attain the 'correct' standards. Sometimes the criteria seem a little obscure (why was Don McLean's 'American Pie' banned?), but usually they reflect the obvious concerns of the apartheid regime. All suggestions of freedom or equality for the black population are censored. Indeed, any idea which seems to disturb the status quo is viewed with suspicion. The result of such practices is that both the musicians and the industry develop a system of self-censorship. Because lyric sheets have to be submitted in advance, many artists regard it as pointless to attempt to write overtly political songs. Nonetheless, the censor's work may still be in vain. An exiled South African poet said of the music made in his country: 'It cannot be explicitly political, so it is subtle. It expresses in its tone, in the sound of the voice and sound of the instruments, the soul of the black South African.'[12]

The effectiveness of censorship depends on the power the government has over the system by which music is heard or distributed. Without extensive control, the objectives of censorship are defeated. Hence in Britain, the BBC can ban Frankie Goes to Hollywood's celebration of sex, 'Relax', but cannot prevent it being a hit. In South Africa, the establishment's control is tighter. The prime agent is the South African Broadcasting Corporation (SABC). When Stevie Wonder dedicated his Hollywood Oscar to Nelson Mandela, the South African government called for the banning of all Wonder's songs on SABC stations. Not only does the SABC implement the government's censorship policy, it also oversees the broadcasting system which, like all else in the country, is divided on racial lines. The SABC is responsible for maintaining the separation of South African society through the creation of a 'white', 'black' and 'coloured' radio service.

The SABC decides on the content of each service, and the system operates exclusively to the benefit of white South Africans – there are no blacks in positions of real power in the black broadcasting service. The SABC decides what records get played on which service; it discriminates, for example, between 'coloured' (i.e. mixed race) and 'black' artists in deciding who should appear on 'white' radio. Records are sometimes deliberately scratched and their titles obliterated to prevent them from being played. As well as worrying over the political and sexual content of any particular music, the SABC's censors categorize records in terms of how 'black' they are: if they are 'too black' they will not get played on the white radio services. Thus success in the white market, for black artists, will depend largely on the current state of government policy. This form of broadcasting discrimination reflects and reproduces commercial divisions. Just as the American music industry has helped to maintain a distinction between the black and the white record market, so in South Africa the ethnic groups are treated as separate commercial units.

This relationship between the SABC, the industry and the govern-ment helps to explain why and how the South African authorities have used music to prop up the 'homelands' policy and their idea of 'separate development' for non-whites, employing tribal music to sustain the belief that black South Africans belong in the artificial homelands. By contrast, the music developed in the townships is not encouraged because it suggests the idea that blacks have a right to a normal life in South Africa. A musical, *Ipi Tombi*, which celebrated traditional culture was welcomed by the white authorities; while another, *Poppie Nongena*, which chronicles the cruelties of the pass laws, enjoyed no such support.

It is not only the radio services and the record industry that work to maintain apartheid. Live performance is subject to similar political control. The government encourages visits by international stars (Millie Jackson, Elton John, Cliff Richard, Linda Ronstadt). At the same time, the authorities take a much less benign view of live performances by indigenous artists. Writing in 1981, Muff Andersson explained:

> Inviting the attention of the police is one of the hazards of a non-racial music festival; and not only the police, but the local authorities too, To this day permits are not granted for the non-racial Free People's Concert, traditionally held on the lawns of an English-speaking university. The concerts go on nevertheless, by being closed to the public but open to students and their guests. Invariably, the police are there and sometimes close the concert mid-show.[13]

In 1983 the armed riot police broke up a non-racial concert organised by students at the University of Natal. The concert was described as an 'illegal gathering'.

Challenging this comprehensive system of musical apartheid is not easy. And only a brave few try. The Kalahari Surfers could find no South African record company to release their album, *Own Affairs*, a sharp and politically radical portrait of life in their country. Racial division seems to be accepted by virtually all the whites in the industry – whatever the liberal rhetoric they use to cloak it. Muff Andersson, commenting on her experience of the South African music industry, said: 'Of all the whites I've spoken to in the industry, only one said he'd like to see an end to musical apartheid.'[14]

Not that life is very easy for those brave people who do try to alter the system. When record producer Julius Levin tried to secure a release for a song recorded in Soweto, all he encountered was 'a vicious racist racket of corruption, depravity, plain pig-headedness, infamy and downright thuggery'.[15] A radio presenter who played multiracial music was deluged with abusive letters. The Scratch Club, at which blacks and whites danced together, was constantly being raided by the police, who on occasions used tear gas and beat up the dancers. Eventually, the club was closed down altogether. In 1983, following a Free People's Concert, two members of a reggae band called Splash were detained by the police. Their crime was to call for the release of Nelson Mandela. They were sentenced to four years' imprisonment for 'indirectly further[ing] the aims of the African National Congress'. Avoiding the system can seem sometimes no easier than challenging it. The mixed group, Malombo, encountered some bizarre arrangements during their career: when playing to a white audience, the black members were hidden behind a curtain.

Observing this mixture of the bizarre and the brutal, it is easy to exaggerate the importance of popular music to political control. Clearly, the edifice of apartheid does not depend on the play-lists of the SABC – whatever the insecurities the government displays in its desire to prohibit all that it considers subversive. Just as with the FBI's interest in Lennon, the South African state's political concern with the music tells us more about the government – and the way it understands music – than it does about the actual operation of apartheid or about the real effect of music. Similarly, it would be wrong to confuse government intentions with its true success. Much as any government would like to control everything around it, it seldom does. Music is used to question and challenge the political system. The government is for ever having to respond to unforeseen political and musical developments; as a result it can never relax nor can it confidently claim to be in control of events. When the Argentinian dictatorship organized a musical festival to encourage support for the Malvinas/ Falklands war, they found the event being turned into a peace rally by the musicians and the audience.

But just because the government cannot determine all that happens, it does not follow that all remaining power rests with the audience or the musicians. Apartheid may dominate the context in which the music is made, but how it affects the product is not easily determined. The South African state is dependent on other powerful agencies. In focusing too much on government, there is the risk of ignoring the political judgements being made by other institutions acting in response to, or independently of, the state. The political control of popular music in South Africa depends on the cooperation and contributions of the music industry. The industry does not simply process music; it too gives a political character to the music by the production and marketing decisions it takes in pursuit of its political and economic interests. The industry too depends on the musicians it employs and on the consumers to whom it sells its products. The politics of music are created by a mixture of state policies, business practices, artistic choices and audience responses. How record companies respond to political conditions will vary.

Following the victory of President Allende's socialist government in Chile in 1970, a number of record companies left, while others were nationalized. EMI, however, avoided nationalization, and instead chose to operate as a capitalist company committed to releasing anti-capitalist music. But when in 1973 Allende's government was replaced by a military dictatorship, EMI stopped releasing the radical folk artists from which it had been making its profits. Instead it vetted its catalogue to ensure 'ideological purity' and dropped many of its traditional folk musicians. Under both regimes, EMI appeared to act as the dutiful servant of its political masters, without compromising its commitment to profit-making. The same applies in South Africa. In the US and the UK, on the other hand, government interest in the record industry is confined to economics; the political meaning of the music is of little concern and the industry decides what to release. Where government and the economy are controlled through a single agency, the state, music takes on yet another political form.

Even as China appears to be shaking off the legacy of Mao and embracing elements of Western capitalism, the state has only slowly removed its suspicions of Western popular culture. In 1982, university students were required to hand over all their cassettes of foreign music, and school pupils were asked to produce lists of all their tapes and records. Access to foreigners and foreign culture was restricted. The government wanted to eradicate 'reactionary' and 'obscene' music. The Party issued instructions as to how to identify 'decadent' songs. Western pop music was described as lacking artistic merit, as an anthem to capitalist greed, as undisciplined and as ideologically underdeveloped. Jazz forced 'people to accept the unexpected, the abnormal beat' and ran 'against the psychological needs of man'; and rock'n'roll suffered from 'a frenzied beat, neighing-like singing and a simple melody'.[16] These official pronouncements were part of a government campaign to modify the behaviour of disaffected young people in China who used pop music to express their frustration. Though the state acted to censor Western popular music, it made no attempt to propagate ideologically correct music, a legacy, perhaps, of the Gang of Four who, it was said, 'turned opera into a lecture'.[17] (Mao, by contrast, had understood that propagandist music had to be artistically interesting as well as politically correct.) Recently, even the doubts about Western music seemed to have been allayed. In 1985, Chinese youth was given the chance to hear the British pop band Wham! play a concert in the country's capital. The relaxation was temporary. The barriers against Western pop have been re-erected. A proposed visit by Men at Work was cancelled. Apparently the authorities were worried by the passions aroused by Wham!, whose visit was not reported in the Chinese press.

Where in China state attention has focused on Western music, East European governments have been trying to find ways to manage the emergence of their music industry. In Hungary, one of the more liberal communist countries, bands approved of by the authorities are licensed. Even without a licence bands can survive, although the state restricts their opportunity to thrive. One group, Beatrice, attracted audiences of 20,000, but because the sentiments expressed in their songs did not meet with official approval, they were not given a recording contract. Groups like Beatrice survive by default through a weakening of central state control over popular culture and a lack of agreement over what is acceptable or unacceptable popular music. The official view is that pop and rock are valueless art forms. But this does not lead to an attempt to ban them, only to put financial and practical restrictions on their production.

Yugoslavia, another relatively liberal communist state, also avoids the problems of direct censorship by limiting the opportunities available to rock musicians. Live performances are indirectly regulated by the requirement that all musicians attain a certain level of competence. They are then licensed to tour. As one disillusioned Yugoslav musician said, 'They don't put you in jail, but they try to make you harmless'.[18] Despite Yugoslavia's market socialist economy, access to record-making facilities still depends on the support of the state-owned record companies, and even these are ill-equipped to meet the demands of aspiring rock artists. After a frustrating studio session, one young performer remarked, 'I mean, the engineer was 50 years old! . . . He had absolutely no idea what I was trying to do'.[19] Artists without the blessing of the authorities face immense problems recording and distributing their material. Though it is rare, these difficulties can then be exacerbated by the application of an extra tax on their records by the Republican Committee for Cultural Questions.

However, the state controls exercised in Hungary and Yugoslavia are mild when compared to the practice in some other Eastern bloc countries. In 1975, the Czech authorities denied licences and professional status to 3000 performers in Moravia and Bohemia. Between 1982 and 1984, the same authorities effectively eradicated live jazz in Czechoslovakia by disbanding the Jazz Section of the Musicians' Union. East German officials imprisoned two members of the rock band Pudhys, which was then the second most popular rock band in the GDR. Their crime was to perform a song about the difficulties of leaving East Germany.

An interesting, if superficial connection can be made between the fierceness of the regime, the vigour of the underground rock scene and the politics of the musicians. One Czech told the British rock writer, Barney Hoskyns, that without struggle 'music is sterile . . . that is why today in England your music is toothless and sometimes has no tongue either'.[20] Certainly, state intervention gives a greater political significance to the music. The state sees the music as a threat, and therefore cherishes the hope, in Josef Skoverecky's words, that youth will 'listen to the trimmed sounds of records carefully preselected by an ideological committee, and play low volume rock that will sound sweet even to the ears of the . . . Communist big shots'.[21] In entertaining such hopes and in intervening, the state tries to redefine the musicians' role. Such efforts can be in vain. Vratislav Brabenec, a former member of the Plastic People of the Universe explained how the group refused to play the state's game: 'we never liked singing protest songs. The conflict was artificially engineered by the police and the state apparatus'.[22] The Plastic People neither participated nor protested. They were not opposed to the state; the state was against them. When, in the 1960s, the Polish authorities acquired a reputation for treating musicians harshly, and for attempting to deny the existence of pop, illicit rock performances flourished, as did black markets in Western and local music. The politics of the music emerged through ignoring the state rather than confronting it.

Attempts to control art, it is said, end up killing it, but there are practical limits to the control that can actually be exercised. The state cannot prevent rock fans from listening to radio stations like Voice of America and Radio Luxembourg. This is particularly true in East Germany, where youth have easy access to West German TV and radio, and can, like Polish fans, develop their own rock culture quite independently of the Party line. However drastic the measures used to curb such activities, their effectiveness is always limited, as the state authorities themselves realize.

Rather than trying to stamp out popular music, the state sometimes resorts to using it. A Polish commentator observed:

> Because rock music is so popular with the youth here, the authorities have used it as a way of winning over youth to their side . . . And after so many years in which groups had to struggle to find equipment and with no chance of recording, the new government made equipment available to every young group, gave radio and TV airtime. . .[23]

This policy has, however, had to co-exist with one which also allows the state to ban rock. As Ian Walker wrote of the GDR, 'On the one hand punk is outlawed and, on the other, a group called Pankow has recently been promoted in the vain hope of defusing dangerous desires.'[24]

Before Solidarity, Western music was denied the state's blessing; afterwards, Western bands were encouraged to tour. In a similar vein, the Czech Communist Party argued that whatever punk's failings, it was better to allow it 'than having young people fighting against the system'. A Ministry of Culture pamphlet on 'Entertainment Music' explains official policy:

> If we, on any level, in any place of work, are faced with phenomena that work against the interests of our socialist society, we have to deal with them resolutely, but at the same time also sensitively, so that we would not suppress hopeful talents, hopeful creativity which, after proper redirectioning, can have the prerequisites of successfully asserting itself.[25]

Similar concerns occupy Polish and East German officialdom. Attempts are made to ensure that, when pop is tolerated, the lyrics convey 'positive' and politically desirable messages.

However, all these efforts may be largely wasted, if only because the content of lyrics is of limited importance to the enjoyment and the politics of rock. A band whose lyrics have been censored can still make a rebellious political point by reading from the telephone directory. Such things are possible precisely because of the tensions inherent in the state's position and because of the character of popular music. The meaning of the music cannot be determined absolutely, and yet the state feels obliged both to assert its authority and to establish its legitimacy with alienated youth. To do this, it needs to be able to interpret the music; it has to have ways to categorize the music, otherwise it cannot make rules and laws to control its use. Musicians and audiences are not so constrained. The exiled African musician Hugh Masekela once remarked, 'the South African government looks at [the music] and decides it is political . . . [but] I never know whether a song is political or not until after its out and the people tell me!'.[26]

In Eastern Europe, the direction taken by popular music depends on factors beyond the state's direct influence: the trends in Western music picked up from radio broadcasts, and the ambitions of musicians and the needs of audiences. The state's problems are neatly illustrated by this story about the Polish band, Republika:

> Their live favourite used to be 'I Want To Be Myself', because a slight phonetic change converted the chorus into 'I want to beat a *zomo*' – slang for cop. The group would sing the original and the audience the modification. And though the authorities could hardly condone massed ranks chanting 'I want to beat a *zomo*', it would be equally ludicrous for them to ban a group from asserting 'I want to be myself'.[27]

The state's dilemma is, of course, a consequence of the way its role is structured. As the East German official Political Dictionary says, 'free time must be purposefully deployed by all members of the socialist community.' It is the state's duty to see this happens. It has to act, and yet in acting it may fuel the very rebellion it seeks to curb. Furthermore, all its policies emphasize the limits of its powers, and the vanity or ludicrousness of its pretensions. Worries about the popularity of US Country music in Poland has led state officials to rule that it is acceptable to sing Country songs in English at concerts, but that on record they should be translated into Polish. Sometimes the state's frustration can take on a much more sinister form. The Polish band Brygada Kryzys, were blacklisted by all the official state entertainment agencies. This meant that their career was effectively terminated. Their offence had been to play in support of Solidarity in 1981. Vratislav Brabenec, of the Plastic People of the Universe, left Czechoslavakia after a police interrogation. He recalled how the police had said that 'I should be careful of the edge of the table because I could easily break my teeth on it, which would make playing the saxophone a little difficult.'[28] Such practices are not confined to the Soviet bloc. Fela Kuti, the Nigerian band leader, has been in prison in

Nigeria for alleged tax offences; it is more likely that his confinement was a consequence of his political opposition to the regime.

The fate of Brygada Kryzys or Pete Seeger may seem mild when compared to the treatment of the Plastic People of the Universe in Czechoslovakia or of the Pudhys in East Germany or of Fela Kuti in Nigeria or of black musicians in South Africa. But all of these examples illustrate the ways in which one of the central actors in politics, the state, becomes involved in popular music, thereby giving the music a political importance that it might not otherwise have had. Whether the state over-reacts, or whether it behaves in a ludicrous or draconian way, the effect is the same: a struggle is fought over the meaning and control of the music. Home-taping is just one illustration of this conflict. Cheap technology makes it possible for independent forms of music making and distribution to compete with the established order. In the West, home-taping threatens the record industry and its profit margins; in the East, home-taping undermines state monopoly control of the manufacturing and distribution of music. However these activities are judged, they are inescapably political; they represent competing attempts to manage leisure time.

Politics also appears in the meanings attributed to the music itself. The moods and sentiments conveyed by popular music can be used for explicitly political ends. Sometimes the music can be made to educate people. In Nicaragua, the government's literacy campaign employs popular music. On one record, *Convirtiendo La Oscurana En Claridad* ('Turning Darkness into Light'), the songs speak of how 'a people which can't read cannot progress', and of how it is necessary to 'build our barricades out of textbooks and with slates'.[29] Music's power to enlighten can, however, be turned to a quite different use: to oppress people by propagating false ideas or by censoring true ones. All these different political treatments of popular music testify to the belief that music is a source of power, that it provides a voice for dissent or consent; controlling its use and its meaning becomes, therefore, a matter of political importance – a truth that is eloquently expressed in the Soviet Union.

2

State Syncopations

No one would call Cliff Richard a political activist; nor would they listen to his music for its political content. And yet both the singer and his songs have become part of a political process. In the early 1970s, the Soviet authorities decided that Western pop should receive the official blessing of the state. Party officials gave permission for artists like Cliff Richard and Elton John to perform in the Soviet Union, and for the Beatles' records to be sold openly in Soviet record shops. (The only condition they made, it is said, was that 'Back in the USSR' be re-titled 'Back in Old Russia'). With these decisions, the bureaucracy simply gave formal recognition to the vast black market in Western pop that had been thriving among Soviet youth for several years. In defying the authorities, pop fans had been engaged in a political act; in sanctioning this illicit behaviour, the state too was making pop political by making it the sound of assent, not dissent. So it is that Cliff Richard and his music become linked with politics.

But the Soviet state's involvement with pop music does not end here. It both sponsors and censors the music. Take the career of the rock band, Machina Vremeni (Time Machine). In the seventies, they were an underground group, whose music could only be heard on privately recorded tapes and at infrequent, unofficial live appearances. Nonetheless, they became increasingly popular. In 1980, the authorities, faced with this popularity, decided to take charge of the band. But rather than doing this by restricting the band's activities, the authorities decided to sponsor them. The band was awarded official status, given access to state-approved venues, and provided with the opportunity to record on the state record label. Then, three years later, a decision was taken to clamp down on unorthodoxy in the arts. The Communist Party's Central Committee launched a campaign to ensure Marxist orthodoxy within the arts and to guard against 'alien' Western influences. Under this new policy, Machina Vremeni was forced to disband. In the Soviet Union, popular music can be both a source of political rebellion and a means of social control, a dual capacity that reflects the state's obligations and the music's character.

In the Soviet Union, the state's formal responsibilities – exercised through the bureaucracy or the Party – involve it in almost every aspect of its citizens' lives. This is not done out of an exaggerated or perverse curiosity, but because the principles of marxist-leninism and the practice of Soviet communism demand it. The state presents itself as the embodiment of the popular will, and as the incarnation of the triumph of collectivism over individualism. What is considered 'private' in the West is a matter of public concern in the Soviet Union. The Party has, for example, recently taken responsibility for improving the sexual manners of the young. Such matters are regarded by officialdom as the legitimate concern of the state. Thus it is no surprise to find that other forms of leisure activity, like listening to or making music, are subject to political oversight and control. What is interesting is how the state interprets and implements its responsibilities.

Official policy on popular music has not followed a consistent line since the 1917 revolution. Popular music has been applauded and banned, it has been censored and sponsored; but whatever its treatment, it has always been mistrusted. There is a natural tendency for any institution that takes full responsibility for life in a community to be unnerved by change. What is new is never fully understood; what is not fully understood cannot be controlled. In the case of pop, this combination of ignorance and impotence can have two, quite opposite effects. For the fans, pop can come to represent an aspect of life that is beyond state control. 'Rock', a Soviet emigré once said, 'is a ten times more powerful emblem of freedom and fun and style in Russia than it is in the West'.[1] In the same way, pop can appear as a threat to the state's authority. 'If music fills a football stadium with raving youngsters', Josef Skvorecky wrote, 'it signals danger'.[2] When pop is seen like this, the state acts to eliminate the danger, either by crude repression, or by using the music (and its popularity) to extend the state's control. At one extreme, pop musicians find themselves imprisoned; at the other, groups are required to sing about Soviet technological triumphs. These two responses, and a whole host of variations in between, are what have constituted the history of the state's political involvement with popular music.

A Short History: Jazz and the State

The political revolution of 1917 was echoed in the arts. Artists and writers took the opportunity to experiment with new forms of expression. The Bolsheviks saw this liberalization as necessary to securing links between the political leadership and the intellectual and artistic communities. The freedoms granted to these groups were not to be shared with the masses, who were to be educated before they were liberated. The Bolsheviks tried to ensure that the massed worker choirs, which they had encouraged before the revolution, adopted an ideologically correct repertoire after 1917. But the Bolsheviks' policy raised a number of questions: what was the proper role of art in Soviet society? what constituted a correct repertoire? These dilemmas were expressed in the stark choice between 'high' art and 'proletarian' art (*Proletkult*). The argument was eventually resolved in favour of high art, partly because it was more susceptible to central control. As Frederick Starr explains in his book *Red and Hot*, '*Proletkult* demanded autonomy, so that it could work side by side with, rather than in subordination to, the Party'.[3] For the Bolsheviks, there seemed to be no reasonable alternative to the state promotion of propagandist art. But their chosen course inevitably brought them into conflict with fashions in popular music and required them to make difficult (and potentially unpopular) aesthetic and political decisions. Had the choice been resolved differently, popular music might never have constituted a part of the political process or a source of political protest – or rather, its politics might have been more akin to those of Western pop.

Jazz brought home the lessons of the Party's decisions. Not only was it popular music, it was also American music. Initially, jazz was seen to symbolize Western decadence. But despite official disapproval, jazz developed a devoted following. In the 1920s, jazz's popularity grew, spreading outwards from Moscow and taking root among the educated middle class as much as among the workers. The authorities, despairing of their 'high art' policy, responded by trying to create a mass culture to rival the American one. They failed, and cutting their losses, they took to creating official jazz ensembles to replace the ones that had sprung up without permission. This policy was as short-lived as the attempt to create a Soviet mass culture. It was ended by Stalin's first Five Year Plan in 1928. The Plan required highly centralized state control and a policy of isolationism. Cultural pluralism and American influences were both outlawed – at one stage, this meant that the saxophone was banned and baseball was claimed as a Russian invention.

Jazz was now thoroughly political. Any doubts about this were removed by Maxim Gorky's 1928 article, 'On the Music of the Gross', in which he disparaged jazz: 'The monstrous bass belches out English words; a wild horn wails piercingly, calling to mind the cries of a raving camel.'[4] Jazz represented moral decay and capitalist subversion. Its emphasis on improvisation, on the individual musician, and on physical pleasure, all ran counter to the spirit and assumptions of the

Stalinist programme. Jazz and communism seemed to be incompatible.

But like the attempt to ban the saxophone, this policy of censorship was unsuccessful. Jazz was popular. The state was forced to accept this, while also recognizing that jazz's appeal lay precisely in its ability to evoke a sense of liberation, and thereby to symbolize a threat to official communist puritanism. Instead of trying to eradicate jazz, the bureaucracy attempted to manage it. It began by drawing distinctions between acceptable and unacceptable types of jazz; and then it promoted the approved version. A State Variety Agency was formed in 1935; jazz musicians were given formal training; and encouragement was given to music that fitted the canons of socialist realism. Improvisational music was frowned on, while traditional folk and swing music were deemed acceptable. The campaign failed. But rather than heralding the freedom of jazz, this provided the opportunity for a new phase in its repression. In 1936, jazz was subject to another wave of assaults, which led to the imprisonment of some jazz players. And so the story continues, with changes in policy on popular music mirroring changing political priorities.

Jazz was encouraged during the Second World War but condemned after it, reflecting almost exactly shifts in USA–USSR relations – from allies to Cold War enemies. With the death of Stalin, attitudes change again. But the impetus for this shift did not come just from the elite. It owed as much to a new generation of Soviet youth who took jazz to their hearts and who, in doing so, rejected official Soviet mass culture. This was not just a matter of taste; it was also a matter of politics. The adoption of jazz amounted to a claim to a private world from which the state was excluded. The new jazz, with its long, improvised solos, explicitly celebrated the individual and expressed the personal turmoils of 'social alienation and inner freedom'. But even here in this private sanctuary, the state was not to be excluded entirely. It took responsibility for the registration of musicians, the vetting of venues and the monitoring of repertoires. Jazz appeared on the school curriculum. But this encouragement – or management – of jazz was always set against a pervasive concern about the 'Westernization' of Soviet culture. The point was to co-opt jazz, not to capitulate to it. The establishment remained reluctant to embrace it. In 1963, Khruschev observed, 'when I hear jazz, it's as if I had gas on the stomach.'[5]

Sponsoring the Sound: The Case of Rock

The same fluctuations in policy, the same strategies of control, and the same source of worries that accompanied state treatment of jazz affected the treatment of pop and rock. The young Soviets who had picked up on post-war US free jazz also discovered rock'n'roll, in the very different shapes of Bill Haley and Elvis Presley. The sounds of rock'n'roll were first heard in the Soviet Union in the late 1950s, and gradually gained a wider and wider audience. The USSR, just like the West, enjoyed a Twist craze. A black market in records and musical instruments flourished to accommodate the new fashion. And as popular taste changed, so did the attention of the state. Replicating its record on jazz, it began, horrified by the new sounds and styles, by trying to ban it, but succeeded only in driving it underground. Eventually, after various attempts during the 1960s to eradicate rock, the state turned instead to a policy of sponsorship, giving the music its official blessing. In 1976, the Party's youth paper (*Yunost*) commented: 'Rock music, viewed 15 years ago as devilment or charlatanry, has now become a rather stable musical tradition in our country.'[6] The state turned what it saw as a threat to the social fabric into a means of protecting that same social fabric. Having discovered that 'stonewall resistance to Western pop culture simply would not work', writes Hedrick Smith, 'Soviet authorities compromised on more sophisticated methods for syphoning off the down beat urges of their young.'[7]

Direct government involvement affected all aspects of music making – from the formation of a band to its recordings and performances. Becoming a professional rock musician in the Soviet Union can be a much more demanding process than it is in the West. The Soviet authorities can require that aspiring musicians be given formal musical training. It is not uncommon to find a rock band whose membership is drawn exclusively from the classical music schools. One of the top jazz-funk bands of the seventies contained five Conservatory graduates and four graduates from the Gresino Music School. By making rock musicians into professionals, the authorities have sought to control the process of music making, a control that is further enhanced by managing access to equipment and resources. While no attempt has been made to outlaw the guitar, the state has been able to exercise its influence over the availability of the necessary instruments. In the Soviet Union, guitars and amplifiers are in limited supply. Musicians have had to rely on equipment imported from other Eastern Bloc countries, or they have been forced to make their own. Groups with official support, or with friends in the right places, will manage to get the best of the available equipment.

A much scarcer resource than amplifiers are recording studios. And once again, the scarcity of the resource puts the supplier in a strong position. There is only one record company in the Soviet Union, the state-run Melodiya. It is in charge of four pressing plants and eight studios. Although these are dispersed throughout the country, and though records appear on a variety of labels, the whole operation is centrally coordinated in Moscow. Melodiya's Director General is answerable to the Ministry of Culture for the company's policy. Consumer demand is only one factor to be considered in the release of any given record. Melodiya does not function just to satisfy popular demand. Its responsibilities extend to educating its consumers in matters of both taste and politics. The company's Director explained his duties:

> It is impossible for Melodiya to turn out records indiscriminately, and what's more it is unnecessary. One often sees on the concert stage, groups and individual performers whose repertoires and skills leave a great deal to be desired. High-powered amplifiers, deafening the audience, cannot help banal, primitive lyrics and tunes. A recording is a great honour for both composer and performer . . . Therefore, Melodiya records only works that have won the acclaim of audiences after being performed on the radio, on television and in concert halls.[8]

The record industry acts conservatively: it both reflects and reinforces the status quo.

Melodiya is part of the political process in a quite different way to that of, say, EMI in Britain or CBS in America. Where EMI is motivated by profit, Melodiya is guided by political priorities. For the 60th anniversary of the October Revolution, it released new recordings of Lenin's speeches. These records joined a catalogue which includes Brezhnev's speech to the Extraordinary 7th Session of the 9th Supreme Soviet. (This is not an exclusively Soviet phenomenon. The British Labour Party has produced a series of cassette recordings of speeches to the 1984 Party Conference. The full set of 31 tapes costs £125.) In being committed to making such records, and having limited resources, it is inevitable that Melodiya is highly selective in the pop/ rock artists it records.

The selection is made by a committee, comprising 'leading musicians – not just rock musicians – and artists'. The winners are chosen on merit, but 'merit' appeals to criteria which might not be immediately recognized by CBS's or WEA's A&R (Artists and Repertoire) departments. Contracts are awarded on the basis of the band's longevity and its musical ability, and skill may be as important as inspiration.

The politics of good music are most clearly expounded in the conditions laid down for live performances. Great emphasis is put on the need to avoid the Westernization of Soviet popular music. During the 1970s, a quota was imposed: a band's repertoire was to contain no more than 15 per cent Western songs. In practice, bands offered one repertoire for the official scrutineer and played a quite different one in concert. Not only were such regulations difficult to police, but the rules themselves were always changing as new worries or new 'problems' arose.

The whole process is neatly captured by the experience of a Soviet band called the Blue Guitars. In 1982, the group was assigned to a tour which included a concert for the Soviet troops fighting in Afghanistan. They did not meet with universal acclaim. A letter signed by four Lieutenant Colonels, a Major and three First Lieutenants was sent to the newspaper *Krasnaya Zvezda*:

> In general, one could forgive all the noise that assaulted the audience through high-powered electronic equipment and that for some reason was called music; one could close one's eyes to the affectation – the performer's stage manner as we saw it simply can't be called anything else; to the tactless solicitation of applause when the audience was in the awkward position of not really wanting to applaud; all of this, we repeat can be forgiven. But we ran into something much more serious!
>
> The program's ideological and artistic aspect will not stand up to criticism – it was simply a pale copy of by no means the best Western originals. Granted, there were a few numbers in which one heard lofty words, but the form in which they were clothed in no way corresponded to the content.[9]

Following the publication of this letter, the leader of the Blue Guitars was called to answer the criticism. His admission of guilt was punished by a ban on all group performances in Moscow and any foreign tours, and by the imposition of 'administrative sanctions' on the leader himself.

The power to punish in this way is implicit in the practice of sponsorship, which, while implicating the state in the production of popular music, also allows it to exercise control over the content of the music. The extent of state control, however, does not end with its sponsorship of the music; it continues into the way music is used to sustain a specific ideology.

Rock as Propaganda

The state's concern about the Western content in repertoires is part of a more general desire to use music to propagate a particular vision of the world and to sustain a particular set of institutions. Without resorting to Lenin's use of massed choirs to carry the Bolshevik message, recent Soviet leaderships have fluctuated between using popular music to advance one line and preventing it from delivering another.

Sometimes Western music is assumed to embody Western values, and thereby to undermine the Soviet order. A slavish adherence to American or British pop, with its decadent and materialist values and its 'free and easy style', is said to have a detrimental effect on Soviet youth. Western bands are supposed to 'inculcate bad tastes that are remote from our [Soviet] ethical and aesthetic principles – incidentally, not only musical tastes but also tastes in morals and manners'. Alternatively, Western music can be used more discriminatingly. A 1976 tour by the US country star, Roy Clark, was promoted on the grounds that his music spoke of the poverty and degradation of the 'toilers of the American South'. Roy Clark himself was elevated above 'the "idols" of the vulgar commercial Western variety stage'.[10] Reacting to Western music, however, is only one feature of popular music's connection with propaganda.

In a speech to the Party in 1983, Konstantin Chernenko, then Secretary of the CPSU Central Committee, spoke of the need for socialist culture to mould and lift 'man's spiritual values', and to influence the individual's 'ideological, political and moral make-up'. The artist, in conjunction with the Party, was obliged to work to these ends. This meant celebrating the achievements and heroes of Soviet society, not dwelling on the 'seamy side of things', 'life's troubles', or 'effete and whining characters'. Chernenko also argued for closer Party scrutiny of popular taste. 'Popularity', he said, 'sometimes brings to the surface musical groups with programmes of dubious quality, which causes ideological and aesthetic damage.' The same warning applied to cultural exchange. Works which lacked 'ideological content', and which were vulgar and artistically bankrupt, were to be avoided. Priority was given 'to the political rather than the commercial approach'.[11]

Chernenko's pronouncement had a direct effect on official attitudes to pop music. Articles appeared condemning pop for its bourgeois, decadent associations. Soviet youth was told it was becoming morally crippled 'in the thoughtless and mindless pursuit of chic'. The showing of the film *ABBA* was criticized; so was the fact that Soviet ice-skaters had to perform to the sound of rock'n'roll in international competitions. The journal *Soviet Culture* carried articles attacking Soviet rock bands either for their insensitive 'reinterpretations' of traditional Russian folk songs, or for their failure to perform any songs of Soviet origin. The First Secretary of the Kazakhstan Communist Party attacked the 'half-baked priests of moral nihilism, to whom we must not show excessive tolerance'.[12]

Both the Russian Republic Ministry of Culture and the USSR Ministry of Culture took action. Control over concert performances was increased, and some groups were disbanded – in the Ukraine, the number of professional groups was halved to 40. The most famous of these was Time Machine, but other groups (the Merry Lads, Hello, Song and Album) were refused permission to perform because they had violated 'the procedure for organising concert tours', and because they had broken 'ethical norms of behaviour onstage'. Time Machine were singled out for their pessimism, for their 'murky, bilious reveries' and their 'pointless grumbling'. One band, the Peddlars, were stripped of a prize they had won in 1976. Other bands were required to improve their repertoires, their musical skills, and their standards of perform-ance. Folk songs, it was decreed, should be treated respectfully, and no more than 20 per cent of a group's repertoire should be written by 'group members who are not professional composers'. This new order was to be administered through a review process conducted by the Ministry of Culture and the Composers' and Writers' Unions. Any bands 'not having a sufficiently high ideological and artistic level' were to be denied a platform.[13] But what were the correct ideological and artistic standards? What could and should rock music do?

Ideological Sound or Sound Ideology?

Implicit in all the twists and turns in the states response to rock music is a single assumption: that rock is politically important. The history of state policy is a chronicle of arguments about whether to trim pop's power or to tap it. The course taken by these debates obviously owes much to changing political conditions and requirements, but it is also influenced by ideas about how the music's power is to be understood. Censoring or sponsoring involves first deciding how music works, determining what is 'dangerous' in a sound and what power a song wields. Musical criticism in the USSR has obvious political implications and practical repercussions; the same cannot be said of Western musical criticisms, although it too affects the form and meaning of music (see chapter 4).

Sometimes the standards of criticism are crudely propagandist. For Chernenko, good art was created by singing or writing about good things: 'the heroes of the five-year plan – workers, collective farmers and specialists.'[14] In a similar way, some Western songs are dismissed because of their subject matter – Boney M's 'Rasputin'; while others are recommended – John Lennon's 'Give Peace a Chance' or Paul

McCartney's 'Give Ireland Back to the Irish'. The music is intended simply to educate the Soviet citizen by confirming a view or supporting a cause.

More obliquely, judgements refer to the mood and the emotions evoked, rather than to the precise lyrical content. Criticisms of Time Machine, for example, focused on their melancholic view of the world. The group was urged to be more positive in its outlook. Similarly, certain standards are expected in performance. Complaints have been made about the use of falsetto – 'Men! Sing like men!' (echoing the BBC which, in the 1930s, attacked crooning for being 'effeminate'); or about the excessive use of lights and smoke; or about the sloppiness of a group's appearance.

The simple application of political and personal standards to rock criticism tends to be confined to those with little sympathy for the music. Musical criticism is just another bureaucratic duty. It is directed by the same rules that apply to the five-year plan. Is music made properly? Is it ideologically correct? More sophisticated (if no more sympathetic) criticism comes from those who employ the standards offered by folk or traditional popular music. According to this approach, 'good music' is music which can be traced back to the 'people' and to Russian culture. Its value lies in these roots; modern rock versions are, therefore, forms of desecration. Rock, it is said, cannot substitute for the politically valuable task performed by traditional music – 'Didn't Lenin and his revolutionary comrades-in-arms sing folk songs?', asked one critic, appalled by Soviet youth's ignorance of folk and its enthusiasm for Western music. The First Secretary of the All-Union Young Communist League argued that victory over the Party's ideological opponents involved 'seizing the initiative in musical influence over Soviet youth'. 'Love for one's homeland', he suggested, 'is inconceivable without love for one's native music'. This meant greater participation in choirs and folk-instrument orchestras. The composer, Vladislav Chachin, declaimed:

> I am convinced that the 'musical output' of the majority of vocal-and-instrumental groups is profoundly alien to the national artistic thought of the Russian people . . . and to the whole of our Soviet musical culture, whose role is to serve the cause of rearing the new man.[15]

However, using folk music as the standard of musical criticism does not inevitably mean a condemnation of rock.

Some of rock's sympathetic critics go so far as to compare rock's popularity with folk's relationship with the 'people'. They do this in order to justify a preference for rock over avant-garde music. Where the avant-garde is elitist and self-indulgent, pop is democratic and based in common experience. Aleksei Kozlov, leader of one of the Soviet Union's longest established jazz-rock bands (Arsenal), argued: 'It seems to me that rock music is the most suitable medium for expressing the feelings and spirit of contemporary young people'. But while Kozlov uses the analogy with folk to justify rock, he also feels obliged to include elements of actual folk music in his compositions – 'we make use of old, genuinely Russian harmonies that one can hear today only in the most remote villages'.[16] Pop fails only when it loses touch with its folk character.

David Tukhmanov, a composer and winner of a young Communist League prize, wrote in 1984 of the need 'to channel rock music in the direction of socially active songs with real content'. Tukhmanov accepted that some rock has not always attained the highest standards, but he blamed this on the reluctance of the media to broadcast rock and on the shortage of professional composers within rock. Rather than folk's *sounds* being preferred over rock's, it is folk's *value* as a vehicle for political ideas that forms the critical standard. Rock's popularity is accepted; it is then only a question of ensuring that its lyrics and sentiments conform to the political norms. This obligation is seen as a musical, and not a political duty – good music and sound politics are inextricably linked. Rock, after struggling for recognition and acceptance, has grown into a respected member of the cultural community. It is no longer the voice of irresponsible youth. In its new maturity, rock needs to follow 'proper creative guidelines', which cannot be transposed directly from political tracts. The music critic Leonid Pereverzev argued that rock should not 'be limited solely to accompanying dancing and putting people in "good moods".' But to do this it has to overcome 'the shakiness of its ideological and artistic position and its lack of clear-cut aesthetic ideals and criteria'. Lyrics that dwell on the angst and pretensions of youth should be replaced by more positive ones.[17] State involvement in the making and distribution of music, and political arguments about musical values, leave untouched one further, but crucially important feature of popular music: how it is consumed.

Disco Dilemmas

Following the change in state policy which lead to the break-up of several leading Soviet groups, a number of Moscow discos were closed and dancing was banned in popular clubs. In Uzbekistan, only half the 115 discos offered themselves for scrutiny. Just prior to the purge, a conservative weekly magazine had urged the youth wing of the Party, the Komsomol, to clean up the disco scene and to rid the city of these 'sleazy dives'.

The Kosomol had been involved in the management of discos since 1976, when the First Inter-Republic Discotheque Festival and Competition had been held, and when considerable time was devoted to defining the disco. One newpaper reported the conference under the headline, 'What is discotheque: A Music Club? A Dance Hall?'. There were two answers. A disco was either a place for 'instruction and education' or a place for 'dance and entertainment'.

Whatever the answer, disco was not something to be treated lightly. As a capitalist invention, it was viewed suspiciously; as a source of entertainment, it was regarded politically. (A leading British communist once described disco as the epitome of alienation.) The slogan for the 1976 disco competition was: 'The Planet's Young People Sing About Peace, Friendship and Solidarity.' To win it was not enough just to play records. Competitors mixed theatre, sounds, poetry and politics. One entry showed 'the struggle of Western young people against the danger of war, against social and racial oppression and for equal rights to labour and education'. Another entry was a ballet danced to the music of the radical British rock band, Henry Cow.

The worthy character of the entries for the competition reflected the seriousness with which the Party took the disco. In 1978, the Ukrainian Komsomol conducted extensive discussions of the 'problems' of the disco. Their research had revealed that although the popularity of discos was growing, there was no purpose-built accommodation for them. Instead they were housed in factories, trade union clubs, dormitories and parks. But these arrangements neither deterred their patrons (in a single year, one disco held 128 sessions and attracted 400,000 visitors), nor diminished their political impact. The Komsomol took comfort from the fact that discos were able to both enlighten and entertain, citing the example of a five-evening series of three-hour sessions for schoolchildren which combined both popular and classical music.

These successes, however, did not herald an end to discussion of the disco. The Party, and particularly its youth sections, continued to examine new ways to combine enlightenment and entertainment. At a three-day conference for DJs, the discussion ranged from problems of obtaining reliable equipment, to questions of training. DJs were not to be left to their own devices; instead they were to receive formal tuition. They were to be given instruction on technical matters, on musicology, on public speaking and on cultural affairs. In Novosibirsk, DJs learnt about the theory of entertainment and developmental psychology. The purpose of this training was to create a politically acceptable disco, which maximized audience participation and education, avoided 'primitivism and imitativeness', but retained 'a democratic spirit without reducing sessions to mere record hops'.[18]

Official approval depended on the disco organizer's ability to find the right answer to such questions. In 1980, *Pravda* indicated that the first five years of the disco had been largely successful. The disco provided a legitimate 'leisure-time activity, combining dancing, conversations, and contests of wit and knowledge'. But this welcome was guarded. It was noted that discos were not 'organizationally defined'; they lacked proper regulations for their conduct and for the selection of records.[19] To appease these worries and to institute more order, the Komsomol, trade unions and the Ministry of Culture were encouraged to play a greater part in the running of discos. Two years later, however, the authorities' worries remained. DJs still were thought to lack sufficient training – they were just enthusiasts, or worse 'dilettantes', who relied on their own record collections. The head of the city's Cultural Department recommended that a 'Disco Centre' should be established to train DJs, and that the state broadcasting corporation provide tapes of carefully selected music. But despite these attempts to reform the disco, official disapproval continued and eventually led to the closure of discos in 1983, following Chernenko's speech.

The attention paid to the DJ seems to be symptomatic of the authorities' general approach. The DJ is identified as the source of power and is cast in the role of the teacher or political leader (the dancers are cast as pupils or party members). The success of a disco is determined by the abilities and behaviour of the DJ, an attitude noticeably similar to the formal interpretation of the role of the Party in society at large. Music, it is assumed, is assimilated in the same way that lessons are learnt; and provided that the content of the lessons is correct the desired outcome will be achieved. Whatever the arguments of music critics or disco organizers, it is this attitude which pervades the organization and responses of the established system of music production. It is not only reflected in the state monopoly in the record industry and in state monitoring of public performances; it is also to be found in official responses to popularity and 'stardom'.

Star Wars

Even if an aspiring band has managed to acquire the necessary instruments, has had its repertoire vetted and its stage perfomance scrutinized, and has finally obtained a recording contract from Melodiya, there are still difficulties which threaten to obstruct its path. As Time Machine discovered, a change of state policy can upset the best-laid plans. But even without such developments, a band's position is always politically sensitive.

Popularity poses problems for the authorities simply because it is difficult to manage. The bond between popular performer and audience cannot be entirely manufactured by Party doctrine in the East (or by marketing strategy in the West). Popularity has an element of unpredictability – most records are unpopular. Soviet officials were embarrassed by the near-riot that accompanied Elton John's first performance in Moscow. Not only did the audience scream and whistle, but they also tried to storm the stage. The officials' discomfort at this 'un-Soviet' behaviour was made worse by the fact that most of the ticket-holders were people with Party or bureaucrat connections – many of the much-sought-after tickets were obtained through such contacts. If proof were needed, events at Elton John's performance demonstrated the problem of stage-managing a pop concert; stage-managing a party congress is a great deal easier, as party bureaucrats in the East and West would confirm.

Popular music inevitably introduces uncertainty into the authorities' world, an uncertainty that sets the limits to state control by establishing an area of popular sovereignty in an area deemed politically important. Attempts to control the consumption of music have to concentrate on the outward and visble signs only – in 1985, the authorities tried to restrict the use of the word 'rock' and the use of 'funny names' for bands; the audience's spontaneous and symbolic gestures had to be left to chance. Clubs in which the audience become over-enthusiastic can be closed, but little can be done about the enthusiasm itself. That can only be managed indirectly by penalizing the musicians whose audience 'misbehaves' (just as in Britain, football clubs are penalized for the misconduct of their fans). The task of control falls to the musician, who may have only slightly more control over the audience's reactions than the state. Kozlov once tried to calm a potentially rowdy audience by saying: 'I consider rock a branch of contemporary academic music. We try to treat it that way, so we ask you to react to it in the same spirit'.[20]

In putting the onus on the musician, the authorities give tacit recognition to the artist's independent power. Success in pop is a tribute to the artist's ability to express what their audience cannot articulate; to be what they cannot become; and to give shape to their fantasies. In doing this, not only is pop stardom acclaim for a particular individual, but pop itself works through the private feelings that it makes public. Pop, by its very nature, mixes individual experience with collective pleasure. In the Soviet Union, where individuals are hailed as examples, not as exceptions, and where collective behaviour is the responsibility of the Party and the state, pop's individualism is an inevitable source of anxiety. A further source of concern – in the West and the East – is the way pop links the public and private world. Its use of fantasy and romance, its dependence on the imagination, all work against a realist or literal interpretation of the sound. The standards of truth in pop are not those of the documentary, but of the fiction film. Reality is a work of imagination.

There may be little to be done to counter the individualist character of pop, other than to replace pop with folk music or massed choirs. But something can be done about stardom. By staging rock events that highlight the price of fame and fortune, the medium can be used to deny its own message. The first Soviet rock opera, *Orpheus and Eurydice*, had a clear message, according to *Yunost*:

> Following his victory in the singing competition, Orpheus is surrounded by a chorus of admirers and caught, as it were, in the vice of his own popularity . . . The singer is crucified on the cross of mass culture, bound hand and foot by mass worship.[21]

Perhaps such crude propaganda seems a rather feeble form of control when compared with the vast network of other rules and constraints operating on popular music. What makes it important, however, is that it represents one of the few attempts to manage the meaning and effect of the music. Most other forms of control are exercised over the production and dissemination of popular music. The attempt to manipulate popularity itself was an attempt to intervene in the experience of music. This was what underlay the whole edifice of state involvement in popular music, and yet it was here that its powers of control were weakest. Frederick Starr tells this story of early attempts to manage responses to rock:

> in 1960 the renowned Moiseev folk-dance troupe worked up a satire on American rock music, it was titled 'Back to the Monkeys'. Poor Moiseev must have been thunderstruck when Moscow audiences burst into applause at the rumbustious music and remained indifferent to the satire.[22]

A similar tale can be told today. On a visit to Moscow in 1984, Simon Frith watched a TV show that, in denouncing punk for its degeneracy, contrived to show lengthy clips of the Clash and the Sex Pistols. The official critique paled beside the power of the images.

There would be no such problem if the state outlawed all forms of popular music; or if, in contrast, it treated pop as irrelevant. But efforts to ban the music failed with jazz; and a policy of *laissez-faire* would mean conceding that previous policies had been misconceived, and that areas of Soviet life fell outside the political realm. The state had, in other words, no real choice. It might have handled things differently, but its intervention was inevitable – as were the accompanying dilemmas and tensions.

Once committed to involvement, and despite its own considerable power, the state finds its position defined by the medium with which it is engaged: the state has no control over developments in Western pop and cannot prevent access to them – in Latvia, Radio Luxembourg is reputed to be the most popular foreign station. Even indigenous pop cannot be subjected to absolute control: neither the artist's creativity nor the audience's responses are entirely manipulable. Thus the state is forced to respond to, rather than dictate, trends in popular music. The way it reacts is similarly constrained. Firstly, the state's view of the organization of pop reflects its view of political administration generally. Hence the emphasis put on DJs and musicians: these are the people responsible for what happens. Secondly, the state's understanding of pop is dictated by its understanding of conventional politics or by its borrowed critical standards. Pop is seen as either polemic or propaganda, and is read like a manifesto; or is seen as folk music or high culture, and assessed by reference to its roots or its techniques. But just as responses to pop cannot be dictated, so literal readings of pop systematically misunderstand its meaning. Even attempts to 'professionalize' composers and musicians, or to insist on particular kinds of subject matter, though intended to turn pop into an administratively manageable entity, can only meet with partial success. Pop's meaning is not captured in the lyrics or in the musical notation or the technical dexterity of the players. Pop's meaning depends as much on how it is understood as on what is intended.

However hard it tries, the state itself cannot make music. It has to rely on others, and in this dependence, a rival power is created. DJs and discos may be susceptible to monitoring and control, but the popularity of any given record cannot be assured or denied. Control becomes even harder as fans and musicians acquire the technology which enables them to record cheaply and independently of the state, further underlining the delicacy of the state's predicament. State control cannot extend fully into the process of creation, whether this is the creativity of the musician's intentions or the audience's interpretations. An alternative music scene, despite recent clampdowns, continues to exist and manages to generate, in the words of officialdom, 'unhealthy excitement in the audience'.

In these circumstances, the state sees music either as a threat to its authority or as a means of sustaining that authority. Whichever view it takes, it faces problems. In trying to eliminate the threat, it drives the music underground, and makes it the sound of political dissent; or in incorporating the music, the state either legitimates the independent 'authority' of the musicians or deprives the music of its original meaning, and thereby creates a desire for more 'authentic' (Western) sounds. These dilemmas are characteristic both of state control and of popular music. The state becomes involved in pop precisely because of pop's ability to transcend its immediate context; and it is this same feature of pop which defies absolute control and which leads those who seek to hold or overthrow state power to use it.

3

Party Down

A musician's ability to create an audience can resemble a politician's ability to create a following. The great soul performer, James Brown, once suggested that politicians were little more than parasites upon the skills of musicians; he said that US Presidents speak to him 'because they feel they need me and need my influence'. He added:

> My stage act is so organised the whole establishment want to steal it from me, they want to know how I can command the love of the people.[1]

Mistakenly perhaps, politicians may indeed see in musicians the ability to create a spontaneous and loyal following through the use of music alone, without recourse to favours or promises or policies. Political populism and musical popularity can seem, on the surface at least, to be related. Selling records and winning votes sometimes appear to be similar activities. It is perhaps no surprise, therefore, that popular music is used by those who seek to overthrow the state or by those who merely wish to join it. This chapter is about the politicians and political parties who employ music to win votes and support.

The Politicians

The sight of politicians forging alliances with the pop business is becoming increasingly common in Western politics. In Britain, the phenomenon has taken a variety of forms. The leader of the Liberal Party has made a rap record, 'I Feel Liberal – Alright' ('You can help to change the face of British politics'). The Head of Computer Games at Virgin Records has taken on the task of recruiting rock stars to the Social Democratic Party. At a Conservative Party pre-election youth rally, the faithful were serenaded by Lindsey de Paul ('Vote Tory, Tory, Tory/For election glory/We don't want U-Turns/So we'll vote for Maggie T./Vote Tory, Tory, Tory/The only party for me/Say no to

Labour/And no to the SDP'). The Tories also had their own campaign song, 'Maggie for Me', written by the combined talents of the light entertainment performer, Vince Hill, and the Prime Minister's speechwriter. The Greater London Council sponsored a record, 'The Streamlining Song' by Hi-Jinx, as part of their anti-government campaign; and NALGO, the local government trade union, supported an anti-cuts record by the Appollonaires. These precedents have been followed by the Labour Party, which sponsored a tour by the rock troubadour Billy Bragg and used his voice for a Party Political Broadcast. It was a simple attempt, in the Labour leader's own words, 'to capitalize on the youth vote'.[2]

Such developments are not new. Even the Liberal Leader's rap record has its origins in black American music's use of speeches as the text for songs. Martin Luther King's 'I have a dream' speech most recently appeared on Bobby Womack's *Poet II* album; another black leader, the late Malcolm X, had his speeches re-edited for the single, 'No Sell Out' (a technique that was also used on the speeches of the British miners' leader, Arthur Scargill, for the record 'Strike' by the Enemy Within). In the United States, the recent British developments are almost established commonplaces. The 1984 US Presidential elections brought this home. Not only did both leading Presidential contenders, Walter Mondale and Ronald Reagan, quote Bruce Springsteen in support of their positions, they almost turned the rock star's lyrics into a campaign issue. Mondale commented on Reagan's appropriation of Springsteen, 'Bruce may have been born to run, but he wasn't born yesterday.' When running for President, Jimmy Carter asked Bob Dylan to lunch. From then on, the candidate spoke of Dylan as his friend and recalled Dylan's songs in his speeches. Such examples reflect a much longer-standing relationship between popular music and politicians.

One aspect of this link can be traced to the New Deal era. In the attempt to change the political agenda, to extend the responsibilities of the state, and to establish new political constituencies, New Deal politicians explored different forms of political communication. One of the most famous New Deal politicians, Huey P. Long, was a songwriter as well as Governor of Louisiana from 1928 to 1935. His song 'Every Man a King' captured the New Deal message. Long promised castles, 'clothing and food for all', and a peaceful future in which everyone could share.

The links between politics and popular music forged in the 1930s are reflected in more recent alliances among Democratic candidates for the Presidential nomination. In the 1976 election, while Jerry Brown used the sound of Southern California (Linda Rondstadt, the Eagles,

Jackson Browne) to accompany him, and while Jimmy Carter used his fellow Alabamans, the Allman Brothers, Hubert Humphrey campaigned to the raw soul of James Brown. (This was in the days before Brown took to courting Republican presidents.) Humphrey's urbanity might seem to contrast starkly with Brown's earthy soul, but their alliance was born of their common audience, the poor blacks of the Southern states. Another New Deal alliance was echoed in Senator Fred Harris's use of Harry Chapin and Arlo Guthrie. Harris's attempt on the Democratic nomination for President owed much to the political populism of the New Deal era. It was a populism which was associated with the dust-bowl songs and folk sounds evoked by Chapin and Guthrie.

It is interesting, if not altogether surprising, that the use of popular music is a habit most commonly found within the Democratic Party. Its traditional constituency among the underprivileged and the exploited inclines the party towards the use of popular music. The Republican Party's association with popular music, by contrast, has not stemmed from the common characteristics of the music and the politics, but has tended to reflect the conventional political beliefs and social aspirations of the musicians. The Osmonds' Mormon faith, Frank Sinatra's desire for social status, and Pat Boone's personal political ambitions: these are all better explanations for their links with the Republican Party than any analysis of the party's political strategy and style or their musical roots. However, it is noticeable that as the Republican Party has adopted a more populist politics under Reagan, it has turned to popular music. Springsteen is evidently seen as the patriotic voice of white working-class America, and 'Born in the USA' is interpreted as its anthem. In the same way, the decision about whether to use the Beach Boys for the White House 4th of July celebrations caused controversy precisely because senior Republicans started to worry about the kind of populism the group represented. Did the Beach Boys represent the family and fun, or drugs and decadence? However misguided, such questions are provoked by the desire to tap music's ability to evoke a feeling and capture an idea. But politicians are not just concerned about images and ideologies, they are equally concerned about money and votes.

The lowering of the voting age to 18, and politicians' growing awareness of the need to capture young voters, has increased the incentive to use pop's images and stars. Not only can pop provide a young audience, it can also provide money. Musicians can act as a valuable source of cash, a particularly important advantage since the change in US electoral regulations in 1974, which limited the size of individual contributions to the ever-increasing campaign costs. Rock concerts allowed large sums to be raised without infringing the law. If artists waive their fee, the takings from a concert can go straight into the campaign fund. This is not deemed to be a donation by the artists themselves but to be a contribution by the individual ticket-holders.

Even before the change in law, musicians had given their services to candidates. Before he began serenading the Republicans, Frank Sinatra sang for Kennedy in the early sixties. In 1968, Simon and Garfunkel performed for Senator Eugene McCarthy. They were followed by a festival of stars who joined the 1972 McGovern campaign. The film star Warren Beatty, acting as broker, coordinated a series of concerts (from Barbra Streisand to the Grateful Dead) which raised 1.5 million dollars. Although the musicians were essentially being used to manufacture money for McGovern, it is clear that their association with his bid for President reflected their own political feelings. The war in Vietnam, and Nixon's failure to end it, were highly salient issues with both musicians and audiences. Popular musicians who are traditionally wary of associating with established political parties and politicians, for fear of alienating their audience, saw in Vietnam a moral issue which allowed them to distance themselves from typical political infighting and which was of direct relevance to their fans. Paul Simon performed because he opposed Nixon, not because he was for McGovern. It is noticeable that once the US had left South-East Asia, rock stars were much less prominently represented on the campaign trail. They were still there, but for a very different reason.

It was the record business, not the performers, that initiated the new political connection. Instead of artists volunteering their services to a politician, they found themselves being volunteered by powerful figures in radio and the record industry. The help given to Jimmy Carter by the Allman Brothers was instigated by Phil Walden, the head of their record company, Capricorn. Walden became a fulltime worker on the Carter campaign. Jerry Brown was helped by the man responsible for record programming on RKO radio stations, Paul Drew. Drew's decisions could determine whether a record was a success or a failure. If he chose not to play it, it might never be heard of again. That, at least, was conventional wisdom, and only the most confident of stars was likely to put it to the test. So if Drew asked a favour, it was difficult to refuse. Drew managed to bring together an impressive roster of performers to support Brown, and at the same time to dissuade other artists from helping Tom Hayden . . . or so it was rumoured.[3]

The ability to deliver audiences and funds was highly valued by the campaign managers. Gary Davis, Brown's Chief of Staff, remarked:

> Entertainers can attract contributions, particularly smaller ones,
> which would not otherwise be available to a candidate . . . People
> go to one of our concerts basically to see the Eagles perform.
> Frankly, we'd have trouble getting one-fifth the people there just
> to see Jerry.[4]

It was reported that Jimmy Carter acquired a new impetus after a
concert by the Allman Brothers. The candidates recognized their debt;
they also recognized their own (limited) role: they confined themselves
to introducing the artists, whose music they did not much enjoy
anyway. The business's involvement was similarly instrumental. The
record executives wanted to purchase influence in the political
establishment.

The politics of the music become the politics of the campaign trail.
What matters for the politicians are the tangible gains they make. For
the individual politician, the music itself is marginal; it is just a device.
The politician is parasitic upon the music. Politicians borrow its
powers to bring people together; they do not use that community or
create it. The music's popularity has only a tangential bearing on the
politicians' political populism. They may hope to acquire the right
image; they are certain to acquire the money. What happens is that
both the politics and the music are reduced to their lowest common
denominator. As Jerry Brown's finance chairman remarked: 'There
isn't much difference between plugging Donna Summers or Jerry
Brown. You have a product to sell and you do it'.[5] Or as the President
of a Nashville entertainment agency said, after signing up the right-
wing Southern politician, George Wallace: 'You're looking at some
basic qualities, whether it's a singer or a politician – believability,
glamour, supply and demand'.[6]

Rock stars who use their audience to support a cause find themselves
in the same role as does the politician: concerts given as part of an anti-
nuclear campaign or to help the miners tend to attract people who care
more about the music than the cause. Both the musician and the
politician borrow (or steal) from some prior relationship, built of a
kind of trust or of a common fantasy, or whatever it is that disposes
people to like a particular music. To *create* an audience musically and
politically, to make a political community of them, requires a quite
different relationship to exist, one built from within the idea of
'popularity' itself. In this new context, politicians and musicians are
replaced by less well-defined entities – parties, movements and
audiences – in which musical taste and political judgement become
confused.

Parties and Movements

It is almost as if the differences between the world of the conventional politician and the world of the political movement are precisely those that make it necessary for the latter to depend more on popular music. While the politician works through established channels of communication, with recognized policy goals and with the support of traditional institutions, political movements, almost by definition, work without this help. They have to impose their will on the status quo; and their ability to do so is determined by the strength and unity of their members. Music can generate the sense of solidarity and community which movements need.

Popular music is a good medium both for expressing dissent and creating unity. It is easily transmitted; everyone can remember a tune, few can recall a tract (as the old joke has it: 'You know "The party is the vanguard of the proletarian revolution"? No, but hum the tune and I'll soon pick it up'). It is also much harder for the authorities to control music than it is for them to control the written or spoken word: in a song, the meaning is opaque; and in mass singing, the crowd gains strength in its harmony. Furthermore, pop musicians share with political movements the preference for a politics organized around a cause rather than an ideology or an electoral campaign. In the USA, it was Vietnam, and not the Democratic Party, that inspired them; and after the war, it has been nuclear power, Nicaragua, famine and apartheid which have galvanized them. In Britain too, it has been the fights against racism or Cruise missiles that have mobilized musicians. They have been much more reluctant to associate themselves with political parties, even where the parties share the same policy aims. Why musicians adopt one issue and not another, and what the music itself contributes, are matters for later chapters. For the moment my concern is with the way movements adopt particular types of music and musician. Two examples seem most interesting: the racist right and the socialist left.

The Racist Right

Writing of the state of rock in Britain in 1980, Marek Kohn argued 'that the most committed political tendency among the various kinds of rock audience is now "*fascist*" '.[7] Certainly, if this faction did exist, the late 1970s provided the images – punk's use of Swastikas and SS armbands – and the bands to satisfy them. Oi groups, like the 4 Skins, seemed deliberately to court the racist audience, while other groups, like Sham 69 and Bad Manners, attracted racists even when the musicians themselves denounced racism. Elements within the National Front (NF), Britain's neo-fascist political party, saw punk as providing a real opportunity for propagating the racist message. Others within the NF saw rock as, at best, an irrelevant distraction, and at worst, a dangerous intrusion. Roughly, the divide was between the old guard and the youth of the party.

For the youth faction, punk, and its later variant Oi music, were seen as the voice of 'white resistance'. Groups and records were singled out for the sentiments they expressed, for the challenge they posed to 'the reds and rich bosses in the music industry', and for the encouragement they gave to 'white culture'.[8] For the old guard, pop music was a decadent art which encouraged 'yobbos', not white resistance. The music, far from being free of 'alien' cultures, was an expression of them; it was 'jungle garbage' produced by a 'zionist-controlled' record industry.[9] What both sides appeared to accept in their dispute was the importance and power of popular music; what separated them was their interpretation of its effect and their understanding of its origins.

The old guard saw rock music as both symbol and cause of a moral and political decline. One NF magazine subtitled a picture of the New York band, the Ramones, with the words, 'These useless looking erks are typical soft society products.' Rock fans were treated with similar contempt, being bracketed with all those groups for which the NF had most contempt. Such attitudes stemmed from the belief that age and tradition were more valuable than youth and fashion, and that 'high art' was better than popular art. Pop found itself condemned on both counts. But the attack did not end there. 'Black rhythms' and the disco were also castigated. Not only did the disco represent an unpalatable alternative to healthy outdoor activity, but young people were seduced into a state of 'emotional frenzy' by the beat: 'the dancers are dominated by their instincts, they are victims of irrationality and unbridled sensuality'. Behaviour at the disco was likened to 'certain religious dances of aboriginal peoples of Africa [sic] or even . . . the gregariousness of some savage animals'. A similar contempt was showered on the rock stars. John Lennon was described as 'a multi-racialist, exhibitionist junkie and professional peace-creep', and his former band, the Beatles, were said to display a

> basic unmanliness: castrated tones emanating from weak faces, topping puny bodies prancing the stage in the manner of comic ballerinas, while overworked guitars placed in front of the unmentionable regions received the attention of limp wrists . . .[10]

Musical criticism became a sub-discipline of Physical Education. The only popular music that escaped attack was country and western. Country music was acceptable because it was said (inaccurately) to derive exclusively from 'the rich heritage of the White peoples' and to originate in British folk songs of the Elizabethan era. Only in country music could they find, the racists said, the values and the community which accorded with their politics. The music was seen, again mistakenly, to embody their racist populism. That same populism was given a quite different musical setting by the NF youth section.

'Generalized nonsense' was how the youth faction described the views of the old guard. Despite this, there are notable similarities in their approaches, even though they reach different conclusions. Traditional folk was acceptable because of its origins in some (mythical) British past; modern folk was unacceptable because it purveyed 'boring neo-marxist ideas'. Rock'n'roll passed, thanks to its country roots; its debt to rhythm'n'blues was conveniently forgotten, or reinterpreted – it was even suggested that the blues had been stolen from white European music. Early Beatles' songs, being free of drug references and Eastern influences, were favoured over later works with their celebration of drugs and Eastern mysticism. Pink Floyd were denounced for their attacks on 'British Nationalism and the so-called establishment' in *The Wall*; while David Bowie was applauded for the 'Nietzschean spirit' to be detected in songs like 'Changes', 'Quicksands' (from *Hunky Dory*) and 'Starman' (from *Ziggy Stardust and the Spiders from Mars*). And so on.[11] The criteria were vague and various, but like the assessments made by the old guard, they drew on matters of content, style and origin. The most systematic discussions of the politics of popular music by the racist right centres on punk and its subsequent development into New Romantic and Oi music.

All three forms of music were identified as 'white'. Punk and Oi, with their shouted vocals and furious beat, were interpreted as the sound of white working-class frustrations; while new romantic bands like Ultravox, the Human League and Spandau Ballet, who employed new electronic techniques, modernist imagery, and melodramatic vocal styles, were said to represent a contemporary version of 'classical and traditional Aryan music', and to reject 'disco style music, which is truly multi-racial and anti-white'. Such judgements are not made on the sound alone. Assumptions are also made about the communal character of the music, about who it belongs to. An Oi band like Screwdriver is praised for 'never having sold out to the establishment'. For the NF, this idea of loyalty is reinforced by Mafia-like threats. When Bad Manners, who had acquired some racist fans, denounced racism and the NF, they were warned in the NF's youth magazine,

Bulldog: 'Our attitude is that bands who are not our friends are our enemies, and will be treated as such.' The emphasis on the communal character of the music extends beyond any given group's fans. *Bulldog* defined Oi as 'the music of the ghetto. Its energy expresses the frustration of white youths.' In its sociological origins the music also acquires its political character. Being the expression of white frustration, it becomes 'the music of the white rebellion'. Oi is about 'fighting the government, about fighting the whole system'. The sleeve notes to the album, *Strength Thru' Oi*, declaim: 'The Union Jack is our flag not theirs. Not the rich's. It's our country, not theirs, our work that makes them wealthy.'[12] The national identity sits uncomfortably with the class identity, the unity of nation being questioned by the divisions of class.

For all the stress on the music's communal roots and origins, the dominant feature of the NF's relationship with popular music is determined by the ideas and values which the songs or the singers appear to promote. (The right's 'class' approach to popular music may owe more to the way in which the pop papers, in particular *Sounds*, wrote about the rise of punk and Oi, than it does to either reality or the right's understanding of it.) The right's ideological analysis of music revolves around four different, if related, ideas: nationalism, racism, anti-communism, and fascism. Each is used, together or separately, to establish the value of the music.

It was nationalism which explains the choice of songs like the Last Resort's 'Red, White and Blue' or 'English Rose', the Angelic Upstarts' 'England', or the Enid's versions of 'Land of Hope and Glory' or 'The Dambusters' March' (a tune also used by the Conservative Party for their 1983 election press conferences). Nationalism also provided the basis for rejecting songs and sounds from other countries. Some NF members boasted of their attempt to disrupt a performance by the US band, the Dead Kennedys, by shouting 'fuck off yanks'. The Ramones, another US group, were exempted, partly because of their song, 'Today Your Love, Tomorrow the World'.

Racism also furnishes a list of 'approved' songs: the Cure's 'Killing an Arab', the Stranglers' 'I Feel Like a Wog', or the Clash's 'White Riot' and 'White Man in the Hammersmith Palais'. Often, as in the case of 'White Riot', the song itself expresses no racism whatsoever. It is the title, or the interpretation to be made in defiance of the lyrics or the band's intentions, that determines its selection for NF approval. This explains the choice of Bing Crosby's 'White Christmas'.

The selection of songs for their anti-communist sentiments is equally tendentious. They single out Steve Harley's 'Red is a Mean, Mean Colour', David Essex's 'Imperial Wizard', Carl Gustav's 'I Want to Kill Russians', and Maddy Prior's 'Wake Up England'. Just as with 'nationalist' and 'racist' songs, the anti-communist songs are selected almost exclusively in terms of their lyrics (and occasionally on the basis of their title alone). The music itself, whether its sound, its audience or its origins, merits relatively little attention. The exception is the treatment of so-called 'fascist' music, although the attention is on the style, rather than the sound.

Fascist associations are identified in the images evoked by such post-punk performers as Spandau Ballet, the Skids, Ultravox, David Bowie, and Joy Division. These musicians were said to have drawn on the sounds and ideas of 'white European culture', to have rejected black American music, and to have used the Futurist imagery of the 1930s. These resources are linked by the racist right directly to the politics of Nazism and the idea of an Aryan race. Occasionally, the musicians themselves even added weight to these ideas. David Bowie once said, 'Hitler was the first superstar . . . I believe Britain could benefit from a fascist leader.'[13]

In all these attempts to define fascist or racist music, the music serves an essentially peripheral role in the movement itself. It is used to reinforce or identify opinions already established by other means. The music is assessed ideologically and stylistically. There is little attempt to link musical popularity with political populism; minimal effort is made to appropriate a musical form or to build a political movement out of an audience. Such attempts are more characteristic of the American right.

In the US, just as in the UK, the right has also seen in pop a threat to the established order, either by direct communist conspiracy or by simple moral degeneracy. The Reverend David Noebel once wrote,

> The Beatles' ability to make teenagers take off their clothes and riot is laboratory tested and approved. It is scientifically labelled mass hypnosis and artificial neurosis.[14]

This power, Noebel concludes, is part of a communist 'master plan' to subvert 'all age brackets of American youth'. However, Cold War delusions of this kind are much less interesting than the process by which the right wing has allied itself with popular music in the US.

Although folk music has been used to provide a medium for the right's traditional nationalism, it has been country music that is most commonly linked with the right. Country songs have been used to give voice to right-wing views on such issues as Vietnam, the teaching of Darwinism, bussing, federal government, taxes and race. Country music has also accompanied the campaigns of right-wing southerners like Lester Maddox and George Wallace. The Klu Klux Klan went much further in their attempt to link music and politics. Not only did they sponsor fiddling competitions to attract crowds to outdoor meetings, they also founded their own record company in the 1920s. Its catalogue, according to Nick Tosches, included such items as 'Why I am a Klansman' and 'Wake Up America and Kluck, Kluck, Kluck'.[15]

But why have country music and the right coexisted like this? The obvious explanation is that country music is the native music of the right's southern white constituency. But social conditions and political views do not simply translate into musical form. The transposition depends on the character of both the politics and the music. The populist element of the politics is as important as the adaptability and appropriateness of the music.

Country emphasizes the voice. The lyrics are easily comprehensible; and in the space allowed to them, it becomes possible to address a whole variety of subjects. These features do not dispose country to fit any particular ideological position. The specific links with the right are a consequence of the sounds and associations which help define the music. Country music works with a sense of history: the present can only be understood by reference to the past. Rock, by comparison, celebrates the moment only. Country also addresses an audience for whom age and fate – the sense that life is beyond your control – are important realities. The rock audience is younger and less attuned to disillusionment. The sense of community is stronger too in country. The rock community is just an audience. Seeing racial integration as the action of unsympathetic, northern politicians, seeing yourself and your community as the victims of an unfeeling, all-powerful central government, creates an attitude upon which country music can work, using its mournful evocation of fate, of embattled communities and its sense of loss. Only because the issue takes a particular form can the music work; and only because the music adopts a particular sound and style can the politics work. The explanation for the connection cannot be couched in political and sociological terms; there must be a musicological element (see chapter 10). The superficiality of the British right's relationship with popular music has as much to do with the musical resources available to them as to the paucity of their political analysis. It is interesting, therefore, to ask whether the same is true of the British left.

The Socialist Left

The Rock Against Racism campaign, benefit gigs for the miners, John Lennon's 'Power to the People' or the Redskins' 'Unionize', all of these would seem to indicate that, in Britain, the left has many links with popular music. When these examples are taken with the traditional ties between the labour movement and popular song, it is easy to conclude that there is a 'natural fit' between socialism and popular music. The truth is, of course, more complex, as is revealed by socialist attitudes to pop itself.

Many socialists regard pop as either trivial or exploitative. These views typically divide between those who are devotees of socialist realism (and favour folk music) and those who are loyal to high culture (and favour classical music). There is a third version of the argument, represented by anarchism. In a pamphlet called *The End of Music*, an anarchist group launch an attack on popular music and, ultimately, all forms of music. Their particular target is punk, precisely because of its associations in the popular mind with radical causes and frustrated, unemployed youth. Punk, argues *The End of Music*, reinforced a spirit of desperation; it did nothing to provide liberation from it. Punk clung parasitically upon real frustrations; the appearance of anger avoided the reality of exploitation:

> Punk is the admission that music has got nothing left to say but money can still be made out of total artistic bankruptcy with all its surrogate substitute for creative self-expression in our daily lives. Punk music, like all art, is the denial of the revolutionary becoming of the proletariat.[16]

Punk used the rhetoric of the working class to deceive that class. It is not just the music industry that is responsible for this process; musicians are accused of failing to challenge the organization of 'musical capital'. Music is treated by everyone as a commodity, and as such it serves the status quo only. A similar argument has been deployed by socialist musicians who believed that experimental, non-commercial music was the only way to make music which advanced the causes of progress and communism; any other music supported regress and fascism. In the early 1970s, Peoples Liberation Music used to involve their audience in discussion in an attempt to demystify their music.

Other socialists tend to take a more pragmatic view of popular music. I remember attending a seminar on the politics of popular music at which an earnest member of the Communist Party asked the speakers to give him a list of records suitable for a Young Communist disco. Like his Soviet colleagues, he was not just interested in records that were good to dance to, but in ones that raised the dancers' political consciousness. It was requests like this that caused Johnny Rotten/John Lydon to remark: 'Those hard line lefties have always hated rock music. They despise it, they're just using it.'[17] But not all the left is either as dismissive as the anarchists or as crudely instrumental as some members of the British Communist Party in their view of popular music.

Rather than discounting all popular music, socialists discriminate between types of popular music. 'Authenticity' and 'realism' are among the most common standards used. Popular music is 'good' if it has genuine working-class roots or if it avoids the taint of commercial exploitation or if it paints an accurate picture of reality. The argument runs like this:

> Music, like any other art produced within capitalist society, is consciously or unconsciously affirmative of bourgeois ideology unless it somehow succeeds in subverting or making visible this ideology.[18]

What this means in practice is best illustrated by a single case, the Socialist Workers Party (SWP), a Trotskyist group bent upon building a revolutionary consciousness out of existing struggles.

The SWP's political strategy inclines it to link with all populist movements that seem to offer possible recruits to the socialist cause. Hence its involvement with Rock Against Racism and the movement's magazine, *Temporary Hoarding*. For the SWP, one question is uppermost: what does a particular trend or style represent in terms of political consciousness or political change? Under this kind of analysis, pop can either be 'plastic dross' (Abba, Olivia Newton-John), or bourgeois ('white funksters' like Spandau Ballet), or radical (The Beat or Gil Scott-Heron). These judgements are responses to the commitment of the artist or the character of the audience, rather than the sound of the music. When a performer like Adam Ant's brief career took him from punk politics to showbusiness stardom, he is seen to sell out musically *and* politically. The road from Rock Against Racism gigs to shows in West End theatres is the road to political reaction, from a politically conscious following to an audience that resembled a 'young SDP fancy dress ball'. Adam Ant swapped 'dangerous electricity, no toilets, no changing facilities, . . . and £10 for a night's work for four people and a roadie and a hire van' for appearances on *Top of the Pops* and for the opportunity to shake hands with the Queen.[19] Artistic and political integrity are linked, and together they are tied to the idea of independence from capitalist enterprise. Good music is music made from the results of struggle and suffering, and away from the world of 'capitalist entertainment'. Musical criticism, on this account, becomes a branch of political biography. Gil Scott-Heron is hailed as the maker of 'revolutionary records' and as the composer of 'the greatest jazz-funk ever laid on vinyl' because of his lyrics and his personal political commitment. His music is radical, the argument goes, because he is radical. Rock musicians are judged as political activists. Take this tribute to the Clash:

> In 1977 the Clash talked militant, played benefits, sang about unemployment and riots, complete control and fightback, and stood their ground whilst outside the demoralisation set in, the downturn began to bite.[20]

Music and musicians are valued in terms of their contribution to a previously identified and specifically located political struggle. Music contributes to the fight, but is not part of it. And its contributions are measured by the topics it addresses, by the commitment of the musicians, and by the character of the audience. For the SWP, it often seems as if lyrics are manifestos, groups are cadres, and the audiences are movements.

Not all SWP analysis follows this line. Traditional leftist suspicion of mass-produced Western music, and its corollary, enthusiasm for local folk culture, are questioned by Noel Halifax, who argues that ideas of 'folk' or 'national' culture have, despite appearances, reactionary features. Emphasis on 'authentic' ethnic music can be used either to reinforce Western ideas of the 'exotic' character of oppressed peoples or less developed countries. It can also divide national workers by imposing false boundaries on their common experiences of exploitation by multinational capitalism. Popular music, it follows, can serve as one basis for the emergence of transnational comradeship amongst urban proletariats. In a similar vein, David Widgery argues that pop music also allows socialists to go beyond reliance on 'the printed word and the public procession'. With pop, and particularly with records like the Sex Pistols' 'Anarchy in the UK' and the Specials' 'Ghost Town', political argument can become part of everyday life. Music can communicate, educate and motivate; it can be a force for 'extraordinary emancipation'. Looked at this way, music is not assessed in terms of what the lyrics say, or what the performer believes; instead, it is a matter of what the music represents and expresses. Popular music becomes 'an example of working class creativity in their struggle against passivity and alienation'; disco is, 'like it or not, a form through which hundreds of working class kids express themselves'.[21]

However, for all its criticism of 'folk-ist' views of music, and for all its delight in the sound of rock music itself, this version of the SWP's line still rests on traditional assumptions about both politics and music. Not only does it asssume that capitalism and the proletariat have some basic universal form, it also assumes that popular music is a direct expression of the oppressed. While it may be true that some kinds of folk music do emerge from particular struggles, it is also true that our ability to identify these instances depends on the direct, visible link between the struggle and the music. In *Absolute Beginners*, Colin MacInnes gently mocks left 'folkism':

> This Ron Todd is a Marxist, and closely connected with the ballad-and-blues movements, which seek to prove that all folk music is an art of protest . . . [and] that this art is somehow latched on to the achievements of the USSR, i.e., Mississippi jail songs are in praise of sputniks.[22]

As soon as the nature of the political issues becomes confused and as soon as other factors (record companies, studio technologies, broadcasters) are involved in the making and distribution of the music, the links become blurred.

The difficulties are most neatly highlighted by the problem of musical criticism: what distinguishes the good from the bad in music? when are we hearing the sound of 'working class creativity'? The answer tends to come in the familiar language of SWP politics . . . and the sophistication of the sympathetic approach is lost. Music is assessed in the same way as political movements: how closely do leaders/musicians represent their members/audience – 'It is this direct contact with the fans and bands that can give music such political relevance.'[23] The politics of the music becomes linked (and confused) with the occasion at which it is performed – Ray Charles singing at a Civil Rights demonstration or Steel Pulse playing at a Rock Against Racism rally somehow make the performance 'radical'. But as another member of the SWP, Dave Harker, once asked, does singing 'White Christmas' at a striking miners' benefit make it a radical song?

Similar doubts are raised by the SWP's tendency to attribute political meaning to a music's form and associations. While musical innovation may be no guarantee of political insight, a style of music (country or heavy metal) which fails to change, or a new style which is commercialized, are labelled conservative and reactionary. Disco music, for all its popularity with working-class kids, is observed to 'gloss over the real social position of blacks'; and discos are implicitly criticized for putting the emphasis on 'escapism, not on rebellion, on consumerism rather than challenging the system'.[24] Underlying these comments is the expectation that pop should be 'enlightening', and that it should be judged by its ability to describe reality. Polemics about the need to fight racism, argues Widgery polemically, are redundant 'after Steel Pulse had played 'Klu Klux Klan' '.[25] But this judgement seems to confuse musical meaning and political argument.

A song, however powerful its performance, cannnot win an argument. The song is a mixture of sounds, references and images; its meaning cannot be stated in the same way that a political view can be articulated. Understanding 'Klu Klux Klan' involves more than agreeing with its lyrics. The song does more and less than any conventional piece of political analysis. When Widgery lists his least favoured brands of music – 'depressing band-wagons of near-rapist heavy metal music, vogues for arty nihilism and . . . militant flippancy, . . . and pseudo-Latin vocalists keener on getting down and boogying than standing up and fighting'[26] – he is itemizing his own particular political values, his own opposition to sexism, nihilism, egoism, hedonism and cowardice. However reasonable these judgements are, they do not constitute an analysis of the sound itself. We can agree with the politics without in any way being committed to the musical assessment. The meaning of the music is not determined by the politics of the party. The categories and language used to describe music do not coincide with those used to analyse and organize politics. When Steel Pulse compose their songs, and when David Widgery writes of the need to oppose racism, they may share a goal but they are engaged in different activities, with different questions to resolve: how does it sound, how does it read?

The problems socialists encounter in making political sense of popular music are most sharply focused and most interestingly revealed not by socialist music critics, but by socialist musicians. They show how what goes down easily on paper comes out awkwardly in concert or on record. As Tom Robinson, a musician associated with Rock Against Racism and socialist causes, explained, political commitment and musical creativity are uneasy companions:

> Well, the danger, which I walked straight into with TRB [the Tom Robinson Band] was becoming a kind of *Socialist Worker* set to music. And I ended up . . . well, being backed into a corner. I was getting letters that actually said, Dear Comrade, we notice that you have not yet written a song to commemorate the murder of Comrade Peach by the imperialist forces of reactionary . . . honestly, I mean *heavy* letters. And at the same time cynics in the music biz were saying, uh huh, Blair Peach is dead, bet Tom Robinson'll write a song about *that*. So . . . If I wrote the song, it was tokenist. If I didn't it was a cop out.[27]

Robinson resolved the conflict by shifting the focus of his politics and the style of his music. The songs became more personal, the politics less hectoring.

The same solution is not available to the socialist with a particular ideological and party allegiance. Although there are not many musicians with this problem (see chapter 7), there are two interesting examples to consider: Leon Rosselson and Chris Dean. Both are radical socialists (Rosselson belongs to the left of the Labour Party and Dean to the SWP), both have written about the links between politics and music (Chris Dean as X. Moore or Chris Moore), and both are musicians. The important difference between them is not their politics, but how they combine their political and musical lives, and how this is reflected in the styles of music they adopt – Rosselson is a solo singer-guitarist and Dean is a member of a rock band, the Redskins.

Leon Rosselson: A Folk Socialism

In some ways, Leon Rosselson's views on pop and rock recall generations of parents who complain about the noise and the inaudibility of the words. For him, pop, as opposed to folk, is of little value to socialists; it is more likely to turn their brains into 'instant mashed potato' than to enliven them. But Rosselson's argument is not as unsympathetic to popular music as it first seems. He does not, for example, share the views of the former General Secretary of the British Communist Party who saw pop music as just another weapon in the armoury of US capitalist culture:

> Cowboys and indians; country and western; horror comics; Coca-Cola; juke boxes; rock; ten-pin bowling; bingo; electric guitars; flower power; American-speaking disc-jockeys; Radios 1 and 2.[28]

Nor should Rosselson be confused with those who see the 'politics' of pop music as nothing more than a clever marketing strategy or as another twist in fashion's cynical path. Rosselson believes that there is something called 'socialist music', and that not all rhythms beat time to capitalism. But creating it depends on meeting two conditions. Firstly, it means avoiding the tentacles of the music business; it is a hopeless task to try and take it on:

> For socialist musicians to challenge this industry with their creativity and their music and still survive on their terms seems to me as likely as walking on the water in a thunderstorm.

Secondly, the music has to be of a kind that

> gives space to the hearers to think for themselves, that involves words rather than sounds, that asks questions rather than provides answers, that allows for some humour, humanity, gentleness, subtlety, wit, irony, thoughtfulness, allusiveness, silence.[29]

In short, socialist music cannot be rock music because that is inextricably bound to the industry. Rather it must be music which uses simple instrumentation, which emphasizes the voice and the lyrics, and provides 'space' for thought and argument.

Rosselson combines his understanding of politics with his appreciation of the limits of popular music. The political demands of socialism cannot be satisfied by the musical format of most commercial popular music. Socialism has to fight ingrained prejudices and assumptions, and conversion to it takes time and patience. Pop and rock do not allow for this; their impact is slight and swift; they allow no space for thought and exploration. They can only 'make statements, rhyme arguments or chant slogans'.[30] Furthermore, rock depends on high technology for its performance and recording; these technical requirements force musicians into the arms of the record companies, which in turn leads to putting commercial success above artistic intergrity. These limitations are compounded by the character of pop's audience. Pop is for the young at play, but, for Rosselson, socialism is made for and by organized labour at work. So commercial pop is incapable of discussing socialism and of addressing socialists. Only folk – or music which is neither commercialized nor dependent on high technology – can perform for socialism because only it can be democratic, relevant and subversive.

Rosselson's resolution of the tension between politics and popular music is not, however, an unqualified advocacy of folk. He is no friend of 'protest' music; because of its tendency to acknowledge no view other than the singer's, it lectures the listener and leaves them no 'space'. The same point is made by Greil Marcus, who wrote of protest songs, 'they refuse to allow the listener to make any decisions'. A song was 'right', not 'good': 'there isn't any way you can talk about "digging" a protest song – first off, you had to agree with it'.[31] For Rosselson and Marcus, good music works through its ability to converse, not to berate; the opportunities it leaves for argument and imagination, ambiguity and exploration. Effective (i.e. popular) socialist music explores the doubts and confusions of its listeners; it does not give answers, it shares problems.

The same argument, with interestingly different conclusions, can be heard elsewhere within the socialist movement, where the tyranny of rock is not to be replaced by a different music, but is to be reorganized from within. This approach is most evident in the work of feminist writers and musicians. Their concern has been, like Rosselson, with the sound of the music, but for them the question has been whether rock is irrevocably 'male' in its sounds and its styles. Is it the case, as one critic argued, that in dispensing with drums, the Young Marble Giants 'proved once and for all you don't have to make macho noises to be interesting'?[32] Women musicians have found different answers to this question. They have, for example, found new ways to play drums – by redistributing the kit and by using the drums to carry a melody. A similar challenge has been directed at many other traditional rock ideas. The Raincoats, for instance, tried to undermine rock assumptions about the priority given to the voice over other instruments. In doing so they managed to expose and upset a range of preconceived ideas about the relationship between a band, a song and an audience. As Sue Steward wrote, 'in common with other instrumentalists in rock, they [women musicians] are not willing to be dictated to by a tradition of sweat and unsublety which they didn't help to create'.[33] Their efforts are part of an attempt to alter the meaning of rock, not by giving it a new set of (socialist/radical/feminist) lyrics, but by altering the sound itself. Where Rosselson looks back to pre-rock forms, these artists are working at post-rock forms. Both, though, are critical of the idea that rock itself is capable of carrying their message. These approaches contrast starkly with those which use an unrevised rock format to convey their socialism.

Chris Dean: Rock Socialism

Like Rosselson, Chris Dean is a passionately committed socialist. But unlike Rosselson, he sings and plays guitar in the Redskins. Using the familiar format of guitar, bass and drums, and drawing on punk and Tamla Motown for inspiration, the Redskins sing in a spirit of comradely exhortation – 'Unionize', 'Lean on Me', 'Kick over the Statues'. Chris Dean said of his band, 'we're not just toytown rebellion. We're the sort of people who should be shot'.[34] These politics are in the style and the lyrics, rather than the sound. Hearing the Redskins for the first time on record, it is possible, if you fail to decipher the lyrics or catch the chants, to miss the politics. But seeing them live during the 1984–5 miners' strike you would have little doubt about the politics. It is there in obvious ways – the back of the stage plastered with 'Coal Not Dole' posters, and the song introductions ('the miners' fight is our fight'). The politics of the music became the politics of the miners' strike; politics and music were linked in a single slogan, a single sentiment, 'no sell out'.

Musicians, the Redskins imply, have the same duty to their followers as socialist and labour leaders have to theirs. They must not flinch from the truth, and they must not compromise. A band, argues Chris Dean, should have 'a cohesive drive'; musicians should not 'wallow', and we should all 'expect the world of everyone'. Bands should not waste time with photo-sessions; instead they should give interviews in which they talk about 'life in all its wonderful glories'. Reporting a meeting with the Redskins, Adrian Thrills wrote, 'The talk is mostly of tactics, of *how* a blunt and unequivocal and political standpoint can best be projected from a rock'n'roll platform'. For Dean, music-making and politics are public activities which both aim to create a community with a common identity and a common set of interests. Dean does not try to entertain his audience; he needles, challenges and unites them. He does not see his audience as a group of people linked by age and leisure. Youth, like style, is 'ephemeral' – 'It's not concrete reality, it's too abstract'. A band has to lead and be loyal to an audience united by their political interests. The band has to become, for Dean, a show of '*collective* strength' in which its audience can share. They have to play a music that must not just challenge by criticism but by offering hope. Dean makes no distinction between the populism of his politics and the popularity of his music.[35]

It is the politics that sets the standards for the music. Understanding the Redskins' sound involves understanding their belief that politics is essentially about the relationship between classes, not individuals. The Redskins don't write love songs. Asked if he'd ever written one, Chris Dean said: 'No! I don't want to bore people with details of my personal relationships.' For the Redskins, what defines both rock's responsibilities and politics' concerns are what happen in public:

> What really guides The Redskins is the political situation . . . We try and sing about whatever is at the forefront of current political debate and at the moment that is the confrontation between the government and the working class. We're not a little band that live in our little world.[36]

The Redskins use rock because of its public power and for its ability to carry a slogan. Just as 'We'll never walk alone' unites football fans, so the Redskins' rock is intended to give a sense of identity and strength. The Redskins try to build a political solidarity out of a musical community. Where Rosselson looks to the politics of private doubt and argument, the Redskins look to the politics of public certainty and action. And where Rosselson looks to a folk style for its ability to allow for the questions in his politics, the Redskins look to rock for the platform it allows to their defiant answers. In seeing rock and politics like this, as propaganda rather than argument, the Redskins not only set themselves apart from folk socialists like Rosselson but also from those rock socialists who want to modify the musical form of rock. The Redskins are interested only in using it.

What is interesting, however, is the way that their exclusive concern with public issues, and their insistence on turning their audience into comrades, can work against their ability to communicate. There is no room for the ambiguity and doubt which Rosselson argued was essential to effective socialist politics and which others say is crucial to good music. Simon Frith once suggested that this problem is captured in Chris Dean's singing.[37] Dean's voice is used to declaim the certainties of his politics; in doing so, there is no room for exploring the realities and myths that fuel those politics. The doubts, confusions, and difficulties which underlie the rhetoric and which form the bridge between audience and singer, are sacrificed in the use of a voice that belongs to the political meeting. At the meeting, the speaker is preaching to the converted who want to know that they are right. At the concert, the band is singing to the politically confused who need to be convinced. And for this, you have to begin with their doubts and intuitions; you cannot hand out your convictions.

Because concerts and meetings are not identical, and because rock and politics do not fit exactly, compromises are necessary. Populism and popularity are not automatically compatible, and it is, therefore, necessary to 'sell out' in order to sing out. Something has to give. Billy Bragg, who toured with the Redskins, has had greater popular success subsequently. Though there is a musical explanation for this, there is also a political one. As Bragg said of the Redskins, 'They have a revolutionary path, I have an evolutionary path.'[38] Bragg belongs to the Labour Party, and Labour's gradualism is more conducive to rock's musical conventions.

On stage alone, with only an electric guitar for company, Bragg might be mistaken for one of Rosselson's socialist folk singers (he has even recorded one of Rosselson's songs). However, he thinks of himself as a rock musician, not just because of the punk thrash of his guitar playing, or his avowed suspicion of folk, but because of his relationship with his audience. The audience share in the illusion that there is actually a drummer and a bass player up on stage. Bragg describes his own performance:

> When I go out [on stage], I still think I'm the Clash. And I think I've got a band behind me, and I should make as much fucking racket as that.[39]

Bragg and his audience enjoy a common fantasy about the kind of event they are at. The audience become a community through their imagination. It is not a community based on some collective class consciousness or some shared political understanding; but this does not mean that politics become irrelevant. It is just that politics must come in a particular form, mixing uncertainty and ambiguity. It is the politics of 'which side are you on?' or of 'there are two sides to every story'; it is not the simple politics of protest: they are wrong, we are right. Bragg tries to engage his audience, not lecture them. He uses the personal relationships that Dean dismisses to give us a picture of his 'New England'– 'I don't want to change the world/I'm not looking for a new England/I'm just looking for another girl.' His music draws together the personal and the political. He can play to an audience that does not necessarily share his views – 'you want people who don't agree with you to listen'.[40] Both his politics and his music are, in this sense, reformist. Bragg is not alone in his approach. Ranking Ann's 'Kill the Police Bill' was given a dance beat with the deliberate intention of getting it across to people not normally interested in politics.

The doubts that Bragg plays on may be anathema to Dean and the Redskins, but to be effective musically there may only be certain kinds of politics that can be addressed. Crudely, socialism and rock can be linked, but it is an alliance marked by compromise, by a recognition that the relationship between audience and popular music is importantly different to that between political activists and political change. It's a tension which sometimes the Redskins seem to recognize, but which they can only resolve through the SWP, not through rock: 'playing in a band', says Chris Dean, 'you are bound to get politically frustrated, because rock and roll can never achieve enough.'[41] Bragg's frustrations are different and perhaps more easily resolved, partly because of his politics, and partly because he recognizes that only certain musical forms can carry the message, and only certain messages can be relayed.

As the miners' strike came to dominate British politics through the winter of 1984–5, people were forced to take sides; there was no alternative. Bragg was caught up in this too. He played benefit concerts all over the country, and as he did so, his music seemed to change. The ambiguities and doubts of 'New England' were replaced by an air of certainty and resolution. The songs on his 'Between the Wars' EP captured his (and the country's) new mood; and they did so by adopting a folk sound and style.

Not only does Bragg's change of style suggest a connection between musical form and political content, it also suggests that the political context in which the music is made determines how it is heard and how effective it is. 1984–5 was a good year for the Redskins. But their musical career may be much shorter than Bragg's because their success has been tied to the miners' strike; the NUM's defiance made sense of the Redskins' politics. The problems in their music were compensated for by its context. The Redskins may fail to convert people to SWP socialism, but they provided a brilliant soundtrack to a particular political struggle. Where there is no such backdrop to focus the music, then the sounds themselves, and the ideas associated with them, may be lost as the audience draws its pleasure from being just that, a mere audience, musical tourists, not witnesses to a struggle between right and wrong. Rock seems unable to sustain the political communities it creates; the rhetoric seems to fracture from the rhythm. But not all popular music in all circumstances is like this; sometimes the rhythm has a rhetoric of its own.

4

Moving to the Music

Between Christmas 1984 and Summer 1985, three charity records were at No. 1 in the charts in the US and the UK. Each one – Band Aid's 'Do they Know it's Christmas?', USA for Africa's 'We are the World', and Mick Jagger and David Bowie's 'Dancing in the Street' – was made to raise money for the victims of starvation in Africa. Musicians all over the world had also joined in, making records for their national markets to raise more funds. There have been countless benefit concerts, of which Live Aid is just the most famous. Together they raised sums of money which almost dwarfed the Foreign Aid budgets of some countries. The Band Aid single alone raised £7 million.

Not all charity records are this successful. On the same shop shelves that were laden down with copies of 'Do they Know it's Christmas?', there were two other charity records: the Council Collective's 'Soul Deep' and the Enemy Within's 'Strike'. They were made to raise money for striking miners in their year-long dispute with the National Coal Board and the British government. Neither record made such impression on the charts, and the sums they raised were small in comparison with Band Aid. 'Strike' collected £1,332.

Why did these different records with their different causes, but with the same purposes (to raise money and awareness), meet with such different degrees of success? The answer seems to lie both in the character of the cause and in the nature of the music. The medium and the political message appear to be inseparably linked. A good cause is no guarantee of good, and hence effective music. The question is, therefore, about how some forms of politics match with some forms of music. Where in the last chapter we saw the (often cynical) use of music by political activists, this chapter examines some of the ways causes and chords, music and movements, have become united without deliberate intervention.

The British labour movement's struggle for trade union rights and decent working conditions has been charted and accompanied by popular music of all kinds. A typical song is 'The Colliers' March', written in 1782:

> The times were oppressive and, well it be known,
> That hunger will strongest of fences break down.

The US labour movement boasts a similar tradition. The Wobblies (formally known as the Industrial Workers of the World) used song in their attempt to organize US labour at the beginning of this century. Recalling how a group of Wobblies walked from Montana to Chicago to appear at an IWW convention, Melvyn Dubofsky wrote:

> These Westerners sang their way across Montana, eating in the 'jungles', preaching revolution in the prairie towns they beseiged, and singing constantly. Walsh [their leader] conceded that the Industrial Union Singing Club's lyrics 'may not be as scientifically revolutionary as some would like, but it certainly has its psychological effect upon the poor wage slave'.[1]

Ralph Chaplin, a prolific writer of Wobbly poetry and songs, explained his song, 'Solidarity Forever': it was meant to be 'full of revolutionary fervour and to have a chorus that was ringing and defiant'.[2] The songs drew their power from being sung together, which was why they often borrowed familiar tunes from hymns or popular songs.

The music served a variety of purposes: it united the singers, it distinguished them from their enemies, it encouraged them, and it communicated the movement's values. Movements and their causes, almost by definition, are the object of great hostility and are often denied access to established channels of influence. Songs can help to strengthen resolve and create a sense of community. The Wobblies, whose ambition was to found One Big Union, came from very different backgrounds – there were socialists, anarchists, revolutionaries and trade unionists – and the songs provided a bridge which conventional rhetoric could not always build. And where communication is specifically denied or actively discouraged, then song provides an alternative form of language. This was the case with the slaves who sang to set the pace of their work, to satirize their masters, and to scold their colleagues. Slave songs had their own code and vocabulary, which created barriers against the intrusion of the slave-owners. The slave's singing became 'political' by its use and its context, without its politics ever being the result of the self-conscious deliberations of political activists. The songs, both in the slave community and the labour movements, take on a political meaning as a consequence of the immediate political experience and needs of the performers and their audience. The music does not substitute for the politics, but seems to be integrated into it.

The populist character of political movements, taken together with the particular difficulties that they and their causes face, points them towards popular song. Music is not just used as a matter of convenience, as the most easily available tool; there is also an element of reciprocity: both the music and movement benefit from their mutual dependence. Gospel music is a classic example of this reciprocity, but to see its full significance, it pays to see the way other forms of music and other religious practices fail to integrate sound with sentiment.

Praising the Lord

Music is used for celebrating most religions. However, it is perfectly possible to be a practising Anglican without uttering a note: celebrating the Anglican faith does not depend on *Hymns Ancient and Modern*. Strange though it may seem, this has interesting consequences for the role of popular music among Anglicans. Anything goes; the only limits are those established by taste or propriety. Somehow, in church, the strum of a folk guitar is acceptable, but the feedback of an electric guitar is not. The choice of music is only tangentially connected to the act of worship. Neither the religion nor the music are called upon to change significantly, because the rites of worship are already established and the sounds are merely appended to them.

At a religious pop festival in the UK, musicians sung of their beliefs in a variety of musical forms. The most peculiar example was a heavy metal band, who appeared to have no difficulty in singing of God while using their guitars in an unashamedly secular, phallic fashion. The only concession to God was in the lyrics, although here too He was harangued in much the same way as Thin Lizzy announced that 'the boys are back in town'. The music was merely a vehicle for conveying the religious sentiments. No connection was made, and no tension perceived, between the meanings implicit in the music and those explicitly stated in the lyrics. Yet rock in general, and heavy metal in particular, seems to establish little common ground with religion. Rock's focus is on the individual, its sexual imagery is concerned with male conquest and adolescent angst, and its obsession is the moment and immediate gratification. Religion offers sacrifice and redemption (deferred gratification), and regards sex with suspicion. The integration of protestantism into popular music requires more than the addition of suitably reverential lyrics because the whole character of the music seems to work against the ways of worship. Or to put to it the other way round, rock only allows for certain kinds of ideas and attitudes.

Religious imagery is scattered throughout rock, most noticeably perhaps in the music of Big Country, U2, and Bruce Springsteen. Springsteen's 'Adam Raised a Cain' and Big Country's 'Harvest Home' ('as ye sow, so shall ye reap') use the language of religion to convey their meaning, but they are not in the business of conversion. The religious allusions are devices for capturing a spirit which owes little to church, and much to the images of rock; they borrow the other-worldliness of religion to evoke the myth of the rock community, freed from time and responsibility, living through the music. Religious ideas of good and evil are employed to validate the pleasures of the audience, not to enjoin them to renounce sin. In his live show, Springsteen acts out a version of Satan's temptation, except he gives the devil the best offer, a pink Cadillac. None of these performers use their music as an act of worship, even where they are, in the case of U2, practising Christians. Religion's place is determined by the demands of the music; they are not equal partners. And, as we have seen, where rock artists do use the music to convey religious commitment, both the music and the faith suffer. Only in gospel do religion and music have equal status.

When Capital Radio organized a gospel competition, they used Cliff Richard as a judge and the winners were the opening act for Al Green's 1984 concert in the Albert Hall. What the winners (and Capital Radio) meant by 'gospel' was clearly pop music (Duran Duran style) with religious lyrics. It was not what either the London Community Choir, the other supporting act, or Al Green might recognize as gospel. The important distinctions lay in the way black gospel fuses music and religious celebration. Gospel, whose influence can be heard throughout black music, is church music; but it is not just music to be sung in a particular building. It is the sound of prayer and has its origins in 'the musical practices of the slave "invisible church" '.[3] The sound of gospel emerged from the way preacher and congregation extemporized around the themes of Protestant hymns. The sounds of praise were defined by the music and created by each church. The call-and-response of the music were the call-and-response of preacher and congregation. Form and content were integrated, without ever becoming the exclusive province of the church. Gospel's sounds have been able to take on a wealth of meanings because there is no literal meaning to be taken. 'Black religious music', writes Simon Frith, 'articulates religious awe and fervour through an apparently spontaneous struggle *against* words'.[4] The release promised by religion and that delivered by sex are easily confused; both deal in ecstacy. Al

Green's love of God doesn't *sound* that different from his love of women.

Gospel forms have been integrated into black politics. When Jesse Jackson sought the 1984 Democratic Presidential nomination, he did not make speeches so much as conduct services. Jonathan Raban describes a church meeting in Memphis addressed by black candidate for Mayor, Otis Higgs:

> Higgs's speech wasn't his alone: it belonged to all of us. Everyone was helping it along. Some were clapping its rhythm on the off-beat; others were providing punctuation marks for it with their *Amens* and *Yes, sirs*; the organist was turning it, line by line, from talk into music. The whole event was more of an improvised service than a political address.[5]

But if black politics have a gospel element, then gospel has a black political element. In her book, *Black Gospel*, Viv Broughton describes how the Clark Sisters casually drop the line 'God's economics beat Reagonomics' into a gospel song. This ability, says Broughton, is characteristic of gospel music, and part of what distinguishes it from white religious music:

> When gospel singers open their mouths to 'make a joyful noise unto the Lord' they sing out of an experience of salvation but they also sing out of an experience of being cheated and downgraded as all black people have been. White Christians tend to sing and speak from the other side of the fence, with their vision impaired.[6]

More generally, what gospel demonstrates is the way in which popular music and politics can be integrated; it is the example against which other links between music and politics can be judged.

Flower Power: Music as the Movement

Rock music has its own rites and rituals, but they do not spring from the same source, or have the same politics, as gospel. In his book *The Death and Resurrection Show*, Rogan Taylor links rock stardom and rock performance to a quite different religion, shamanism. Like the shaman, the rock star, says Taylor, provides a vision of the mystical pleasures and powers of heaven and hell, in a world where science and technology seem to deny the existence of both.[7] Whether Taylor is right about rock's shamanism, he draws attention to the strangely 'religious' character of the links between fans and performers; and contained within the bond are the ingredients of rock's political uses.

The Flower Power or underground or counterculture movement of the late 1960s was conceived as a politicized rock audience. The music was the means by which people were brought together and through which they expressed their common identity. The politics dissolved into the music:

> The bands, pure primal power, our first deities, the sources of our new myths, metaphors, and anecdotes. If there was any social organization in the Haight in those days, it was that of a big, anarchistic family, with the bands as a sort of primal father and we as happy, naive children.[8]

For a variety of personal and political reasons, the movement's members resisted the appeals of formal organization – even to describe it as a 'political movement' is to attribute to it a purpose and self-consciousness that it neither possessed nor sought. But almost precisely because of the movement's vagueness, rock music came to play a central role. It voiced the sentiments and forged the links that any movement needs, but which this particular one could not generate by conventional political means. The movement's politics (or anti-politics) made possible the prominence of the music and the musicians. The movement found its most lasting symbol in Woodstock, a free festival of rock and collective pleasure, proof that music could turn an audience into a self-sufficient community. But it is all too easy to confuse the myth-making with the reality. Woodstock was also three days in a muddy field, without enough food or proper sanitation.

Woodstock's image owed as much to cynical calculation, media attention and the self-aggrandisement of the participants. The organizers seemed deliberately to exploit the romantic idealism that the music suggested. When the festival's title was being discussed, one of the impressarios came up with 'An Aquarian Exposition'. It was acclaimed:

> It's got everything. Nature, art, the counterculture, music, freedom, tripping – it's terrific. And it'll look great in the underground papers. It's got no Establishment ties to it.[9]

Later, when the discussion shifted to ticket prices, it was agreed that 'you've got to set a fair price, one that's going to turn a profit at the gate and yet won't offend the hippies'. When Woodstock was made a free festival, this was a consequence of administrative mistakes (the ticket booths were not built in time); it owed nothing to political commitment. The movement's own politics (or lack of them) had raised the music onto a pedestal, at which point the industry moved in to sustain the music's elevated position.

The hippies trust in the power of love and understanding, their belief that the world's problems were largely a result of 'attitudes' and ideas, explains the emphasis put on music (and drugs), but it also accounts for the movement's demise. It was no coincidence that the more hard-edged political movements like Black Power, or the more sharply focused anti-war campaign, both of which flourished at roughly the same time as the rise of Flower Power, were more politically effective, and less reliant on music and musicians. Any politics which relies on rock will be affected by the strengths and weaknesses of the music, as John Lennon discovered.

Lennonism: The Movement as Music

Lennon had very different dealings with the radical left in Britain and the US. Lennon's disillusionment with the hippy dream engendered a curiosity in politics generally, and a sympathy for left-wing causes in particular. While in England, he arranged meetings with Tariq Ali and Robin Blackburn, who were then prominent figures in the new marxist left in Britain. Lennon learnt about Marxism, appeared at demonstrations against the British presence in Northern Ireland, and gave money and interviews to radical papers like *Red Mole*.[10] When in New York, he continued his involvement in politics, but there he associated with the Yippies. There his political lessons came from Jerry Rubin and Abbie Hoffman (who had been two of the thirteen defendants accused of disrupting the 1968 Democratic Convention in Chicago), and from the radical street musician, David Peel. Just as in England, Lennon used these people as sounding boards for his ideas and sources for his political education. What is interesting, however, is that Lennon was much more at ease with the American brand of radicalism than with their British counterparts. One of Rubin's colleagues told Jon Wiener:

> Lennon always said he was more comfortable with us than with Tariq and Robin because our style of politics was similar to show business, which he was used to and could understand.[11]

Ali and Blackburn's International Marxist Group (IMG) had little sympathy for show business. The rigorously Marxist character of both the IMG's analysis and its organization left little opportunity for music to play anything other than a peripheral role. For the IMG, revolutions were not the result of spontaneous eruptions of popular feeling, but were a consequence of the deliberate strategies of a revolutionary elite. The IMG were, in this sense, avowedly anti-populist. In contrast, the Yippies, in so far as they had a political strategy, were determinedly populist and unrepentently destructive. They were not interested in building revolutionary cadres, but simply in destroying the established order, an order which they saw as being sustained by the media's ability to propagate certain ideas and values. They showed little interest in Marxist assumptions about power's location in the ownership of capital and its expression in class struggle. For the Yippies, power came out of a cathode ray tube. Lennon was more comfortable with a politics based on mass communications. 'Henry Ford knew how to sell cars by advertising,' Lennon once said, 'I'm selling peace'.[12] Just as Lennon felt more at home with Jerry Rubin than Tariq Ali, so the differences in the movements seemed to explain the differences in their emphasis on music. And if variations in political approach affected the emphasis placed on music, then the character of the music also influenced the form of the politics.

Punk and Rock Against Racism: Politics and Style

Once the hippies' trust in music's ability to set them free had been disabused, music's political significance would always be different but it would not necessarily disappear. Punk was proof of this. Here was the semblance of a political movement, organized around unemployment, whose voice was expressed almost exclusively through a series of angry three chord roars. Like Flower Power, the politics were vague, being more concerned with feelings than policies; and once again its vagueness was crucial both to the movement's popularity and to the role played by the music. In terms of organization (or lack of it) and in terms of political precision (or lack of it), punk and Flower Power were very similar, but the concerns of their politics and the quality of their sounds were importantly different. The benign hopes of Flower Power contrasted starkly with the disconsolate frustration of punk, a comparison that is reflected in the dreamy melodies and pastoral sentiments of psychedelic music, and in the staccato roar and defiant slogans of punk – 'No Fun', 'Pretty Vacant', 'Anarchy'. While Flower Power spoke of the alternatives to work, punk talked of the absence of work. But though these differences in style and content are easily observed, they do not explain how a particular sound connects with a particular politics. What these comparisons make clear is that the links between music and movements cannot be understood simply by exclusive reference to either politics or sounds. Although some forms of political organization and analysis provide more convivial lodgings for popular music than others, the type of music that fits in, and how it works, will depend on a variety of 'musical' factors.

The Rock Against Racism campaign, which brought together 80,000 people in Victoria Park, London, in 1977, illustrates the delicacy of the relationship between a cause and its music. RAR was started in 1976 to organize rock events to fight the spread of racism. The focus of the campaign was racism, but the vehicle for it was music. RAR was set up after Eric Clapton had made racist comments while performing in London. It was fitting, therefore, that it was music which gave expression to the politics, whether literally in specific songs (Steel Pulse's 'Rock Against Racism'), or visibly in the use of bands with black and white musicians (the Specials, UB40, the Beat), or physically in an audience singing 'black and white united tonight' and 'One-two-three and a bit, the National Front's a load of shit'.

Just as the Wobblies used songs to unite their disparate supporters, each with their own distinct political persuasions, so RAR brought together 'punks, rastas, gays, trade unionists, the Left'. But while in both cases music helped to bridge gaps between the supporters, the divisions were of very different kinds. For the Wobblies, the differences were explicitly political – anarchist versus socialist; for RAR, the divisions were stylistic – rock versus reggae, and, superficially at least, the political differences were either unrecognized or unimportant. It was almost as if the lack of any divisive internal politics, and the presence of considerable stylistic differences, forced the reliance on music. Where the Wobblies shared a commitment to direct action and spoke to each other in the language of politics (albeit in very different dialects), RAR united around their common language – music, and addressed their objective in these terms: they rocked against racism. For both movements their strengths and weaknesses lay in these facts about them. Crudely, what they won in unity they tended to lose in political effectiveness, and RAR's weakness was all the greater for their dependence on music. The paradox is that the RAR's relative fragility was not a result of political division (no one disagreed with its aims), but was a consequence of stylistic affiliation; the very lack of any politics was what led to the reliance on music as the source of unity and strength, making the differences more important. RAR's problem stemmed as much from musical meaning as political interpretation.

One such difficulty arose in 1981, when a concert was organized under the banner of 'Oi Against Racism'. Oi music had acquired links with racism, whether deliberately or by default. It had been an Oi gig that had provoked Asian youths into burning down the Hambrough Tavern in Southall, West London. Proponents of Oi, who defended it as working-class music, not white music, wanted to polish its tarnished image through links with RAR. But RAR were wary of such moves, and they turned down a suggestion for a gig under the RAR banner in Southall; the bill was to have included a reggae band, an Asian group, and the 4 Skins, who had been playing when the Hambrough had been set alight. RAR were suspicious of both the interests of the organizers and of the motives of the 4 Skins, and made their own counter-suggestion: an Anti-Racist Skinhead concert in Sheffield, where local skinheads had been vocal in their denunciation of racism. RAR also suggested that none of the Southall bands be involved, preferring an Oi group with proven support for RAR.

Very similar arguments occupied US versions of RAR. But there activists refused to ally the movement exclusively to punk. Punk appeared to be a predominantly white music which seemed, in phrases like 'Disco Sucks', to deride black music. For Boston RAR, it was important to use all forms of music in their anti-racism campaigns.

Political strategies and arguments were, therefore, played out and resolved in terms of musical choices. Musical images, affiliations and sounds were part of RAR's politics. And while some critics saw this as thwarting the movement's political impact, others regarded is as a real advantage; the music allowed RAR to 'capture people's imagination [and] not just make a lacklustre appeal to their consciences' – one of RAR's slogans was 'All power to the imagination'.[13] The argument reflected the tensions between musical popularity and ideological purity, between the power of the imagination and the power of direct action; it raised questions about what 'success' meant – what did it mean to have fun at an RAR gig? what did it achieve? Support for the National Front did decline, but it is not clear what contribution RAR made; what is clear is that while RAR illustrated the limitations of a politics organized around music, it also demonstrated a new way to involve politics in popular music: it created new roles and platforms for musicians, and it seemed to suggest new methods by which music could change the way people thought and acted. Its example stands, albeit slightly obscured, behind the subsequent use of popular music to raise money (rather than consciousness) for the victims of famine in Ethiopia.

Raising Money and Raising Consciousness

Band Aid's success with 'Do they Know it's Christmas?' owed much to both the cause and the way the appeal was made. Although the origins of the famine provoked much argument, few contended that raising money for those who suffered was wrong. There was agreement about the worthiness of the cause. And it was easy to contribute: for the musicians, it meant a day in the recording studio; for the public, it meant five minutes in the record shop. The largest sacrifice was made by the record companies who gave up their profits, although they gained favourable publicity for themselves and their artists in compensation. Band Aid raised few awkward questions of ideology, commitment and action. All of this was important to the project's success, but there was one final, crucial ingredient: the medium itself.

'Do they Know it's Christmas?', like the US equivalent, 'We are the World', was a pop song; Live Aid was a pop spectacle. Neither had much to do with the rock; and this mattered. Live Aid was not, despite Joan Baez's claim to the contrary, an 1980s Woodstock. Woodstock was a rock myth, a fantasy about the possibility of creating a self-sufficient musical community. However unreal its aspirations, however cynical its organization, Woodstock's success lay in its exclusiveness, the barriers it created between 'them' and 'us'. Woodstock was about being there. Live Aid created no such barriers, being there made no difference to the character of the event; it was just as important to watch it on television. The point of Live Aid was to attract as many viewers (donors) as possible. Rock's exclusivity works against such an ambition; pop, on the other hand, thrives on it. Pop works through its universalism – 'We are the World'. The choir format used by both the British and US records symbolized the communal, all-embracing spirit of the project. They were attempts to create a sense of global community, even if the techniques used did not always work. The tradition of gospel choirs that runs through US pop, argued Robert Christgau, is lacking in British pop, thereby diminishing Band Aid's musical effectiveness.[14] Similarly, the use of irony in 'Do they Know it's Christmas?' – 'Thank God it's them not us' – and the distinction between 'them' and 'us' that the song trades on, has been interpreted as complacency rather than compassion. But it can be countered that the passionate conviction of the voices obscured the ironies and distinctions in the song.

What also can be heard in the voices is a desperate sincerity which belies the idea that all we are hearing are the smug sounds of Western self-satisfaction. The singers' passion may owe something to their realization that singing and raising money are all they can do; the songs give expression to a sense of frustration and inadequacy as much as one of self-congratulation. Certainly, the popularity of the song needs to be explained musically as well as politically. And their effectiveness depends on how they work as music.

Because Band Aid was a pop event, it also becomes easier to talk about money. Rock disguises the money making side of the business, except to disparage it; pop makes money part of the show. Rock hides its wealth (Springsteen's tattered jeans); pop flaunts it (Elton John's diamond-studded glasses). Pop lacks any guilt about the money involved. It can simply demand it. When the Supremes played at 'Anglia for Africa', East Anglia's version of Live Aid, they inspired many more donations than the rock acts. Whether or not rock's concern about money, or its ability to give audiences a sense of collective identity, make it more exciting music than pop is beside the point. Given the cause and the campaign, pop provided the best method. As Midge Ure, one of the co-founders of Band Aid, said, 'All we're trying to do is get the money from A to B.'[15]

In contrast, the records released to raise money for the striking miners (by the Enemy Within and the Council Collective) met with dramatically less success. Support for the miners, just like support for RAR, needed more from their audience than a willingness to pay; backing the miners meant a show of commitment, however feeble. Where the media worked with Band Aid – Geldof's idea for a charity record came from watching a BBC News report from Ethiopia – it worked against the miners, not just by favouring the status quo, but by emphasizing the political conflict involved. Winning over an audience to the miners in such circumstances made considerable demands of the music and musicians. It was not just a matter of writing ideologically correct lyrics; the sound itself had to be persuasive. Why the Council Collective's song for the miners made little impression requires a musical explanation as well as a political one. 'Soul Deep' was a sullen, rather worthy record, whose dance beat worked much better than its lyrics ('Where is the backing from the TUC?'). It lacked the inspirational qualities of another profoundly political record, 'Free Nelson Mandela', by the Specials Aka. Political seriousness need not necessarily result in musical dullness.

'Free Nelson Mandela' was No. 1 in the British charts in 1984. It had an irresistable chorus which made it a great summer pop record, but its message was straightforwardly political. And its success as a record was dependent upon the way it treated the politics. The people who bought the record may not have known of the song's eponymous hero; but what knowledge they had would have disposed them favourably towards him – an ageing, brave victim of a cruel system. This natural sympathy was enhanced by the way the song concentrated on a lone individual and his unjust treatment; it was not about the African National Congress or about the morality of terrorism; it was not really about apartheid either. It was about a man, 'twenty-one years in captivity/his shoes too small to fit his feet'. The record, with its infectious chorus and its rousing horn riff, won the listeners immediately, and then made a brief, fragile political movement of them. Where a movement already exists, or where prejudices or feelings are already well established, as was the case with the miners' strike, then the music has less scope to work its own magic. The record then simply provides a service, an excuse for the faithful to get together. It confirms, it does not convert.

'Do they Know it's Christmas?' was a success as a record and for its cause; 'Soul Deep' failed on both counts; 'Free Nelson Mandela' was a musical triumph, but had no discernible political impact. What these examples confirm is that the nature of the cause and the character of the music are mutually dependent. The singer and songwriter, Ian Dury, remarked once, that a political song is likely to be 'a very ugly song', in which case it wouldn't work.[16] What makes a song 'ugly' is not just a matter of how it's written and performed, but also the circumstances in which it tries to work. The political context in which the song is played shapes the way it is heard. Where a song is used by a people already united by their politics, then it merely has to confirm their sense of unity. Where a song wants to encourage people to act in a particular way, then it depends on them *not* having any particular political commitment. Neither accords exactly with the example of gospel, where commitment and music are almost inseparable. The closest political parallel to gospel seems to exist in the meaning music can acquire in Eastern Europe.

Blows Against the Empire

The authoritarian state can generate conditions in which music can *be* political dissent in the same way that gospel *is* worship. The imprisonment and punishment of pop musicians, and the censorial restrictions on the production and consumption of popular music, are not simply the paranoid delusions or the megalomaniac aspirations of autocrats. Their sense of insecurity may be justified. The Soviet regime, for example, has real cause to worry about the young in its country. Soviet society has a long tradition of rebel street culture which is based on Western styles and music, and which flout accepted notions of good socialist behaviour. Although these youth subcultures rarely exhibit an explicitly political character, they demonstrate an independence of mind which can, in certain contexts, take on an explicitly political dimension. In the USSR, one youth group, the New Romantics, express dissent through an interest in prerevolutionary clothes and fashions; another group shares a taste for the unsocialist pleasures of a hippy lifestyle; and there are 'skinheads' (*fashisty*) who take their fun in sympathy for fascism. Each clan, by its allegiances or its accoutrements, sets itself aside from the dominant political culture, and thereby dissents from it, whether or not their dissent is effective or deliberate. Even without the adoption of a distinct life-style, the state creates the opportunity for dissent by its own involvement in the consumption and production of popular music. Musical taste is made into a political issue by the state.

Music also becomes political through the way dissidents tie their dignity and independence to what they choose to listen to, dance to or play. They challenge the state's authority to organize their leisure. A slogan at an off-limits East German rock concert, a 'blues fair', read, 'We're a powerless generation, governed by angst, but the blues fair gives us strength.' At the blues fair, the punk band, Excess, sang of anarchy, of their political impotence, and of state surveillance. In doing so, they were not just conforming to punk conventions: they were taking a real political risk. One leading East German rock group, the Klaus Renft Combo, was disbanded and two of its members imprisoned after they had sung about the restrictions on their freedom.[17] Because leisure is explicitly politicised, how you enjoy yourself becomes a political question. The paradox built into the heart of Eastern bloc regimes is that to ignore politics, to have fun instead, to refuse to be involved, is to engage in politics. It is often the apolitical citizen who participates.

Music does not substitute for political dissent, just as gospel music does not replace religious faith, but the music does become the *form* of that dissent and not a mere appendage to it. Music's use in repressive regimes cannot simply be reduced to the machinations of political activists who cynically use music for their own ends; nor can it simply be attributed to the fact that in totalitarian states all areas of life are politicised by the state, thereby making musical 'dissent' a creation of officialdom. Instead the audience and the musicians together conjure a political community and a political statement out of the music, in response to, but independently of, the state. Music becomes the language of freedom. The Plastic People deliberately avoided collaboration with the state. In doing so, they were following the precedent set by an earlier Czech band, the Primitives Group, who 'created, outside a corrupt society, its own independent world with a different charge of inner energy, a different aesthetic and, as a result, a different *ethic*'.[18] The music was the focus for the creation of an alternative, 'free' community.

The rules of the music shape the dissent. East German groups do not write about food shortages, but about alternative ways of living, although these alternatives are only vaguely defined. The music is the sound of protest, not policy. 'We hate the bastard Russians, of course,' said one Polish fan, 'but that doesn't mean we want Western capitalist shit instead. We have our own way to go, our own thing to do.'[19] Pop celebrates the rebel's hope for independence and self-sufficiency. At one time, the most popular song of Poland's Republika was 'I Want To Be Myself'. It is no coincidence that it was Flower Power, the archetypical anti-authoritarian, libertarian pop movement, that was taken up by Eastern European youth. In its Polish incarnation, it led to riots and then a clampdown by the government on Western music. In Czechoslovakia, the psychedelic sound was deliberately used, according to Ivan Jirous, 'to create in the listeners a particular mental state which temporarily at least, liberated them'.[20] Jazz and punk were able to express a similar longing for freedom and mistrust of authority. However, the fact that music is used like this, to express political dissent, begs a further, important question: how the sound and the sentiments become linked together. The state may create the conditions for dissent, and dissidents may express their protest in music, but why do they choose one form of musical expression and not another?

The ability of particular musical styles to express political feeling is observable; it is not easily explicable. Why is reggae such a common feature of the musical repertoire of oppressed peoples all over the globe? Why do white South African dissidents draw on the work of rock avant-gardists like Frank Zappa and Captain Beefheart? What does punk mean in East Germany? A full answer to this question will have to wait until later (Part Three). One aspect of the riddle, however, can be unravelled by examining the way in which music is interpreted, the way its political significance is attributed. From the earliest days of modern popular music, writers have imposed categories which shape the music's meaning. And just as the state sometimes creates its own dissidents, so the press has created its own rebels (and traitors).

The *NME* Within

Punk's political character was shaped as much by journalists as by musicians. The political rationale and rhetoric of Oi music owed much to Gary Bushell's pieces in *Sounds*. Journalists help to establish the relevant critical criteria; they find a format for the fans' curiosity and they define the musician's role and responsibilities. Political activists try to do the same. Abbie Hoffman once commented cynically, 'Rock was only "revolutionary" because we said it was.'[21] When Stanley Kubrick chose 'Thus Spake Zarathustra' for the soundtrack of his film, *2001*, he influenced the way generations of people would hear the music: who does not think of outer space as the drums roll? Similarly, rock journalists forged the link between a three-chord rock song and unemployment. It was the writers, rather than the musicians, who gave punk its social meaning; they acted as rock's social anthropologists. Mark P. explained to the readers of London's *Time Out* magazine:

> The Sex Pistols are not a new 'fashion craze', they're reality. Life is about concrete, the sinking pound, apathetic people and the highest unemployment figures ever. The Pistols are helping kids to think; that's why everybody's scared. They reflect life as it is on the council estates, not in the fantasy world that most rock artists create.[22]

These ideas were – or became – part of the music's sales pitch. Malcolm McLaren told *The Observer* (with his fingers crossed and his tongue firmly in his cheek), 'Punk rock players are nearly all ex-Borstal or unemployed lads.'[23] It was nonsense, but it was the right image. But why were such responses given credence? Why was it acceptable to talk like this about music?

Though there is no simple answer, the recent history of the *New Musical Express* gives a few insights. In the early seventies, the paper revamped its style and sought a new market. It left behind its pop (early teens) readers, and replaced them with a rock (sixth form/ student) readership. It brought in a new generation of journalists, in particular Nick Kent and Charles Shaar Murray, whose musical tastes were for the rock bands of the late sixties (Cream, Velvet Underground, Jimi Hendrix Experience) and whose journalistic experience had been acquired on counterculture magazines like *Oz* and *Friendz*. Their approach, borrowed from a US school of rock journalism (Lester Bangs, Richard Meltzer et al.), made the writer as important as the musician, and placed personal feelings above objective analysis in judgements of the music. Under the influence of Kent and Murray, the *NME* came to interpret rock, firstly, as the voice of a community with a common set of beliefs and experiences – good rock told it like it was: it was the sound of rebellion – against authority, against stereotypes, against parents; and secondly, as the expression of individual feelings which meant that musical taste was a matter of subjective taste – whatever turns you on. Readers were treated as part of a close-knit community which valued music for the skills it deployed in expressing what the audience felt. It was an interpretation of rock and the readership which initially left little room for politics, at least in the conventional sense: anyone in authority, anyone outside 'the community' was not to be trusted; and political values were simply a matter of taste. Gradually, however, politics became a more prominent concern.

The critical standards, and the interpretations of rock they rested on, were reorganized to accommodate each new musical fashion. With each new style, the interpretation increased the emphasis on politics. Reggae was seen as the authentic expression of black protest. The voice and the lyrics spoke of black anger (*NME* writers always favoured what they saw as the 'raw' emotion of black music – Stax rather than Tamla; the Isley Brothers rather than the Stylistics). Punk's style and sociology were subjected to a similar reading. Punk was the voice of an alienated, unemployed youth. Musically, the old values were adapted to the new sound. Punk was a re-assertion of rock's *traditional* virtues: honesty, rebellion, integrity. Punk was a release from the technical blandness and superficiality of the mid-seventies music. The *NME* no longer believed that music could change the world, but it could change the musical establishment. Tony Parsons, who, with the splendidly vicious Julie Burchill, represented the new guise for the *NME*'s critical voice, wrote:

> The most important weapon the Pistols had going for them was that they carried real rage. For the first time in years a band was directly reacting against the music business monolith . . .[24]

The critical standards were still those of authenticity and commitment. But where Kent and Murray looked to the music alone to carry these virtues, Parsons and Burchill examined the behaviour of the musicians as well: who they signed for, what they said.

For both generations of writers, the price of their view of rock was gradual disillusionment. Writing in the famous *School Kids' Oz*, Murray was still clinging to the hopes that the sixties had inspired.

> It's precisely because the music is such a vital, integral part of our movement that what's happening to it at the moment augers so badly for the whole Underground Community. The whole point about the early Underground music scene was that it was an honest experimental, no bull-shit service provided by and for artists and consumers whose tastes were ignored by the media.[25]

That same mixture of promise and disappointment was also felt by Burchill and Parsons, although this time around there was a note of cynicism. First there was the promise: 'The Pistols had crystallised widespread repression, giving it form, style and direction. Single-handed, they had instigated a movement'; then the disappointment: 'What were once sharp, angry fangs are rendered soft, ineffective gums . . . Punk started as a movement born out of No Fun and ended as a product whose existence was No Threat.'[26] Or as Jon Savage reflected on his own punk experience: 'I still like records and things, but I don't make the mistake of thinking that they'll fuel the barricades: for in pop there is no Youth Rebellion, only Youth Consumption'.[27] For all these writers, a movement that emerged from authentic feelings and needs was incorporated and then marketed. What started out as rebellion ended up as entertainment.

The political implications of these views of rock are fairly obvious. Rock is only political when it speaks with an 'authentic' voice, when it expresses the anger of an oppressed group; and it can only do this when it maintains some distance from the machinations of the music industry. Good rock is the music of a community: it is the sound of a movement. The idea of a movement applies to both art and politics. It does not just refer to shared tastes and styles, but also to a common cause and a collective political identity. In the same way, ideas of authenticity, integrity and honesty have an artistic and a political meaning, captured in the injuction not to 'sell out'. Music making is judged aesthetically and politically; musicians are judged by their creativity and their commitment. The *NME*'s interpretation of rock is premised on the idea of a rock community out of which different artistic and political movements emerge, in response to changing cultural and social conditions. The populism of the music ('our music') is translated into a political populism which in turn shapes the critical criteria applied (not selling out to 'them'). Whether the community actually exists is another matter; its existence is (or has to be) assumed by the press in the way it addresses its readers: we are altogether, we share the same values, judgements etc. It is these assumptions which make the links between the people and the music. Ideas of 'community' and 'authenticity' are the categories which enable journalists to make sense of the music. Categories of some kind are, of course, essential; what matters is that the particular ones chosen to analyse rock automatically give a certain shape to the music's political significance.

Different papers, with different categories, give rock a different political meaning. *Rolling Stone* readers and writers are not the same as *NME* readers and writers; they do not share the same cultural and political experiences. More importantly, a different kind of community is involved, and as a consequence the political language of the music is not the same. Simon Frith argues that *Rolling Stone* continued to assess music by reference to a community ('1960s youth culture') long after that community had ceased to exist; the music was judged by its ability to re-form or to recapture those now dispersed individuals. The *Rolling Stone* approach was 'essentially conservative: it looks to music to recreate the past'; and rock music became 'the art that guarantees the community.' *Rolling Stone* has more recently adapted to a new market and a new community: the young professional class. Rock music is now part of the life-style of the upwardly mobile; rock stars join film stars, not as representatives of a generation, but as models of self-advancement and style. Music's meaning is determined by its contribution to club life and the private pleasures of the affluent (or those who aspire to affluence); its politics are those of stylish consumption. *NME* writers also have a community in mind, but its concerns are the present – not the memory of youth, but its immediate experience; not the promise of affluence, but the threat of poverty. The *NME* explains present experience through the music, and as a result 'it is the community that guarantees the art'.[28] The politics of the *NME* are, therefore, determined by how it interprets the lives of the young: during punk, youth was seen as alienated and unemployed; during the miners' strike, the miners' struggle became youth's too. The harsh realities of Thatcherism were read, for example, into the cynicism and hedonism of Frankie Goes to Hollywood. Frankie's morality mocked the Victorian morality to which the Prime Minister appealed; but the blatant commercialism, the celebration of hype for its own sake, that was used to sell Frankie was seen as proof of music's political impotence. The same attitudes explain why the *NME* has turned its attention to conventional left politics, and why it published stories about the miners' strike or nuclear weapons without any reference to music. It also explains why questions of political commitment feature regularly in the standard interview of musicians.

The rock press, therefore, imposes a political meaning on the music, through its creation of a community, its understanding of that community, and its interpretation of the music's relationship with that community. This is important, however, not just for what it tells us about writers and the press, but for its effect on the meaning of the music itself. The press plays an important part in actually defining the politics of the music. It is not that musicians and audiences believe everything they read. After all, they do not read much – the papers are used largely as consumer guides – but even in this capacity, the press represents an important source of the language by which music is made sense of: in arguments between fans, in musicians' self-image, and the business's marketing strategies.

The press both helps to create and articulate the idea of a community. In this sense, the music press contributes to the music's political significance. But though the music press has the power to create certain 'political' meanings for the music through its role as intermediary between music, musician and audience, it too is part of another relationship which also has consequences for the politics of the music. Making pop music is also about making money. The press cannot avoid its mediating role: it is forced to reconcile commercial values – what sells – with aesthetic values – what is 'good'. The rock press, as Jon Stratton points out, is caught between the two worlds of music and business. In attempting to bridge the divide, the press imbues rock with a communal and a political character. But important elements of the music and its politics are lost from view in the process. Emphasis on authenticity and integrity, while establishing important aesthetic and political standards, tends to obscure the fact that all popular music is part of a system of commercial production. The politics of pop are also the politics of mass production.

The links between popular music and politics clearly vary according to the political context, the nature of the cause, the form and traditions of the music, and the way the sounds are interpreted. Sometimes music is merely appended to a political movement, at other times it can lie at the heart of a movement. Popular music has the ability to forge links, create communities and express passionate dissent. However, it is an ability that can only be deployed under particular conditions. The extent and the effectiveness of the music's politics are mediated by a whole range of political and musical factors, many of which we have mentioned here, but the whole relationship is framed by the fact that making popular music is also about making money.

Part Two
Profits, Programmes and Performers

5
A Sound Sales Technique

There was a time when Jerry Lee Lewis's 'Great Balls of Fire' was the excuse for teenage rebellion and parental horror. Now his song advertises Edam cheese – 'Great Balls of Cheese' goes the jingle. What was once exciting, even radical, is now neatly incorporated into consumerism and made safe. John Sinclair, radical polemicist for the White Panthers and manager of the rock band MC5, once declared that it was 'the rock and roll imperialists of the mother-country music industry who destroyed the power of rock'.[1] It sometimes seems as if this is all the record industry does, and that emphasis on rock's explicit politics and its links with established political activities obscures the one crucial and consistent feature of popular music: money. The film of *Woodstock*, the free festival, had taken $50,000,000 at the box office by 1979. Perhaps this should come as no surprise, for as Phil Hardy has written: 'With the gimcracks of the counter culture finally discarded as inefficient marketing ploys, the whole of the music business will stand revealed for what it always has been: Business.'[2] Or as the Managing Director of EMI once explained:

> We live in a capitalist society, and until that changes the motive is money. Experimental music will continue to be financed by the business, not because of a wide-eyed belief in the rightness of the music, but because there's a commercial potential there. It's childish and naive to say the opposite.[3]

It is clear that the politics of popular music are inseparable from the politics of the record industry.

For some writers, it is the selling of the music that shapes its politics. The politics of popular music are those of the market. Simply stated the argument runs like this: the demand for popular music is created and managed by the industry. Music has been transformed into a product, and quality has been replaced by quantity in the measurement of value – a good record is one that sells well. The industry builds immediate obsolescence into the product while at the same time it busily recycles past artificial fashions and styles. In this world, and from this perspective, the addition of 'politics' to music is just a marketing ploy. Making music is only about making money. What concerns record companies is how they can sell their product; and this is not just a matter of what band to sign or what song to release, but also how the performers and the music should be packaged. Arista Records, for example, devised a novel way to boost sales of a Thompson Twins' single: they put the same song on three differently shaped discs, designed to fit together like a jigsaw – customers got one song for the price of three. In Joseph Smith's novel *The Day the Music Died*, a character says of the record industry, 'this business is ninety-nine per cent hype and one per cent bull-shit'.[4]

Although the cynic might take comfort in such a view, and although it offers an important counterweight to romantic views of the power of rock, the argument that pop is *just* a business is only partially accurate. It is true that the industry is powerful, and that records are manufactured to make money, but to rest the case there would be to ignore the infinite number of ways in which profits can be made and losses incurred. It would also be to ignore the way popular music is used in Eastern bloc and totalitarian countries where political interests take precedence over commercial decisions.

In the capitalist West, most records released are not hits, but flops. The industry lives in a constant state of uncertainty. How it responds to this uncertainty – how it treats its artists, how it presents its products, how it persuades its customers will depend on a whole range of factors. The industry has to make choices, and although all the decisions may be motivated by profit, there is no one answer to every problem. Their uncertainty and their decisions are vital ingredients in the politics of the music.

Just because popular music is commercialized and mass produced, it does not follow that, as a product, it is deprived of all meaning and significance. Mass producing music does not automatically make it bad art; anymore than mass consumption makes consumers mindless. Selling a product, whether it be disposable nappies or Duran Duran, is a complex business. How things are sold (just as how things are written about) has a significant impact on the meaning that item has, and this is particularly true for music where the precise use of the product is not determined in advance (a disposable nappy has only a single use). How music is sold tells us much about the political meaning imparted by the industry to the sound. The fact that different sounds are sold in different ways, and that some ploys work and others do not, suggests that 'commercialization', while affecting the music, has any number of consequences.

Marketing Time

EMI broke its contract with the Sex Pistols soon after the group had, with provocation, sworn on an early evening TV show. EMI's Chairman, Sir John Read, explained the company's decision: 'Throughout its history as a recording company, EMI has always sought to behave within contemporary limits of decency and good taste. . . . It is against this present-day social background that EMI has to make value judgements about the content of records in particular.'[5] Read's moral conservativism appeared to conflict with his other duty, to maximize record sales. Where the conservatism argues for the status quo, the market demands endless innovation. It is an awkward predicament. The Chairman of Capitol-EMI captured the dilemma:

> The support for our recording studios, manufacturing plants, distribution networks, promotional and marketing capabilities enable Capitol-EMI to recognize the increasing abolition of frontiers in public taste, attitudes and life-styles, while retaining a deep sense of involvement with the distinctive cultures and the economic, social and political aspirations of the various world communities to which we belong.[6]

Barriers have to be broken down and respected simultaneously.

One aspect of the politics of the record industry lies in the way these conflicting pulls are accommodated (they can never be resolved). How companies organize themselves, how they select and record their artists, and how they promote their products, are all part of the process by which the industry manages the pressures upon it. It is, in part, a political process. For example, a company with a strong country and western roster can survive an economic decline in the record business much more successfully than a company that relies on the pop market. Country may not be as financially lucrative, but demand for it is relatively stable. Demand for pop fluctuates rapidly and dramatically. Insofar as companies can choose what they sell and who they sign, they can choose to act conservatively, or to take risks.

Such choices do not, of course, exist for everyone in the market. And the politics of the industry do not just involve the choices made, but also the power wielded. Some companies are much more powerful than others. Phil Hardy identifies three different categories of record company: the 'transnationals' (WEA, EMI, CBS) who produce and distribute their own product throughout the world; the 'majors' (Virgin, Island) who record their own artists but who rely on the transnationals to manufacture and distribute the finished product; and the 'independents' (Rough Trade, Cherry Red) who record and distribute their product without relying on the established networks (the Cartel and Backs are examples of independent distribution companies). In Britain in 1982, there were approximately 1500 independents, who between them accounted for 40 per cent of the new titles released in the UK. The majors and the transnationals dominate sales: in the UK market they account for 62 per cent, and internationally 70 per cent. But although this suggests that the independents hold a sizeable share of the market, if sales are calculated on the basis of the products *manufactured* by the transnationals, then, according to Hardy, the independents' share drops to 5 per cent of the UK market. Power is very unevenly distributed in the marketplace, and what the customers get to hear or buy is affected by this inequality.[7]

The word 'independent' is, therefore, something of a misnomer. Independents rarely enjoy freedom of action. They are forced either to sell to a small, dedicated market (the rock revival/re-release market picked up by Charly and Chiswick, for example), or to take the risks the big companies refuse. Although the independents are relatively free of the bureaucratic conservatism of their larger competitors, and therefore can afford to be more flexible and experimental, they are limited by the degree to which they can give effect to these advantages. The creative liberalism of the independent is constrained by the market's tendency to favour the strong. An independent that uses a larger company for its production and distribution may have to make concessions. Ice Records, an independent run by Eddy Grant, was forced by its distributor, Epic, to change the title of one of its albums. Green of Scritti Politi once spoke of the independent scene as a 'ghetto' which 'was never going to present a route for people who wanted to make their music on a wide scale'.[8]

The transnational and majors have the strength to counter the capriciousness of the market; but their power is enshrined in a large bureaucracy. Flexibility comes expensive in a large corporation. Their policy, therefore, is to sell a lot of 'units' based on the work of a small group of artists. Talking of Paul McCartney's contract with EMI, a managing director remarked, 'he practically guarantees volume sales . . . His albums pay a lot of peoples' wages here.'[9] In the same way, RCA depended on Elvis Presley, Capitol (in the US) on the Beatles, A&M on the Police, Virgin on the Human League and Culture Club.

With these bulk sales, the large companies are much more able than the independents to predict and control the behaviour of the market. Their object is to keep tastes constant, but appetites insatiable. They cannot, of course, be absolutely sure of their market. But in the face of this uncertainty, they will tend to stay with what is familiar, rather than experiment. In signing new artists, the incentive will be to favour those acts that resemble existing or earlier ones. Future success in a large and complex organization is planned by reference to past triumphs. The risks of plunging into the unknown are greater than those of recycling the vaguely familiar. 'Breaking new ground' means 'novelty', not innovation. Paul Morley of ZTT Records said of his rivals: 'The record industry cannot bear mockery, and it cannot tolerate ingenuity . . . it is easier for the industry to smother its audience with weaker versions of what has gone before.'[10]

Economic recession has made the innate conservatism of the record industry all the more apparent. After the boom years of the sixties and early seventies, there has been a noticeable decline in the industry's fortunes. Where a 'hit' used to mean sales of a million copies, more recently a No.1 may produce sales of only 3–400,000. As a consequence, factories have been closed and workers laid off. Between 1980 and 1984 in the UK, 5000 jobs were lost in the manufacturing and distribution of records and tapes. Though all sectors of the industry have been affected, the independents have been the ones to suffer most. The majors and transnationals, despite losing sales, have been able to use their greater resources to help survive and to dominate the charts more than ever. Meanwhile, in an attempt to recoup lost sales, the big companies have increasingly turned to an international market. In doing so, not only have they squeezed the smaller, nationally based companies, they have altered their products. Companies look more and more for 'international stars', the sort of performers who appeared at Live Aid. Alternatively, companies constantly search for artists who will 'crossover' markets, bringing together, say, pop and country consumers without offending either. Such artists are often sold through the use of television advertising.

The rock tour, one important feature of the selling process, has changed in accordance with the new economic conditions. The record industry has resorted to outside sponsorship to finance their musicians' tours. Initially, sponsors were used to underwrite the increasingly extravagant demands of the performers. (Rick Wakeman's arrays of keyboards were subsidized by the National Westminster Bank.) But in more straitened times, the sponsors provide much needed financial support. While record sales have declined, the cost of touring has increased. One US tour by Supertramp involved an initial outlay of $16 million, and in charging $12 a seat, it had to sell out to realise a profit of $2 million. Sparkomatic, US makers of car sound systems, contributed $3.5 million to another Supertramp tour. In 1981, Levi Jeans sponsored tours by Roxy Music and David Bowie. Schlitz put up the money for the Who's last tour of the States. The manufacturers of blank cassettes are regular contributors – the Stones have been helped by TDK tapes, Duran Duran by Sony, and Japan by Maxel. The sponsorship has encouraged the industry's conservatism; the support has gone to established artists. The Who's Pete Townshend, a beneficiary of the system, remarked, 'The biggest injustice in sponsorship is that the groups who need it don't get it. The Rolling Stones and David Bowie don't really need the money.'[11] The injustice is compounded by the way support bands, who have yet to establish themselves, are expected to pay for the privilege of accompanying a better known band on tour.

New groups suffer in other ways. As money has become tighter, and the market increasingly dominated by the big companies, the contracts offered have become less generous and more cautious. Maurice Oberstein, then Chairman of CBS, said in 1979, 'there will be fewer shots taken, fewer risks will be chanced'.[12] Often groups are signed to contracts which only guarantee the release of singles; the album is kept as a company option which will only be taken up if a single is successful. Artists are investments. And in choosing new bands, companies may be as interested in their manager as their music. *Melody Maker* once reported, 'Acts aren't being signed, however promising, unless the companies think that they have a good manager and they can be promoted sufficiently well.'[13]

All these practices make sound commercial sense to the companies. Profits depend on the number of copies sold. There is little point in putting much effort into selling a cult artist or a new act, if the same effort could enable an established artist to reach a much larger market. The promotional video has become increasingly important to the selling of music, but it is a costly item. Companies cannot afford to make a video for all their acts, so the money will be directed to those artists from whom a return is virtually guaranteed; the rest are left trapped in a familiar paradox: to be successful they need a video, but without success they will be unable to make a video. This logic is not the consequence of some natural law; it is the result of the organization of the companies and the market they operate in. These dominant assumptions, and the industry's conservatism, are only exposed when someone challenges them, when someone refuses to cooperate.

Chaos and Cash

When EMI signed the Sex Pistols on the strength of the band's reputation and their few live performances, the company was taking a risk, but then it had done that before. Despite their aggressive, rebellious image, the group worked with EMI and recording proceeded normally. The Pistols made suitably disdainful remarks about EMI, but they were never totally uncooperative, and although senior managers were wary of the band (again, there was nothing new in this), they maintained a reasonable working relationship. This all changed after the group's outburst of swearing on television; among other things, they called their interviewer, Bill Grundy, 'a dirty fucker'. The newspapers picked up the incident, and suddenly EMI found itself in the middle of a public row. EMI began to worry about its ability to control its new signing and about the company's reputation. EMI's chairman told the company's AGM:

> it must be remembered that the recording industry has signed many pop groups, initially controversial, who have in the fullness of time become wholly acceptable . . . The Sex Pistols have acquired a reputation for aggressive behaviour which they have certainly demonstrated in public . . . I need hardly add that we shall do everything we can to restrain their public behaviour, although this is a matter over which we have no real control.[14]

In the end, EMI concluded that it could not 'do the normal things' with the group because they would not allow the company to 'operate in a normal fashion'. The Sex Pistols' clash with 'normal' practices exposed the way in which the business created its own 'common sense' of record production and promotion. But it was not just the arrangement of 'normality' that they clashed with and exposed, the Pistols also highlighted the distribution of power and interests within EMI.

The women working in the packaging factory balked at handling the Sex Pistols' material; there were arguments between senior management and the A&R (Artists and Repertoire) department; and then there were the protests of other EMI artists (e.g. Cliff Richard). Keeping the Sex Pistols became increasingly awkward for EMI – and later for A&M. Whatever the deliberate intentions of the band and their manager, Malcolm McLaren, it was evident that the established majors seemed ill-adapted to the demands and behaviour of the band. It was not so much that the Pistols were difficult to handle; it was particularly difficult for EMI to handle them.

Virgin, by contrast, clearly experienced less problems. When the Sex Pistols first looked for a record company, Virgin were uninterested – the group 'didn't conform to the way the label was at the time'.[15] Virgin's 'progressive' image did not fit with punk's simple rock. But by the time A&M had dropped the band, Virgin had had a change of policy. They were in the market for a punk act. However, for the group, Virgin had three main disadvantages. First, Virgin was still an 'album' label, with little experience of singles. Secondly, Virgin could not offer the money or institutional support of EMI. Thirdly, as a 'hippy' label, Virgin had none of the establishment status of EMI, and it did not offer a very good target for the band's abuse – the Pistols disliked hippies as much as pin-striped executives, but there was none of the publicity in attacking 'alternative' entrepreneur style. The difference between Virgin and EMI reflected the divisions within the industry. Without pretending that Virgin is any less concerned with profits than any other record company (whatever the image or the rhetoric), it is more flexible than the larger businesses. The price of this flexibility was paid for in the limited extent of the company's economic power.

While British artists use their relations with their record company as part of their style and image, US artists act differently. It is not that US-based record companies are any less conservative or market-orientated, rather it is that musicians focus their attentions elsewhere. US punk, for example, was less concerned with the institutions that obsessed UK punk (from the monarchy to the record company); US punk dwelt on suburban alienation. More generally, the fact of pop's commercial status causes much less anxiety to US artists; they accept, as befits the nation from which most forms of popular culture have originated, that popular music depends on mass production. The politics of the industry in the US are largely confined to the way the companies organize themselves, package their products and manage their artists.

Economic and organizational differences between companies and within companies have a direct impact on what gets heard and sold. The market is a crucial factor in the making of music; and market competition tends to favour the strong; and the strong have good reason to behave conservatively. But there is more to the politics of pop production than the market. How the music is sold also matters.

Shifting Units

Selling to the pop market, with its emphasis on the charts, on singles and on a fast turnover, is not the same as selling to the rock, soul or country and western markets, where the pace is less frenetic and the product less changeable. Each market has different consumers who differ in their expectations, habits and sources of influence. The business, while wanting for commercial reasons to create a uniform mass market, is compelled to recognize the distinctions. Pop music is sold on the strength of its novelty and its immediate pleasures. In selling rock, the industry attempts to create some kind of 'brand loyalty'. Where both rock and pop emphasize the performer's appearance, different criteria apply in each case. The selling of Bruce Springsteen neatly illustrates the differences. Since the chart success of 'Born in the USA', he has been sold both as a rock star and a pop idol. When being sold to the rock audience, the photographs were simple: Springsteen as blue-collar worker; Springsteen as a 'regular guy'. For the pop audience, a new style emerged, captured in the video for 'Dancing in the Dark'. Springsteen was shot in soft focus, miming to a backing track. The film used several shots of the young girls at the front of the stage. Where the rough-edged live performer suited the rock market, when it came to selling to pop audiences the 'live' performance was blatantly staged and directed to a new audience. Springsteen was presented as a different kind of artist; he was a pop star with an aura of unattainability. CBS's strategy was intended to reinforce a set of views about what the product meant and how it should be consumed. It was another attempt to win over consumers by inducing them to think and respond in a certain way.

Selling records involves the industry in a struggle to impose a particular meaning on music, and thereby to ensure a demand for their product. Consumers and companies are engaged in an endless series of ideological skirmishes. With no apparent irony, record companies use political radicalism ('the Revolutionaries are on CBS') or transvestism or showbusiness superficiality to disguise the commercial process. More recently, exposing the cash nexus has itself become part of the sales technique. Heaven 17 were sold as businessmen with pony tails. With Frankie Goes to Hollywood the process was taken one stage further. The selling was celebrated as much as the music. And just as this myth faded, it was replaced by another, more familiar myth: music for music's sake, the sound of 'authentic' US rock (Jason and the Scorchers, John Cougar Mellencamp etc.). And so it goes on. Every company tries to sell by convincing people that they are doing something else. Even when they appear to make no effort at all. This is the technique used by the Manchester-based Factory label, best known for Joy Division and New Order. New Order albums are displayed with virtually no identifying marks; the group performs rarely, and hardly ever speaks to the press. But whatever appearances suggest, the intention (and the consequence) is substantial sales. All sales techniques are attempts to persuade the customer that they are buying something more than they can see and hear, that they are buying a share in a particular group or experience.

Not all forms of popular music are sold like this. The selling of country music, for example, seems to change little, and the same basic image applies to all artists, the differentiation being made in their personal character and their voice. Only with artists like Waylon Jennings and Willie Nelson was this approach changed. They were sold as 'the Nashville rebels', but this image owed less to their behaviour than to the fact that they were being sold to a rock audience who would not buy straight country music and were not convinced by traditional country values.

The packaging and presentation of music is part of the same attempt by the industry to organize the music's meaning and its consumption. Women performers, for example, are sold differently to different markets. Female souls singers are often posed in sophisticated, luxurious settings; female pop singers are given an air of glamour; and singer-songwriters are given a 'natural' look. Each is intended to convey a particular use for the music, and to encourage a particular interpretation and audience. An attempt to enable Dolly Parton to cross over from country to pop has involved a change of image: from sequinned suits or plaid shirts to evening gowns. In selling Tina Turner to a predominantly male rock audience, rather than to the r'n'b/soul market from which she emerged, her record company has stressed her sexual attractiveness. However misguided these record company practices may be, they nevertheless contribute to the way music is understood and marketed; they affect both record company policy and consumption processes – how music is interpreted and where it is played. Only artists who fit into recognized categories will be signed, and once signed they will be sold to the 'appropriate' market in the appropriate fashion – soul artists in the disco, pop artists on daytime radio. All these attempts to manage music are attempts to manipulate responses to the music, to use and reinforce existing assumptions or to create new tastes. Insofar as they affect people's thoughts and actions, these practices are political.

For all the emphasis on novelty, innovation and rebellion, there is an underlying conservatism. Consumers are expected to behave in predictable and consistent ways. There is also a liberal element: record buyers are supposed to have insatiable appetites and to display a willingness to adopt new sounds and ideas. The intention is that this liberalism be constrained by the music's commodity character: consumers are expected to demand only what the company can package. Consumers, however, sometimes break the rules, by rejecting the 'official' image, or by developing tastes and habits which companies neither anticipated nor can control. Scratching, the art of editing and altering the sounds of existing records to create something new, is one recent example of independently created music. This state of 'anarchy' is, of course, usually followed by an attempt to reassert commercial control. Success in these struggles is dependent on any number of factors. For example, changes in technology can cut both ways. The development of cheap, high quality multi-track cassette recorders has favoured the independent music-maker; the emergence of the video has favoured the large corporation.

'I Came, I Saw, I Videoed'

The development of the pop video has made a considerable impact on both selling and sales. In 1983 in San Antonio, Texas, Adam Ant replaced the Human League at the top of the LP charts. Neither record was featured on local radio; both were featured on the national pop video channel, MTV. In Houston, Duran Duran's 'Hungry Like the Wolf' was in demand in areas where MTV was available, and totally ignored where it was not. The video, which emerged originally from musicians' creative indulgences or laziness (Mick Jagger said that the advantage of the video was that he did not have to visit TV studios; he could send the tape instead), has now become an integral part of record company marketing strategy.[16]

Videos, however, are expensive to make, the more so as the competition intensifies. In 1985, the average cost for British videos was £18,000. These promotional films represent an ever larger part of the advertising and promotional budgets of record companies. Not only does the cost of videos increase a company's propensity to act cautiously, it also increases the company's power over the consumers. Choice is limited and alternatives harder to develop. The exercise of control extends into the video's ability to shape what the music means. The video for Ultravox's 'Vienna' turned a long-winded, pompous pop song into a tribute to elegant European decadence. The video suggests a set of images to the viewer, images quite different to those the listener might have conjured up after hearing the song on the radio. Although in both cases the consumer is encouraged to interpret the song in one particular way, and although the video cannot impose a single interpretation, the degree of freedom available to the consumer is reduced, precisely as the record company intends.

This balance of power is never fixed or absolute. The struggles for meaning and commercial success are never finally resolved. They change as markets, industries and technologies change. In concentrating attention on the industry and consumer, there is one factor in the complicated process of producing pop which we have not yet considered: the musician. The business politics of popular music are also contained within the relations between artists and the industry for which they work.

Contracted Creativity

Unless their name is Paul McCartney or Stevie Wonder or Michael Jackson, musicians tend to find that their record company decides whether they are signed and how they are sold. It is the record company that has access to most of the important resources. The Redskins, for all their radicalism, were told by their label, London, which record producer to use. Despite the signs of affluence, record company resources are finite, and they cannot give the same attention to all their artists – even if there was no limit to resources, it would not make sound business sense to spread them evenly. Who to favour and who to keep on ice are, therefore, the decisions which company executives have to make. (It was suggested, for example, that EMI signed the Norwich band, the Farmers' Boys, as security in case Duran Duran failed.)

In signing performers, a company tends to act conservatively. Its natural inclination is to ensure a constant supply of recognizably similar musicians and music, appealing to the same kind of audience and sold in much the same kind of way. Anything that disrupts this pattern is relatively costly, presenting new types of sales, promotion, distribution and packaging problems. In trying to limit changes to a minimum, organizations evolve a structure and ethos which will tend to screen out the new. Hence there is an inclination to see all new fashions as passing phases – initially, rock'n'roll, Flower Power and punk were all dismissed in this way. Acceptance is sometimes forced on the industry, as with punk, sometimes it is more willingly grasped, as with Flower Power. In the mid-1980s, with the industry in the ascendant, it can resist change. The industry's conservative disposition, however, sits awkwardly with its desire to find new sources of profit. When Decca turned down the Beatles, they were dismissive of the group's prospects and talent; when the Beatles were successful, Decca went in search of 'their Beatles' and found the Rolling Stones. The taste for reggae was picked up by companies in the same way. The reggae poet/musician, Linton Kwesi Johnson, described Virgin's approach: 'They think if they sign as much artist as they can for as little as they can, no big moneys, just a few thousand pounds, and hope that one will make it big.'[17] Dave Laing describes this as the mud at the wall approach; the hope is that some of it will stick.[18] Its particular consequence for reggae was to disrupt indigenous local markets, while increasing the dependence of the musicians on the large transnational and major companies. Independent reggae companies were forced into becoming glorified talent scouts for the large labels. Not only were these small companies under-rewarded for their efforts in finding new acts, they also discovered that their home market shrank while the transnationals' grew, making profits which were invested elsewhere.

Although most record company signings are simply attempts to cash in on existing markets and demands, or are based on previous successes, there are artists who do not quite fit into these categories. The people in A&R departments, who are responsible for signing acts, have their professional pride. They believe that their decisions involve more than hunches, intuitions and luck, and that their judgements are not simply based on the image and saleability of the artists. While some signings are intended to make an immediate return through bulk sales, A&R personnel are proud of their 'quality' acts. These are signings who are seen to have a long life span, with sales accumulating over time. Dire Straits are a classic example of a quality act. They play restrained, tasteful rock with considerable skill; they started as a cult band with small sales, and ended up as international stars. With a group like Dire Straits (or maybe in the future, Fine Young Cannibals), A&R personnel can see their professional judgement confirmed by public taste, rather than simply reflecting it. But while every label has its 'quality' acts, which beside flattering A&R egos also enhance the company's image, the contract with the performer, whether they are a 'quality' or 'quantity' signing, rarely resembles an act of charity.

Very few groups enjoy vast wealth. The huge advances sometimes announced at the signing of a contract give a distorted impression. Whatever they seem to promise, the advances get eaten up by studio costs, equipment, touring costs etc. Most bands spend most of their time in debt to the record company, and given the way record company accounting works, a record makes a profit for the industry long before it does for the musicians. As a result, the companies enjoy a considerable power over their artists.

Record companies may like to give the impression that their artists are their partners. But underlying the cordiality is an inescapable conflict of interests. What the company keeps, the artist loses. A display of liberal affability by the company usually belies a ruthless employment policy. Virgin, for all its easygoing image, is as hard-nosed as its competitors. Indeed the company's well-known intolerance of unionization may be possible precisely because it can use hippy mistrust of bureaucratic organization and belief in 'togetherness' to exercise what one commentator described as 'an almost nineteenth-century control' over its workers.[19] Although some artists can negotiate better terms than others, the balance of power and resources favours the companies, whose adaptability to changing fashion, though limited, is greater than that of their artists. While the list of forgotten stars grows, EMI remains.

The apparently arcane issue of copyright illustrates the way in which power is distributed. The ownership of property is a crucial determinant of the distribution of power in capitalism. It is property that enables some people to make profits and forces others to sell all that they have, their labour power. Within the music industry, property comes in a variety of forms. There are the studios, pressing plants and so forth, but these are useless without the sounds to be sold. These are the products of the artists: the result of their labour power. It is ownership of this that determines how profits are distributed. Copyright law provides the means of attributing the rights of ownership to music. Importantly though, the rights of ownership apply not to the recording itself but to the musical manuscript. It is the order of notes that is 'owned' by the artists, not their reproduction on tape or in the digital computer.

In the earliest days of rock, unscrupulous record producers claimed for themselves the copyright on the songs they recorded. All subsequent royalties, therefore, accrued to them, and not to the people whose work it was. In pop, where music is rarely 'composed' in the formal, manuscript sense, the performance is as much part of the song as the crotchets and bars. When, in the 1950s, cover versions of songs proliferated, it was the composer who benefited, while the black groups who gave the original performances received money (if they were lucky) only for the records sold, a figure that was severely depleted by the white cover. (A similar kind of theft has occasionally been practised by the musicians who have taken blues songs, rearranged them slightly, and claimed sole authorship for themselves.) Sometimes, instead of taking the copyright, the industry has simply ignored the original author. Arthur 'Big Boy' Crudup is said never to have received any of the royalties due to him from Elvis Presley's hit version of 'That's All Right, Mama'. Even when authorship was acknowledged, it sometimes happened that the publishers, who were also entitled to royalties, took more than their agreed share. These crudely corrupt practices are now uncommon, but disputes continue to arise over the ownership of, and rights to, musical creations. Recently, Sting of the Police received an out of court settlement of an estimated £1.5 million from Virgin Publishers; Gilbert O'Sullivan successfully sued his ex-manager, Gordon Mills, for £3 million and Elton John and Bernie Taupin were judged to be owed as much as £5 million by their publishers, Dick James Music. Bruce Springsteen commented wryly that when he signed contracts with his ex-manager, he 'didn't even know what publishing was'.[20] He was unable to record for two years while he fought these original agreements.

Musicians, managers, publishers and record companies are just some of the prominent participants in the struggle to own and control the music. When Andrew Loog Oldham negotiated the Rolling Stones' first contract with Decca, he recalled the advice given to him by Phil Spector. Spector had told him not to let the Stones use Decca's studios and producers, because this gave Decca copyright over the finished tape (but not the songs themselves, which continued to belong to their composers and the publisher). Oldham was advised to record in an independent studio and to lease the tape back to Decca. This way the Stones kept some control over the tape and the songs (and made more money). In fact, Oldham had to use Decca's in-house facilities, and the Stones lost and Decca benefited.[21]

Recently, the character and effectiveness of copyright laws have been highlighted by a quite different development. The advent of home taping has led to attempts by record companies to reassert their rights of ownership – and profit – over their products. The battle for ownership of music is not just being waged between artists and the business, but also between the business and the audience.

Though the copyright laws are now operated much more scrupulously than they were, they remain an evocative symbol of the way the record business is organized. Lawyers are as important to the success of a record company as producers. The rights of ownership establish a tension between the interests of the composer and the company. How the profits are distributed will reflect how power is balanced. Importantly though, this conflict of interests is paralleled by the mutual dependence of the relationship. Owning the rights to a song is of limited value. Money can only be made when that song is available on the mass market. For this, the musician needs the company. The company, on the other hand, depends on the artist for the 'raw material' which it converts into a marketable commodity. The conflict and the dependence in the relationship varies over time and with a variety of factors. To understand how they change is to understand the politics of pop.

Some musicians can dictate to record companies. When the Stones left Decca, record companies queued up to sign them. When Decca asked if there was any little thing they could do to persuade them to stay, they were told that they could pay the group's bill for their stay at the George V Hotel in Paris. The bill was vast but Decca paid, and the Stones signed with Kinney/Atlantic. But it is notable how few musicians can command this sort of power in their relations with record companies. When Simon Booth of Working Week wanted to use an artist from another label on one of his records, he found that 'the record company treated her as their property'. [22] Even immensely successful groups like the Beatles and the Rolling Stones have been overruled by their record companies, if only on apparently trivial matters like the design of a record sleeve. The popularity – and wealth – of musicians is what gives them the freedom to ignore the power of the company to which they are contracted. Thus, the Stones could afford to give Decca the unpublishable 'Cocksucker Blues' to fulfil their contractual obligations. Few other groups could behave in the same way. For them, the experience can be quite different: the world is filled with uncertainties, about whether the company will release their record, whether they will promote it, whether they will finance an accompanying video, whether they will back a tour, whether they will make the band available for *The Tube*, whether they will pick up their option on a second contractual term. While the industry too is subject to the vagaries of the market, it never suffers in the same way as the artists, whose cause is not helped by the absence of any very effective unionization among rock musicians.

For a company, the failure of any individual record means very little; for a performer it may mean the end of a career. A lawyer for the record company, ABC, put it more graphically: '. . . one fucking little band just doesn't matter in the whole scheme of things . . . There are lots of good bands.' Or as one executive said after the departure of a band from his stable, 'there are thousands more bands where they come from.' When an album by Commander Cody and the Lost Planet Airmen proved to be a relative failure, their record company, Warner Brothers, who had promoted the record enthusiastically, seemed unperturbed. Having followed the record from inception to release, Geoffrey Stokes observed,

> Warner Brothers were used to hits, flops and everything in between, and though the Airmen felt that their album was a flop, for Warner's it was at worst a high in-between. While the Airmen were still reeling in pain, Warner's was gearing up for the next album. [23]

This very different experience of the same event sets the tone of company–artist relationships. The artist's uncertainty is paralleled by the company's sense of security. The musician Robert Wyatt said once: 'I noticed right from my beginnings with the bigger record companies that the people who were slowly and steadily building a position for themselves weren't the musicians. They were the people running the companies.'[24] But even the careerists within the companies are prey to some of the worries that beset musicians.

While the company as a whole may be relatively secure, the workers within it are caught by conflicts and anxieties very similar to those which afflict the performers. The constant need to replenish the supply of products, to keep the customer satisfied, creates a set of interests which run directly counter to other interests within the company. The A&R department is responsible for finding new artists and discovering (or creating) new trends. Not only does its future depend on their discoveries' success, but their interests conflict with other sections of the industry. At EMI, senior management's wariness over the Sex Pistols caused considerable frustration in the A&R department. When he worked for the Warners' A&R department, John Cale found that the company's lawyers were always able to veto his choices.[25]

Paying Pipers and Calling Tunes

For all the attempts to control its market and its musicians, for all the disparities of power, and for all the conservatism, the industry is unable to dictate the creative process itself. Although attempts have been made to standardize and control creativity, the industry is always dependent on the ideas and inspiration of others. This is partly because the industry has no particular wish or interest in controlling the sound itself. It rarely has the vested political interests that governments and broadcasters share and which inclines them to censor music – it censors only when the stock market is offended. The business's liberalism owes little to any political commitment; it is like the liberalism of the pornographer who says he is only catering for a market. EMI's dropping of the Sex Pistols, though appearing dressed in the clothes of moral indignation, owed as much to the marketing problems they posed, to the complaints of the label's other artists, and to the possible damage to the company's image. When censorship is exercised it tends to apply only to the literary or visual content. EMI insisted that the work 'fucking' be removed from the lyric sheet of John Lennon's 'Working Class Hero'; they made no objection to its appearance in the actual song (though no radio station in the US or UK would play it). Atlantic insisted that the Stones re-title 'Star Fucker' to read 'Star Star'; the song itself remained unchanged. The Stones were also refused permission by Decca to use their chosen design for the cover of *Beggar's Banquet*. Lennon and Ono had a similar problem with their sleeve for *Two Virgins* – EMI and record shops objected to them posing in the nude on the cover. And while companies display an occasional puritanism, they seem little concerned about sleeves, lyrics and videos which glorify violence or sustain a crude sexism.

It is of course true that the absence of overt censorship is not proof of no censorship. Censorship may take place in the decision not to sign a band, or not to release a particular track as a single. It can also be identified in the decision of artists who, in anticipating the company's reaction, do not include a certain song. What happens is that companies sign 'political bands' when politics is fashionable; when it is not, such acts get ignored. It is more likely that a popular political band will choose not to sign, than it is that companies will not sign them because they are political. On the other hand, a band which has its own ideas about the internal politics of the industry, about how music should be sold, about who owns it, is more likely to find itself in conflict with the industry than a band that sings about revolution, but signs on the dotted line. It is the way in which the industry structures the conditions of work for musicians that constitutes the politics of popular music production. It is the way the music is produced, packaged and marketed that matters.

The left's concern with the way rock'n'roll rebels have been turned into showbusiness entertainers or with the way bands like the Clash, the Gang of Four, Scritti Politti and Stiff Little Fingers, lost their explicitly political character, leads them to attribute these changes to the industry's conservatism and its power. But even if their overtly political stances or their 'raw' sound were what constituted the politics of their music, which, as will be argued later, are dubious claims, it is not clear that the industry's politics work in quite the manner the left imagines.

Emphasis on the industry's intention and ability to eradicate political radicalism cannot explain those artists who change little during their career, like Bob Marley. Nor can it explain the behaviour of those musicians who acquire political radicalism during the course of their career (for example, Stevie Wonder, John Lennon, Marvin Gaye and Paul Weller). The argument's main weakness, however, lies in the exaggerated importance it attaches to the musician's views, and the little interest it takes in their music. In terms of the consumption and production of popular music, it is not clear that either the political values of the rebels-turned-rockers or the rockers-turned-rebels are of any great significance. The real political questions for them as musicians are not who they vote for or what they think about nuclear weapons, but how they use their music to communicate with an audience who are their political, but not musical, equals.

But even in looking at the effect of the industry on the music itself, the left's argument can be based on shaky grounds. The idea that the music is 'sanitized' in the process of production rests on some claim about what 'unsanitized' music sounds like and about what virtues it embodies. It means demonstrating that the Beatles in a Hamburg night club played better rock than they did at Shea Stadium; or that 'Twist and Shout' is better than 'Eleanor Rigby'. The Beatles' music clearly changed while they were at EMI, but did it become, as the left sometimes suggests, more respectable? Being applauded by *The Times*' music critic does not of itself make the music 'respectable', especially as most people who listened to the Beatles were blissfully ignorant of changes in fashion among Britain's cultural elite. It may just be that rock has exhausted its repertoire of shocking gestures, and all that is left is plagiarism and parody. Music and musicians are changed and manipulated by the business, but it is not best understood as a process of incorporation.

The industry is not much interested in the political views and activities of its musicians, who reciprocate by showing little concern for the industry's accounts. It is the music which provides the setting for their conflict of interests: how it is to be produced and presented. It is here that the important struggles are acted out. And one way the industry is able to impose its own will is in the use of technology.

The making and recording of music cannot be understood independently of the technology used. Studio technology is not just a way of converting sounds into a tape or digital recording. The technology creates and limits opportunities for musicians. Observing the world of the rock musician, Stith Bennett wrote: 'It is important to see that the studio's inherent sound control possibilities lay the groundwork for the intricacies of the musicians' relationship with it, its owners and its operators.'[26] 'Good' music comes to be defined in technical terms, and bands are left with little choice but to accede to the new standards. The important fact about the changes in the Clash's music is not so much their desertion of politics as the increasing studio costs of their albums. Their first record was made for £4,000; their second for £150,000. The escalating costs increase dependence on the facilities and the finance provided by the industry.

Technology can also appear to set musical standards. The idea of 'progressive' music, which emerged in the late sixties and early seventies, was as much a technical as a musical judgement. Progressive music was technically sophisticated music. Subsequently, definitions of 'good' music have referred to the quality of the recorded sound. A clean, high-fidelity recording, which came over well on expensive equipment and on FM radio, was valued for the clarity of the music. Sandy Pearlman, who produced the £150,000 Clash album, explained why he had been hired:

> There is a real revolutionary, anti-authoritarianism, subversive consciousness in The Clash songs. I've been asked to produce their next album to bring their sound more in line with what's acceptable to American ears.[27]

Many a true word is spoken in jest.

The emphasis placed on technology has important consequences for the ideological character of the music (see chapter 10). Technology, for all its appearance of neutrality, sustains values and interests which run counter to the virtues and intentions of musicians. It is used, for example, in the record industry's discrimination against, and exploitation of women.

In the record business, women are not only in a minority, they are also confined to a limited number of roles. Women may be singers, but not instrumentalists; they may package records, but they do not produce them; they may work in PR, but rarely in marketing. One of the exceptions to the rule, Carol Wilson, Head of A&R at WEA, recalled her interview with Richard Branson at Virgin, where she wanted to work as a studio tape operator:

> He thought it was hugely funny and refused. Then I suggested I do marketing, again he refused. Finally, he offered me a job as head of the publishing company, Virgin Music. I didn't know a thing about publishing either, but he was prepared to let me try because it was traditionally a woman's job.[28]

This pattern is, of course, not greatly different from that found throughout society, but it has the added consequence of affecting the music as well as those who produce it. Some musical forms allow more opportunities for self-expression to women performers than others, folk and country being more hospitable than rock. The rock guitar works against women's involvement: the style of playing that has emerged tends to require the player to regard the guitar as a phallus or a gun (or in Jimi Hendrix's case, both). For women, playing the guitar in this way may seem entirely inappropriate or inadequate. But in trying to find an alternative they have to work against a dominant ethos and structure sustained by a record industry which is reluctant to change. Women are forced into particular roles and images because, for the most part, the industry has defined its products and organized its production process in ways which preclude women from playing any different part.

Equally insidious and equally pervasive discrimination can be seen in the attitudes and structures which work against the opportunities of black musicians. Racist employment practices have been supplemented by the division between 'black' and 'white' music sustained by the record industry. Eddy Grant, owner of Ice Records, found that it was much harder for black labels to get a bank loan than it was for white ones.[29] The creation and maintenance of separate markets, and in the early days of rock, the use of white cover versions of black songs, helped to maintain a discriminatory system. Bobby Womack, reflecting on his own treatment, once said:

> The Rolling Stones copy my songs exactly and go to number one, and that makes me ask myself, what is it about my colour that makes me different? . . . I think the record industry perpetuates a lot of racism in music – you can see that in the different ways they market music.[30]

Not only do practices of this kind have an affect on the music itself, they also affect what is released and what is heard. The industry is an important contributor to the meaning and the politics of the music.

What should not be forgotten, however, is that the organization and behaviour of the industry are not fixed and immutable. Capitalism no more 'dictates' than the Soviet state simply 'rules'. There are choices, and there are, therefore, alternatives which those inside and outside the industry can adopt. Each decision is part of a political struggle to determine how the production and consumption of music is organized. Though the industry in general, and the transnationals in particular, tend to have it their own way, there are those who question the status quo. Rough Trade has challenged the assumptions of a business hierarchy; Stiff and Factory have devised new ways of presenting music and musicians; the Who put money back into the industry and built up their own independent touring and recording facilities. The list may not be endless, and may apply to only one end of the company spectrum, but there are enough examples to allow the conclusion that the old way is not the only way; that the old way involves a choice, a political decision, and that an alternative exists, and with it a different political decision. Tony Wilson, head of Factory Records, claims that

> Factory . . . behaves with what I would call an egalitarian anarchic expression of anti-business or whatever. In our actual moments of working in the market place we make that stand every single day. The stand one makes against business and its commodity fetishism.[31]

Against this perhaps over-blown ambition, there is a harsh reality. Simon Draper of Virgin recalls what happened to the same rhetoric when his company began,

> I thought 'Let's start a real alternative record label, with total freedom of choice for the artists, and a sharing of the profits'. That was a kind of naive ideal. It didn't last very long at all.[32]

Certainly, the conflict is never resolved. Record companies work to eliminate that idea of the alternative or its prospects of success, but record buyers, musicians and others occasionally manage to ensure that – sometimes – the companies fail. Both sides learn, and the prizes change. In 1984, the balance favoured the industry (as it will always tend to). Paul Morley, reflecting on the success of the band he had helped to promote, wrote: 'The industry has arranged itself well since punk. It will not allow Frankie [Goes to Hollywood] to be anything more than a minor embarrassment.'[33] But Frankie Goes to Hollywood have, in Mary Harron's words, exposed 'the process of manufacture, distribution, and marketing . . . as an intrinsic part [of the] product's effects'.[34] Self-conscious commercialism can have a subversive effect by its ability to reveal the commonplaces of business and practice, even if in the end it too is incorporated into the industry's normal marketing methods.

So the struggle for control and meaning goes on. What is certain is that the record industry can never follow Frankie's advice and 'relax'. Much as the industry would like to lapse into a conservative complacency, it cannot afford to. Neither the commercial demands upon it nor the character of musical creativity and consumption will allow it.

6

Radio Plays and TV Exposures

That record companies bribe DJs with money (payola) or drugs or anything else is part of pop's folklore. A DJ in the film *Songwriter* remarks 'payola isn't dead; hell, it ain't even sick.' Bribery makes sense because of the importance of radio and TV to success in the pop world. Broadcasters, standing between the production and consumption of popular music, are in a position to decide what is heard. They can act as gatekeepers – or perhaps more appropriately, as bouncers – regulating the flow of music. Their importance is testified to by the lavish attention paid to radio and TV by the record industry. And because the media are organized around the chart sales, the industry has devised ways of influencing those charts. Initially, the hit parade was introduced to provide market research for companies who needed to organize their marketing, stocking and promotional activities; and only later did the charts assume their importance at the heart of pop broadcasting policy. Now the values of radio shape record company policy. Richard Lyttleton of EMI makes the connection clear: 'Radio is incredibly important. It probably does more to influence public taste than anything else . . . I'm sure there's a direct correlation between airplays and sales.'[1]

Politically, the conservatism of radio reflects and reinforces the conservatism of the record industry; but the relationship is not as simple as it sounds. Firstly, the media's conservatism, like the industry's, is ambiguous; it is caught between the need to lead and the need to reflect public taste. Where such tensions exist, there can be no single 'correct' policy. Secondly, radio and TV's power is not all-pervasive; record buyers have other sources of information: clubs, discos, music papers, and so on. Nonetheless, the broadcasters play a vital part in the process by which pop's meaning, and hence its politics, is shaped. And as with governments, the media's most obvious role is as censor.

On Air/Off Air

There are many examples of records being denied exposure or air-time because their content was deemed unsuitable. The excuse for this censorship varies, but it usually falls within the obvious categories of 'sex', 'religion' and 'politics'. In Britain in recent years, the BBC has publicly banned a number of records, most commonly for their sexual content. Not wishing to offend its audience, the BBC banned 'Wet Dream' by Max Romeo, several Judge Dread records, 'Je t'aime, moi non plus' by Jane Birkin and Serge Gainsbourg, and 'Relax' by Frankie Goes To Hollywood. It also refused to let the Gang of Four perform on *Top of the Pops* because they would not remove the word 'rubber' from 'At Home He's a Tourist'. Politics has provided the reason for banning Paul McCartney's 'Give Ireland Back to the Irish' and the Sex Pistol's 'God Save the Queen'. In 1984, Dave Wakeling of the Beat remarked wryly that 'it seems easier to get sexual innuendo through . . . sex is okay on Radio One, but politics has to be very subtle to get through'.[2] The Rolling Stones' 'We Love You' was banned because it was thought to advocate drugs; the same was said of the Beatles' 'A Day in the Life'.

Censorship is not the exclusive prerogative of a state-sponsored broadcasting corporation. Dave Harker points out that although the USA has over 5000 radio stations, they are almost all owned by conglomerates such as NBC and CBS. The power of ownership has been used to control the output of the individual stations. In the early days, the censorship was explicit. Harker quotes a 1939 manual which itemized taboo subjects for popular songs: 'Direct allusions to love-making, or the use of words such as 'necking', 'petting' and 'passion' must be avoided . . . Direct references to drinking, and songs that have to do with labor and national and political propaganda are also prohibited on the air . . .'.[3] In the 1950s, control was exercised more subtly. It was quite common for records which had originated in the black market to be toned down in the process of crossing over to the white market. Some records were considered too strong even for this sanitization. According to Charlie Gillett, Johnny Ray's version of 'Such a Night' (originally performed by Clyde McPhatter and the Drifters) was deemed 'offensive to good taste' and banned from the radio. Other songs were rewritten for the white market. Hank Ballard's 'Work with me, Annie', a pleasantly rude, and only slightly ambiguous song about sex, received an equally raunchy, if marginally more ambiguous reply from Etta James, 'Roll with me, Henry'. Gillett remarks: 'Although [Etta James'] song was more respectable than

"Work with me, Annie", it was still not considered suitable for the general public – that is, the white audience.'[4] A new, cleaned-up version was recorded for Mercury by Georgia Gibbs. The song was now called 'Dance with me, Henry'. And dancing, not sex, was the song's unambiguous subject. In the 1960s, it was protest songs that worried radio stations in the States. Barry McGuire's 'Eve of Destruction' was banned by a number of stations.

Despite these examples, censorship remains a relatively rare practice in Britain and America. There are a number of reasons for this. Firstly, much popular music thrives on euphemism and thinly veiled analogy ('Little Red Rooster', 'Let's Get it On'), and this means that a song's message has to be *interpreted* by the censor. Songs do not mean what they say – 'Little Red Rooster' is not about chickens. The would-be censors have, therefore, to become party to the furtive thoughts of the songwriter; otherwise there is no cause for banning Chuck Berry's 'My Ding-a-Ling', and finding a reason can be difficult, as Mrs Mary Whitehouse found when she tried to have Chuck Berry's song excised from *Top of the Pops*. The censors always risk making fools of themselves. Derek Chinnery, former Controller of Radio 1, justified the banning of 'Relax' with this argument:

> The lyric is 'If you want to relax suck it/Relax if you want to come'
> – which the group seemed to confirm as referring to fellatio and
> ejaculation, which are not exactly subjects which I think are
> suitable for broadcasting on the radio . . . when the performers
> themselves confirmed it was referring to these sexual aberrations
> then it didn't seem to me appropriate that we should play it at all.
> And most of my colleagues agreed.[5]

Censorship's weakness is also exposed by what the censors and their colleagues miss. Johnny Bristol's 'Hang on in there, Baby' was a hit, whose sole lyrical concern was with the delights and details of making love, so was the Pointer Sisters' very obvious 'Slow Hand'. Lou Reed's 'Walk on the Wild Side', which also survived the censors and was a hit, referred to the 'sexual and other aberrations' of fellatio, drugs, transvestism and more. It was in code, but one understood by any mildly curious listener. Not only can censorship make the censor seem slightly ridiculous, it is also ineffective. It is now a cliché to refer to the commercial success that seems to follow the banning of a record. It seems unlikely, for instance, that 'Relax' or 'Je t'aime non plus' would have enjoyed the same success without the BBC's timely intervention.

But for all its inadequacies, censorship continues. However, to concentrate on the overt, public banning of records is to miss a much more important form of control. The censoring of records usually occurs after they have acquired a certain notoriety or some chart success. What is of greater concern are the records that disappear before they even reach the public. It is radio's and TV's ability to act as a gate-keeper for public taste that identifies the real site of political control. The BBC is just one example of the gate-keeper in action.

The BBC: Public Service and Commercial Success

Commercial success, as defined by the charts, has been the main basis for record selection operated by the BBC. Though the emphasis has varied over time, the BBC has always tied its daytime pop broadcasting to the charts. In doing so, it has both reflected and shaped public taste. It has reflected it by simply responding to the choices of some record buyers. It appears to be quite happy in this capacity; it does not have to make difficult decisions, except where popular taste conflicts with the code of 'responsible broadcasting'. It is less happy – and less honest – in its role as shaper of popular taste. Rarely will radio or TV producers admit that their decisions actually affect the content of the charts. (This unease is more common on the pop channels, Radio 1 and 2; on Radio 3 and 4 broadcasters fit more comfortably into the idea of educating their audience.) But however uncomfortable Radio 1 feels with its role, and however much it pretends to be the people's radio, it does exercise choices and it operates under constraints which reflect its place as guardian of popular taste and morals, and its concern to avoid public fuss.

This does not, of course, mean that it agonizes over every record and every DJ link. No institution could survive like that. The process of selection is established in the 'common sense' of the organization. It is part of the routine; it is part of the definition of 'good' radio; it is part of the job of a 'professional' broadcaster. DJs are expected to show an indiscriminate enthusiasm for all the records they play or for all the acts they introduce. This enthusiasm, combined with their friendly familiarity ('hello mate'), creates the impression that they are simply cyphers for the people's choice. But the records they play are selected by their producers, who themselves depend on the charts. What the listeners receive is a highly selective populism.

The biases in the selection process are best demonstrated by looking at the foundations of the BBC's claim to objectivity: the charts. If the BBC really does reflect popular taste, and if it does this by relying on the charts, then the charts ought to reflect popular taste. Even the BBC's 'minority' or specialist shows (John Peel during the week, and whoever gets put out on Saturday and Sunday evening) are defined by reference to what is *not* included in the charts.

The complaint that the charts can be rigged is a familiar one. Until 1983, record companies could get a record into the charts by making various underhand deals with the 'chart-return shops', the outlets whose sales were sampled in order to construct the national picture. Obtaining a list of these shops was not difficult, and once armed with one, the record companies could focus their attention on these retailers. These shops could be certain to get any available special 12-inch mixes or they could expect to get records at considerably reduced costs. Alternatively, companies organized teams of 'shoppers' who would be sent out to create an artificial demand. Steps have been taken to guard against such practices, but they remain obstinately difficult to perfect. Nonetheless, Gallup, who took over the chart business from the British Market Research Bureau (BMRB) in 1983, claim that their scheme is 'unriggable'. Instead of the written returns used by BMRB, Gallup have installed electronic return devices. But they are still using a sample, based on 250 shops.

Even if the charts are a reliable reflection of sales at the 250 selected shops, there still remains the question of the representativeness of the shops themselves. It is noticeable how little black music, particularly reggae, there is in the charts. Only in 1985 was a reggae shop included. This should not be taken as proof of racial bias, at least not in itself, but rather of the geographical distribution of buyers of certain kinds of records. Some kinds of music sell in vast quantities in very specific regions. A chart system based on a cross-section of the whole nation will tend to under-represent large sales in any one area – indeed, this is precisely what the chart system seeks to guard against. Where this phenomenon happens as a result of legitimate local demand, the charts fail to reflect it. Despite selling 67,000 copies, an album by Tim Chandell received neither airplay nor a chart placing. Sonny Roberts, Director of Orbitone Records, Tim Chandell's label, explained the problems of getting national recognition for his artists: 'I mean take "Gypsy Love" . . . Now that record – the only radio station that is playing that record is the pirate DBC [Dread Broadcasting Company] – that record came out two or three months ago, and has sold over 7000 records.' Without mass exposure or the backing of a major label, this represents a considerable success – especially since, with exposure, some records sell less than a 1000 copies, and yet still make the Top 50. Roberts' problems do not end with airplay and commercial backing. Even word-of-mouth recommendation among record buyers may be frustrated by the unavailability of the record. Small companies are caught by the notorious paradox of the music retail business: record shops will only stock 'hits'; and the only way a record can become a hit is if record shops stock it. A record that is not played on the radio will not create the demand to which shops could then respond. Orbitone Records are just one of the many victims of this logic. To the independent record company, it is a logic which seems to create impenetrable barriers. Sonny Roberts recalled, 'I phoned many white shops in this country to say "Have you heard of this artist?" "No." "Are you interested in taking some of these records?" "Oh, no." '[6]

Distortions in the charts create distortions in radio programming, and these biases are underpinned by the assumptions made in the name of 'common sense' or 'good broadcasting'. One such assumption links record sales to popularity. Charts provide only a table of relative sales, so that in the summer, when record sales tend to fall, a chart record is required to sell fewer copies to be a No.1 than it would have to in November. Furthermore, a record that sells many copies quickly has a briefer chart residence than a record that sells a more modest number over a longer time, and yet it is the second record that will enjoy the most airplay. The Beatles' 'Can't Buy Me Love' sold at least a million copies within a week of release and stayed in the charts for nine weeks. Ken Dodd's 'Tears' took five months to sell a million and yet it was in the charts for 21 weeks. Relying on the charts is to act conservatively, to mirror consumer habits rather than to lead them; and it is to depend on a particularly crude measure of popular taste: the number of units sold.

But while the BBC relies on the charts, it does not accept them unconditionally. The BBC has to honour its dual commitment to both reflect public taste and to protect or educate the public. The banning of chart records is one way in which these roles conflict. It is apparent that even within the selection of morally acceptable chart records, the BBC does not act entirely even-handedly. Not every chart record receives the same airplay; some records are promoted at the expense of others. Although Steel Pulse's 'Klu Klux Klan' entered the charts, it was ignored by Radio 1. 'Radio', said one reggae company boss, 'will never allow more than one reggae record in the charts at one time.'[7] The habit of favouring certain chart records is simply a more subtle (or less easily detectable) version of the process by which new releases are selected for airplay. Where a record has no chart placing, it is up to the producers to decide whether it should be played. The criteria employed are, once again, essentially conservative: if the new record is by an established artist, or if it is by someone whose last record was a chart hit, then it will get initial exposure. On the US chart-oriented radio similar criteria apply, a new record will get played if the artist sold well the time before or if the other stations are playing it. There is, therefore, an inherent bias in favour of the established record labels.

The independents, like Orbitone, are less likely to succeed than their multinational rivals. Otherwise, new records depend on the particular enthusiasms or interests of the DJs and their producers. On Radio 1, Peter Powell's infectious enthusiasm for Duran Duran was clearly a help to them in the early days of their career. Thus, when record selection is not based on conservative principles, it is based on liberal–individualist principles – which are vulnerable to the manipulations of the unprincipled.

Bribery and Convention

There is a fine moral line between being paid cash to play a record and being invited to lavish parties or exotic places to meet the stars. For all the signs of profligacy, record companies do not deliberately waste money. They clearly regard there to be value in fêting DJs and producers. Even if each company throws a party because their rivals do the same thing, this too testifies to the fact that *not* throwing parties is presumed to diminish the chances of a company's product being played.

The importance of the charts and airplay to the success of a record means that the relationship between broadcasters and the business is a constant source of suspicion and of possible abuse. Ever since selling records has been big business, record companies have adopted fair and foul means to persuade DJs and producers to play their records. Simple bribery remains a standard sales technique. In the 1950s, it was payola, a direct payment for a play; nowadays, it is a little more subtle, if no more ethical. The executive producer of TV's *The Tube*, Malcolm Gerrie, was offered 18 free weekend trips abroad by record companies eager for him to put their artists on his show. He refused them, explaining: 'This kind of thing happens in all businesses, of course, but it's beginning to go beserk in the record industry. If you fall for it and get wined and dined and everything else that goes on, you don't have to be that bright to see there's some sort of commitment there.'[8] In the US, payola is a commonplace, but responsibility is diffused. The magazine *Rock and Roll Confidential* voiced its suspicions:

> record companies, or managers, are paying fees in the neighbour-hood of $100,000 to promo men or groups of them. The fees are then farmed out to subordinates and programmers on the take, though no one seems to know about how much changes hands and how much sticks to the promoter's hands.[9]

The straightforward bribery aside, most record companies allocate a budget for entertaining DJs. Here favours and corruption shade into each other. A Jamaican company boss explained once:

> A person might drive a car. His tyres are worn. He's done a good
> job, he's broken a couple of records for you. You give him a new
> set of tyres. Or a nice cassette to listen to, but with your
> product.[10]

More typically, the relationship between the industry and the
broadcasters is cloaked in a spirit of mutual dependence. The industry
provides broadcasters with records to play, artists to interview, and
videos to show. The radio and TV provide the outlets. But the
relationship is less benign than it seems. The growth of the
promotional video, for example, has led to changes in the character
and format of television shows. MTV, the US TV music channel,
could not exist without videos; and videos could not survive without
MTV. *Top of the Pops*, Britain's long-standing TV pop show, added a
new element: the chart run-down. Bands with a video will feature in
this section of the show, where bands without one will not. So an
innovation is once again turned into a device for ordering the
consumption of popular music. The development of FM rock radio in
the US resulted from the need to find a suitable outlet for the high
fidelity, stereo rock records which were being made in the late 1960s.
FM radio's development began with the industry's technical innovation, but subsequently FM radio came to influence the character of the
products made by the companies.

All this might not matter were we dealing with typical manufacturing
products, but where the product is music, then the selection process
takes on a new importance. Radio programming involves trying to
impose a particular meaning on the consumption of music. There is an
ideology at work, one that is conservative in its preference for the
established or the familiar, and liberal in its reliance on market
performance.

It is not enough just to observe that judgements are being made and
that they can be fitted into broad political categories. We need to be
more precise about the content of these categories. If the broadcaster
acts 'conservatively' in reflecting the charts, and if the charts are
partially of the broadcaster's own making, what determines which
records are favoured: how does an established artist come to be
'established'? The answers lie, once again, in the 'common sense' of
broadcasting.

Sounding Good and Good Sounds

Broadcasters are very concerned about the technical quality of what
they transmit. But an obsession with technical perfection can make

Above Billy Bragg on the Labour Party's 'Jobs and Industry' Campaign tour.

'STRIKE'

MAKE THIS RECORD NUMBER ONE !

'STRIKE' is a record made by a group called THE ENEMY WITHIN in support of the miners' fight to save their jobs, pits and communities.

ALL PROCEEDS FROM THE RECORD WILL BE DONATED TO A MINERS' SOLIDARITY FUND.

Set against the harsh sound-track of today's streets, the record uses quotes from speeches by Arthur Scargill and the voices of miners to confront issues raised by the dispute.

The record has been made to help raise badly needed cash for the miners and their families. Seeing it high in the pop charts would also be further evidence of the British people's support for the miners.

The Enemy Within recognise that the attitude the media has taken towards the dispute so far will make it very difficult to promote the record by normal means.

They therefore urge all those who can to buy the record in its first week of release. If this happens it will break into the charts and it will be impossible for the press, radio and TV to ignore it.

The record has already proved too hot for any major record company to handle. It is finally released on the Rough Trade label (catalogue number RT 151) in both 7" and extended 12" versions on FRIDAY NOVEMBER 16, though copies should be available from November 12 onwards.

If you have any difficulty in obtaining the record ask your local record shop to contact The Cartel, Rough Trade's distributors, on one of these numbers:

LONDON : (01) 833 2133
BRISTOL : (0272) 299105
EDINBURGH : (031) 225 9297
LEAMINGTON SPA : (0926) 26376
NORWICH : (0603) 26221
YORK : (0904) 641415

Top Henry Cow, a group who explored the political and musical boundaries of popular music. *Above left* Rock musicians and members of the Socialist Workers Party, the Redskins. *Above right* 'Unionize' the B-side of an early single by the socialist band, the Redskins. *Left* An advertisement for the Enemy Within's 'Strike', a record which used speeches by the UK miners' leader Arthur Scargill, to accompany a hip hop beat.

К 2 АПРЕЛЯ
Жиртрес 4:57
Смелый 5:20
Автопортрет 4:09
Сельская песня 6:32
Танец 1:59

ОРКЕСТР
ДЕВУШКИ

Голубая звезда 7:52
Печаль 3:39
Жуть 5:00
Вошь 2:27
2ª АПРЕЛЯ 2:30

AVANKITCH RECORDS
℗© 1984
стерео

Top A Leningrad audience at a concert by Strange Games. *Above left* The Soviet group, Time Machine, who have been both censored and sponsored by the Russian authorities. *Above right* The cover of a recording made by an unofficial Soviet punk band. *Below* The Vicious White Kids – Nancy, Sid Vicious, Glen Matlock, Steve New and Rat Scabies at the Electric Ballroom.

Images of women in popular music:
left page Annie Lennox of the
Eurythmics; *above* Tammy Wynette;
left the Slits. *Below* 'Turning
Darkness into Light': an album
released by the Nicaraguan Ministry of
Culture to promote its literacy
programme.

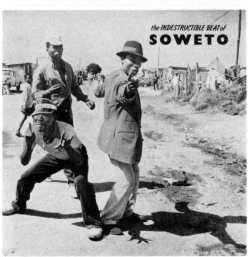

Above Richard Branson, head of the Virgin empire, poses in front of a new venture. *Left* The sound of black South Africa. *Below left* 'No Sell Out' a dance record built around the speeches of the black power leader Malcolm X. *Below right* The Specials Aka's No.1 British hit, Nelson Mandela.

Above John Lennon and Yoko Ono perform for peace. *Below* the myth of the rock community, Woodstock 1969. *Overleaf* Live Aid 1985.

form more important than content. (It affects all kinds of broadcasting. I remember watching someone editing out of a news interview an extraneous (and barely detectable) noise; it changed the sense of the speaker's sentence, but it was technically perfect.) Music can get judged technically rather then aesthetically. The quality of the broadcast signal can become confused with the quality of the original source. The record with high 'production values' – lengthy stays in the studio, extensive overdubs etc. – sounds 'better' to the technician. Hearing a record technically will create a bias in favour of music of a particular kind and from a particular source. It will give an advantage to musicians who themselves are more concerned with form than content, to singers more concerned with correct notes than with effectively conveyed sounds or emotions, and to producers more concerned with the individual components than with the overall impact. The ability and the desire to satisfy such standards tend to be found amongst the major companies rather then the independents. The Local Radio Workshop, for example, argue that London's Capital Radio playlist is dominated by records from the majors, and that though the music is of 'a very high technical quality', it is 'uncreative', 'unchallenging and unoriginal'.[11] The apparently neutral concern with technical quality has a subtle but definite effect upon the content of the programming. Punk's disturbing raucousness, when heard on the radio, cannot be explained just by the sound itself; it also reflects the way programmes are organized and listeners' expectations shaped. Radio producers work to create an even pattern of sound, which does not jolt or unnerve the mass audience.

In the 1950s, white cover versions of black hits were another, more crude variant of this approach to radio programming. For white radio stations, the covers had two major advantages over the black originals. They were produced by large corporations with which they had a 'good working relationship'; and, secondly, the sound was produced to standards which white programmers recognized as good radio material. These structural features of radio policy exclude certain kinds of sounds or emotions, sounds and emotions which happen to be characteristic of black music. Carl Belz compares the black (by the Chords) and white (by the Crew Cuts) versions of 'Sh-Boom'. He argues that the Chords' version was a blend of voice and instruments, creating one rhythmic sound. The Crew Cuts drew a much clearer distinction between the lyrics and the backing. Where the Crew Cuts sang words, the Chords made sounds which happened to be based on words. Belz's claim is that the Chords' version 'sounded strange to many listeners' (by which he means white listeners); the audience, he says, were 'accustomed to a cleaner kind of music in which the separate parts were more easily perceptible . . .'[12] Whatever the explanation, the effect is similar: political values and interests affect the radio output.

Biases also emerge in another 'common sense' rule of broadcasting. The charter of British public broadcasting companies require them to appeal to the largest possible audience. Whatever the concessions to minority groups and interests, the emphasis is on the size of the audience. Just as record companies seek to maximize profits, so radio stations seek to maximize listeners. Minorities are allotted the times when the majority are not supposed to be listening.

Simon Frith describes the BBC's view of its duties:

> Radio 1 is to appeal to the biggest possible audience . . . and the BBC would regard itself as irresponsible to its licencees to focus an entertainment channel on a specific minority (Radio 3 is not, in this context, regarded as entertaining).[13]

US radio has adopted a similar strategy. Having rejected Top 40 formats in the 1970s in favour of specialist stations catering for specific audiences, broadcasters have returned to the charts and to the search for a mass audience. But where Radio 1's format stems from its centrally ordained public duty, US radio is led by pressure from its advertisers who want to reach a large market. In either case, the desire to include everyone leads to a programming policy which concentrates on 'lowest common denominator records, sounds that cross categories without offence'.[14] Raucous, awkward sounds are deemed unsuitable; comfortable, smooth sounds are ideal. The BBC keeps its audience not so much by enthusing or startling them, but rather by not offending them, by never giving them a sufficiently strong reason to turn off. The same is true of US radio, and helps to explain why groups like Foreigner, Chicago and Dire Straits are so successful.

Making Common Sense

But what underlies the emphasis on technical quality, mass audiences and inoffensiveness? How do the media define or create a sense of familiarity and acceptability? What is alien and what unacceptable? There are no common sense answers. One person's disgust is another's delight, and the BBC has a particular view on what is disgusting and what delightful. Tied to this view is some notion of who its audience is and how it should be treated. Together these ideas are combined in what Simon Frith calls 'BBC culture'. This emerged in the 1920s in 'response to the fear of Americanization'.

America represented the idea of mass culture, and though the BBC recognized its duty to a mass public, it rejected the American (democratic) solution. Instead, the BBC evolved an approach to light entertainment which pleased the public without being dictated solely by it: 'BBC light entertainment was a "middlebrow" form shaped itself by the idea of public service.' The BBC's first Director-General, Lord Reith, wanted to create an audience that actively chose its entertainment. Teaching how to choose was the BBC's educational role; the choice was the public's. Popular music, therefore, was to be broadcast until the public had raised itself above such things.

BBC culture, however, was not just constituted by how people listened, it was also influenced by where they listened. The home, and particularly the hearth, was central to BBC thinking. The picture was of the family gathered in domestic cosiness around the fire, a vision that contrasted directly with the public and 'unruly' character of working-class culture. The BBC's audience, whatever its true character, was seen as middle class, and in keeping with this perception, entertainment was seen as 'relaxation', which meant that 'no one should be disturbed'. Only certain dance bands and only certain sounds were thought acceptable by the BBC. The rawer, more experimental side of jazz was ignored – or even explicitly banned. The BBC allowed its audience access only to the blander dance bands. The BBC, in defining popular entertainment in this way, had a profound effect on musicians, record companies, and the character of popular music itself.

'It was radio', writes Frith, 'that determined the conservatism of band leaders and record companies.' The BBC's understanding of its audience and its own responsibilities resulted in the 'taming' of popular music, by taking it from its live venue and sitting it next to the fire. The BBC's treatment of popular music established the idea of a mass public: 'The pop audience was seen as a series of individuals, listening and buying privately rather than publicly.' Such an approach established a kind of programming that reflected and fitted with middle-class values. Music was to be relaxing and reassuring, unobtrusive and inoffensive. The BBC's audience was constructed so that it was able to feel part of an established and stable community. The family round the hearth was the nation at large; and the tone struck by broadcasters encouraged a sense that the broadcasters and the audience were united by their ordinariness and their shared tastes.[15]

BBC culture was not – and is not – confined to the portals of Broadcasting House or to the prewar era of dance bands. It helped to shape the form and content of commercial broadcasting. London's Capital Radio, it has been argued, 'has preferred to treat its audience as a homogenous whole with "middle of the road" music tastes', despite the fact that in its planning stage, Capital spoke of London as an 'archipelago of localities'.[16]

The common sense and unspoken assumptions of the BBC's policy contain the heart of radio's contribution to the politics of popular music in Britain. Though the overt and crude manifestations of the politics are to be found in the exercise of censorship, the more pervasive and effective politics lie in the culture and ethos of broadcasting itself. There an institutional conservatism is translated into a musical one. This musical conservatism takes two forms. The central role played by the charts means that the radio reflects (inaccurately) popular taste, which gives rise to the conservatism of giving people what they appear to want. The broadcaster is not just providing a service, they are injecting a set of judgements, an ideology even. Talking of radio generally, Malm and Wallis point out:

> It is foolhardy to assume that the public is 'getting what it wants' because a lot of people watch or listen to a certain programme on television or radio. It stands to reason that the public prefers what it has got used to. Preferences refer only to the available alternatives. When the gatekeepers stick to well-proven formulae, they are in effect restricting the number of alternatives available to the public.[17]

But radio does not in fact just reflect the charts. Though its intuition is to play only chart records, and thereby to stagnate chart changes (airplay being crucial to maintaining chart success), it has to acknowledge the fact that there are new releases to be considered and that not all the records in the charts can receive equal attention. A selection has to be made, and in this there is the second face of radio's conservatism. Records are chosen on the basis of technical quality, inoffensiveness, previous success and so on, all of which serve to maintain the status quo. It is noticeable that though in both respects radio is conservative, precisely the same kind of conservatism is not involved in each case. Reliance on the charts demonstrates a form of liberal conservatism: giving people what they want, letting them stand on their own two feet, and so forth. Whereas the criteria for musical selection are conservative in a more traditional, High Tory way: giving people what they *ought* to want, protecting them from their own mistakes etc. There are clearly tensions between these two brands of conservatism, and broadcasters struggle to find a settled solution to their conflicting ideas and obligations. No such solution exists. When Robin Nash was producer of *Top of the Pops* he told Nick Kent, 'Some people ask me what my favourite record is, and I always tell them "The record that's No.1 this week". The public are always right in these matters.' But when Kent asked him why he had included a Vince Hill record as a 'tip for the top', he said, 'Well, this is really business, y'know. I mean, people like Vince and Cliff (Richard) have series coming up and obviously the BBC think it would be wise that their records get into the charts, and so we . . . I mean, that is business, you understand'.[18]

Meanwhile, amidst the confusion listeners try to make their own sense of the radio's output. Playlists are disrupted by records, bought on the strength of a disco or club airing, which become hits despite the radio; radio programming is subverted by home taping and by switching stations; and broadcasting monopolies are threatened by the growth of independent and illegal radio stations.

Radio and television, like the industry, both make pop available and attempt to control it. They are part of the process of making popular music. The way they act, the attitudes they bring, the power they exercise, these are all part of the politics of popular music. But there is one further element in this process: the musician.

7

A Dime for the Fiddler

Making music is not just a matter of making commercial decisions; nor is it simply a question of making up a tune. Caught up in the world of mass-produced music, musicians have to take any number of decisions. Some of these are about the chords of C, F and G7, about what rhymes with 'love', and about whether to add a brass section; others are about integrity, commitment and honesty; and yet others about contracts and money. Every decision affects what the musician does and what the audience hears and imagines; and all of them are political, even if what counts as politics may take a strange form. After kicking the Yippie leader Abbie Hoffman off the Woodstock Festival stage, Pete Townshend concluded that it was 'the most political thing I ever did'.[1]

For the pop press, it often seems that the only important element in popular music is the musician. Reviews and interviews concentrate on the artists, not on the business or the economy or the radio. The pop process appears as the creative process with added mass production. Understanding pop music seems only to involve asking the musicians about their intentions and influences (once it meant asking them to choose their favourite colour). The only other relevant factor is the audience. The changing tastes and pleasures of the audience provide the setting for the musicians' creativity; audience response is the measure of artistic achievement.

Neither journalists nor musicians are wholly convinced by this view of the pop world. Both are daily aware of the part played by the industry and by the broadcast media, but to acknowledge them puts too much at risk. To accept your role as a small cog in a vast machine does little for your self-esteem. It is difficult to sustain a view of yourself as a creative artist when your art is just another product whose success is largely determined by the policies of complex bureaucracies and the decisions of lawyers and accountants. But the fact that a musician's creativity is part of countless other processes and pressures does not make it unimportant; it just puts it in context.

Being a Musician

In Tom Stoppard's play *Travesties*, one of the characters says:

> What is an artist? For every thousand people there's nine hundred doing the work, ninety doing well, nine doing good, and one lucky bastard who's the artist.[2]

This is a view sometimes shared by artists and their admirers who suppose that artists are able to transcend society and the everyday concerns of ordinary people. It is a view which is expressed in the idea of an 'artistic' life style. The artist is the bohemian, careless of material gain, or the creative spirit, oblivious of mundane matters, occupying a world in which the typical concerns of politics neither affect them nor interest them. The justification for such an existence lies with the belief that the artist is blessed with special talents. Artists are said to have the ability to describe people's lives and their societies; the artist is a sage possessed of insights and skills which are denied to their fellow human beings. In popular music, these common images of the artist exist, but they do not apply universally. In pop, how the musician lives and what they say is of no consequence; in rock, such things may matter almost as much as the music itself.

Flower Power and punk made an explicit connection between artistic and political life. Being a musician meant being a politician (albeit not a conventional one); making music meant making a commitment; and writing a song meant writing a 'manifesto'. Other styles of performance have made different links. The singer-songwriters who flourished at the end of the 1960s (James Taylor, Leonard Cohen etc.) were expected to fill their songs with autobiographical detail. The integrity of the musician-politician was replaced by the honesty of the self-analytic singer. Other genres have created different artistic standards. For writer-performers like Randy Newman or Tom Waits, truth is not measured by the quantity or quality of autobiography in a song, but by the persuasiveness of the fictions they construct. And in yet other genres, none of these issues arise at all. The pop performer, Nik Kershaw, thinks of himself as an 'artist' – he writes his own songs and he cares about what he says. But his audience do not appreciate this. They shout and scream; they treat him as a pop musician; they admire his looks as much as his lyrics. The conventions of pop music do not make much allowance for those who think of themselves as 'artists'. The idea that a rock artist can reflect and comment upon society is itself a legacy of the merging of rock and folk in the mid–1960s.

But even for those musicians allowed or encouraged to speak about society and their own feelings, there were constraints, imposed by how the role of 'artist' was defined. Women in particular have felt these restrictions most sharply, being forced into established stereotypes, most of which are defined in conjunction with male 'needs': good-time girl, lover, mother, goddess. Men too have been bound by convention, even when the convention requires unconventionality. In rock, the male star is expected to adopt the guise of a 'rock'n'roll gypsy' – rootless, free and promiscuous. Not only is the image supposed to convey some feature of the music, but underlying this is the asumption that the sound is intertwined with the style.

While these expectations persist, shaping images and styles of creativity, they are not fixed. Definitions and roles are constantly being questioned or changed, as a consequence of both personal choices and commercial pressures. Though different eras and different musical forms establish their own conventions, they do not determine absolutely what musicians think of themselves or of the world they inhabit. They have choices and exercise them. Often little thought is given to each decision and little results from it. But together these decisions form part of the process by which popular music is made. Their cumulative effect is to mould perceptions of the artist and his/her responsibilities or obligations.

The choices made by musicians parallel the politics of popular music as a whole. As citizens, they are victims, opponents or supporters of governments and politicians. As workers, they are subject to exploitation and abuse. As individuals, their work is bound up with a series of moral decisions about what it is right to do. In all these roles, they have questions to resolve or ignore, decisions to take or avoid, commitments to make or abandon. The consequence of each contributes to the politics of pop.

Musicians as Citizens

In many ways, musicians are not very different from their fellow citizens. Their views, like everyone else's, fluctuate between the crude and the sophisticated, the eccentric and the commonplace. What distinguishes them is the interest taken in what they think. Like other public figures, they are an object of curiosity and sometimes a source of power. The invitations extended by white South Africa to artists and sportspeople to perform in that country are an attempt to acquire the kudos and respect that these public figures have won. Occasionally people take notice of what they say. Normally, however, a musician's political role is confined to expressing an opinion, rather than propping up a regime.

When *NME* conducted a small survey of British musicians before the 1983 General Election, a majority of them said they were going to vote Labour. The list included Gary Kemp (Spandau Ballet), Ben Watt and Tracey Thorn (Everything But the Girl), Steve Severin (the Banshees), Eddie and Sunshine, Mari Wilson, Astro and Robin Campbell (UB40), Jayne Casey (Pink Industry), Marc Almond, Roddy Frame (Aztec Camera), and Mark Bedford (Madness).[3] But such support does not always translate into active involvement in conventional politics. During the 1974 election, the Musicians Union asked for rock artists to support Labour's campaign. They got two replies: Alan Price said he would help; Ray Davies of the Kinks said he was voting Conservative.

Ten years later, Labour represented a more popular cause for musicians. In November 1985, a loose-knit organization, Red Wedge, was formed to provide an umbrella for musicians who supported the Labour Party – Paul Weller, Billy Bragg, Working Week, Madness, Lloyd Cole, Fine Young Cannibals, and others. It was, according to Billy Bragg, a bargain. The performers would help Labour by giving concerts, provided that the party would help young people by devising appropriate policies.

Though supporting socialist causes has subsequently become more fashionable, there is no reason to assume that musicians are natural allies of the left. Roy Carr once said of Elvis Presley, 'when tackled about patriotism and politics, his views make . . . John Wayne seem like a traitor'.[4] In 1983, Leee John (Imagination) announced he was voting Conservative: 'Old Maggie seems to have done very well – she has a glamorous image, great presentation and is obviously a star. I don't agree with all her points, she needs to get her arse moving regards unemployment, and I wish she'd leave school dinners alone. But I'll probably stick by the old girl.' Uriah Heep's Mick Box shared John's admiration for the Prime Minister: 'I'll vote Tory because Maggie Thatcher sticks to her guns . . .' And although Rod Stewart said he wasn't voting in 1983, he supported Mrs Thatcher: 'I think she's here to stay and I think she does deserve another period.'[5]

There are liberals too, though they are harder to idenify, partly because, in keeping with their liberalism, they believe their political allegiances are a private matter, and partly because the liberalism with which they identify tends to be dismissive of the conventional political demarcation lines. Yet despite this reticence, it is probably true that 'liberalism' as a disposition, rather than as an allegiance to a particular party, is the most widespread among musicians. Art Garfunkel epitomized the liberal musician's approach to politics. Asked why he agreed to perform on behalf of George McGovern's Presidential campaign, he said: 'It appealed to my showmanship. Much more than McGovern ever could to my politics. I do believe in the lesser of two evils, and in that spirit I became a McGovern supporter.'[6] The liberal's mistrust of organizations and parties is expressed in Bruce Springsteen's belief that 'people on their own' can change society; it is also in Sting's decision not to belong to a party: 'I deal in specifics and . . . party politics deal in generalities.'[7]

The voting habits of musicians have little obvious direct bearing on their music, but this does not mean that their political views are of no consequence to their art, or their art of no consequence to their politics. All it means is that little can be deduced from a Gallup poll of the rock community. Audiences do not follow a group because of the band's party allegiance. As some skinheads told the politically radical band, the Mekons, 'We hate your politics, but we love your music.'[8] A musician's politics do not link directly with the politics of the music. Steve Jones of the Sex Pistols once remarked: 'I don't see how anyone could describe us as a political band. I don't even know the name of the Prime Minister.'[9] To know the name of the Prime Minister does not make a band political, any more than voting Labour makes a band socialist.

Most pop musicians, even those who are politically aware, are dismissive of conventional politics. Terry Hall (ex-Specials; ex-Fun Boy Three) who has played in bands which have used their music to make overtly political statements, saw little connection between the politics that inspired his singing and songwriting and the politics of parliament. 'People matter more than politics' was his justification for not voting in the 1983 General Election. He added, 'I'm not worried about Thatcher getting in. It's a question of accepting things . . . like nuclear weapons. OK, I'd support CND if it worked but I accept that they'll never do anything about it.'[10] Hall's mixture of fatalism and humanism seemed entirely appropriate to his music, in which a cheerful tune was undercut by his dour delivery. The world-weary cynicism of his voice was offset by the optimism of the pop melodies. Hall talked and wrote about politics, but he was dismissive of conventional solutions to existing problems. Politics were a part of his musical language – a mixture of pop, punk and ska sounds – but they did not fit in easily. Hall had to find a way of resolving the tensions between his political views (what do I believe?), his role as a musician (what can I do?) and his abilities as a songwriter (what sounds good?). Musicians from other traditions do not feel the same pressures.

Simon Le Bon of the pop band Duran Duran shared Hall's opinion on the arms race and his fatalism: '. . . I believe that disarmament will never happen.'[11] But unlike Hall, Simon Le Bon's views had no implications for his music. For Duran Duran, there was no tension to be resolved, no need to introduce politics into the music. The difference between Hall's response and Le Bon's had nothing to do with the quality of their respective arguments (which are essentially the same), it owed more to the contexts in which they work. Hall's musical tradition is built on an ethos in which politics is (at least) acceptable. For Le Bon, his musical links are with the self-consciously apolitical world of glitter rock, itself a rejection of hippy musical politics.

There is no simple connection to be made between musicans' views on politics and their music. A dislike of conventional politics does not necessarily involve a rejection of all forms of politics. The link between musicians' politics and their music is determined more by the character of the music (its history, its audience, its industry) than by their opinions. A manifesto distributed at an Oakland concert by the Stones read:

> Greetings and welcome Rolling Stones, our comrades in the desperate battle against the maniacs who hold power. The revolutionary youth of the world hears your music and is inspired to ever more deadly acts.[12]

But Mick Jagger himself remained aloof from such embraces: 'I never was particularly left-wing, but I'm not very right-wing politically. I'm not a Reagan supporter. I can't vote as I'm a non-UK resident, but I must admit that when I was living here I never voted anyway.'[13] Even in the Stones' most famous 'political' song, 'Street Fighting Man', the words mix radicalism with caution: 'Hey! I think the time is right for a palace revolution/But where I live the game to play is compromise solution.' But if Jagger had been in Duran Duran, he would never have written 'Street Fighting Man'; he wrote it because it was appropriate to the Stones' rebel image. However cynical the motive and however cautious the lyrics, the song remains, of course, a brilliant piece of rock opportunism. The song's meaning and politics lie beyond the control of its author. 'Street Fighting Man' derives its power from the musical conventions which shape how it was written, not from the personal beliefs of the songwriters. There is another side to this argument.

Where musicians with no strong political convictions allow the musical form to shape their pronouncements, musicians with a point to make have to confront the limitations of the music. Jerry Dammers (the Specials Aka), who has consistently used his music to address political issues ('Racist Friend', 'War Crimes', 'Nelson Mandela'), argued that his ability to do so was as much dependent on the musical form as on his own feelings. For him, it was black music that provided the best opportunities to make political points:

> black music is less about being young, being a teenager, more about handing on experience. Cult-of-youth pop [e.g. Wham!] is so divorced from anything important, it's a white American invention. There are better things to worry about.[14]

Where Simon Le Bon's commitment to pop makes his politics irrelevant, so Dammers' commitment to black music allows for the expression of his politics.

Dammers' approach is taken one stage further by those musicans who try to integrate their musical and political practices into a single activity. They try to collapse the distinction between form and content. Bands like the Gang of Four, Crass, Henry Cow have all tried – with varying degrees of political and musical success – to tie together their politics and aesthetics. For them there was little difference between their role as citizens and their role as musicians. Henry Cow, said one of their members, Chris Cutler, were working towards the point where 'the political content of our music, as well as that of our existence, became a positive object of our work'.[15] The choice of musical form becomes an act of political commitment; it is accepted that the political character of the songs is partly determined by the conventions of the music rather than the politics of the musician. Where Henry Cow struggled to find an alternative form to rock through which to express themselves, others, perhaps sensing the tension, capitulated to the existing form. Jagger, for example, excused the treatment of women in Stones' songs (like 'Under My Thumb') by referring to the music's rules:

> Rock and roll is not a tender medium; it's raunchy and macho. There's no such thing as a secure family-oriented rock and roll song. I suppose I'm a bit hidebound by the tradition but I don't really think of them like that.[16]

Where Henry Cow tried to evolve a new musical form, Jerry Dammers tried to match his views and his music, and Mick Jagger accepted the terms of his music. Each was making a political and musical choice. Such dilemmas are not, however, confined to politics; there are moral choices too.

Musicians as Individuals

While their views on politics may not distinguish musicians from their fellow citizens, their views on morality do seem to differ. In their personal relationships, in their financial dealings, in their social activities, they behave differently from (or at least more extremely than) their audience. While living in France in the 1970s, Keith Richards apparently spent 'on average $1000 a week on lobsters, caviar, steaks and other foods, and $1000 a week on alcohol'. The drug bill came to $9000 in one month. Meanwhile, Richards was said to charge the other Stones rent when they stayed at his chateau for the recording of an album.[17] Once, in the space of two weeks, Keith Moon crashed a Hot Rod, a Morgan and a Mercedes. The crashes took place in the drive of his home; he did not have a licence. In a biography of the Who, Richard Barnes records that Moon did about £150,000 worth of damage to hotels. At one time, Moon carried a hatchet in his suitcase for his destruction work; and having destroyed a bed, cupboard, chairs and a TV, he looked on them as 'creative achievements'.[18] When someone asked Janis Joplin whether she had enjoyed a holiday, she said, 'it was just like anywhere else, I fucked a lot of strangers.'[19]

The explanation for behaviour of this kind may owe nothing to the individuals themselves. It may instead be a feature of the peculiar opportunities and pressures which face musicians. Pete Townshend gave an insight into that world:

> After all the excitement of a concert, and after not just pretty girls looking at you like that, but the promoter thinking you're wonderful – everyone thinks you're wonderful if you've made a lot of money . . . To face up to the fact that you've now got to go back to your hotel room, get into bed with yourself, and face up to the fact that just like everybody else, you are fuck all . . ..[20]

Undoubtedly such feelings help to explain some of the self-destructive life styles of people like Keith Moon, Sid Vicious, Jimi Hendrix, Jim Morrison and Janis Joplin. But not every rock musician lives the same way – some are out jogging, while others are shooting up. Some element of choice is involved. What is interesting is how the choice is shaped by musical and commercial factors. Being a star is to live with opportunities and expectations that never enter the world of a singer in a struggling band. Similarly, the constraints on a rock musician are different from those on a C&W performer. The morality of musicians is, therefore, a consequence of the combination of personal choice, opportunity and ethos.

Although there are no sweeping generalizations to be made about the code by which musicians live, this is no reason for ignoring it. Because rock in particular makes a direct link between personal experience and musical expression, the moral world of musicians is important to the way that experience is constructed. Further, popular music in general emphasizes the ties between musician and audience; it therefore matters that the two inhabit different moral worlds. And finally, in so far as morality varies within and between the styles of music, it can both reflect and shape the politics of the music itself. Attitudes to money help to illustrate some of these points.

Contrary to every impression, musicians are not especially well paid. Very few are truly wealthy. Musicians who appear on MTV or *Top of the Pops* may be receiving no more than a low industrial wage. Whatever the sums involved, money, and its distribution, can have a considerable impact on music making. Although bands often appear to be close-knit groups of like-minded equals, they are often divided financially. Sometimes, there will be the simple distinction between the stars and their musicians. On tour, the group will be paid a regular wage (with expenses and bonuses), while the star's earnings are supplemented by a percentage of the door receipts and the merchandise deals for T-shirts etc. In the studio, the group will be paid as session musicans, while the star holds the contract and collects the royalties. Such inequalities may be agreed or imposed; either way they can be a source of tension.

In the early days, Brian Jones used to claim special privileges and benefits as 'leader' of the Rolling Stones (he got more of the door money and better overnight accommodation), while the rest of the group shared their poverty. A more usual source of inequality emerges from the division of creative labour in a band. Mick Jagger and Keith Richards are the financial aristocrats of the Stones because they are credited with writing the songs, and therefore they receive the publishing royalties. As songwriter for the Police, Sting earned considerably more than his colleagues in the group. Even in less successful groups, the financial advantages may be smaller but the differences more acute: it may mean the difference between a mortgage on a house and sharing the rent on a flat. The tensions created by these inequalities are exacerbated by the realities of the composition of rock music. In rock, composing songs is not a matter of writing so much as playing. The writer may have a melody and some lyrics, but what we hear as the finished product often owes much to the way the group has chosen to present the song. Only occasionally will the writer have decided on the bass line or the drum pattern. The same goes for the arrangement. George Martin's contribution to the Beatles' songs were always treated as part of a secondary service industry: they were not part of the composition. Guest performers may be treated in the same way. Is Eric Clapton's guitar solo on 'While My Guitar Gently Weeps' part of the song or an embellishment to it? George Harrison is named as the sole composer. Malcolm McLaren's album, *Duck Rock*, made no secret of the way it borrowed samples of music from around the world. The plagiarism was part of the art, as it is, and has been, throughout rock's history. Keith Richards once recalled how, if he was stuck for a solo on stage, he'd lift something from Buddy Holly; it was meant as a mark of respect, not a guilty confession. Although occasionally writers are taken to court over cases of plagiarism, most of the time a set of unspoken assumptions organize the attribution of authorship. In these conventions lie a set of choices which musicians make or ignore.

A song may justly be described as a collective composition, rather than as the work of a single writer. How or whether the group decide to recognize their different contributions involve moral and political dilemmas. Some groups insist on a joint credit for all songs, whatever the contribution of each individual; and some writers insist on exclusive credit, whatever the contribution of others.[21] However the composition or arranging of a song is done, the question of who is to take the credit (and the money) cannot usually be resolved by an appeal to law; at some point, ideas of fairness and equality will intrude.

Money also plays a part in its effect on a musician's perception of the world and their relationship with their audience. Whether this is significant depends on the music and the musician, but mostly it depends on myths and conventions. The wealth of a rock musician is of more importance in rock than is the wealth of a soul star. Even within rock there are distinctions. Money is more a source of embarrassment to radical populists like Joe Strummer and Paul Weller than to the elegant decadence of Bryan Ferry. The idea that money matters rests on a variety of fictions and time-worn traditions. Rock often celebrates a mythical democracy in which rock stars belong to the 'people' and speak for them. The myths matter to rock's belief in the idea of a rock community; they bear little resemblance to reality. While private wealth may in fact make no difference to the music itself, the idea that it does is crucial to how the role of the rock star is constructed.

Rock musicians have at various times found themselves faced with the need to justify or distract attention from their wealth. John Lennon once felt compelled to argue for the compatibility of radicalism and vast wealth:

> I certainly don't agree with the philosophy that you can't be left-wing because you're rich. I just happen to be rich by a rather dubious process called showbusiness. We're artists, so we're revolutionaries too.[22]

Not everyone was convinced by Lennon's defence. Bob Edmands wrote:

> Eccentric millionaires tend only to be tolerated if they're aristocrats. Lennon's ham-fisted adoption of radical causes hasn't helped close his personal credibility gap. There has always seemed somthing bizarre about millionaire revolutionaries . . .[23]

Lennon too came to recognize the difficulties of using radical politics to change his circumstances or appease his guilt. He discovered a more productive approach: he explored the dilemmas of his fame and fortune through his music. Other rich rock musicians, feeling a similar guilt, have reinvested their wealth. Pete Townshend has financed bookshops, publishing projects and music making ventures. Townshend said that he chose not 'to blow the money I had on mansions or Rolls Royces or homes in LA, because I thought it was much better to create jobs or put money into something which helps other people, and to accept that this was part of my responsibility'.[24] Peter Gabriel invested (and lost) a considerable personal fortune in the WOMAD international music festival. Bruce Springsteen has given money to labour unions and other such causes in both the USA and the UK.

Not all rock stars respond to the pressure or feel the guilt. Sometimes it may simply be that musicians, like anyone else, are insensitive to those less well-off than themselves. According to Philip Norman, one nanny who felt she was being grossly underpaid by Mick Jagger got her revenge by letting his child play with the Stones' gold discs in the bath. In fact, Jagger himself explicitly rejects the idea that he should use his money for good causes: 'Charlie [Watts] always wanted to put money into clubs and things. I was never that interested . . . that's not philanthropy, putting money into rock clubs, that's self-perpetuation . . . I don't wanna be a club owner, I wanna be in a rock and roll band.'[25] Whatever they decide to do with their money, rock stars are subject to a nagging pressure to justify, excuse or distract attention from their wealth. At Woodstock, the stars dined on T-bone steaks and drank champagne at the Holiday Inn, but before they went off to perform they changed into torn jeans. The same need to appear to be unaffected by money persists through rock – even the jeans remain the same, as Bruce Springsteen shows on the cover of *Born in the USA*.

Pop, in contrast to rock, pays little attention to the ethics of wealth.

Elton John is immensely wealthy, and he too redistributes his wealth to Watford Football Club, to Rocket Records, and via simple acts of generosity, but these actions do not appear to be motivated by a sense of worthiness or guilt. Were he not to engage in philanthropy, no one would notice or comment. This is because Elton John is a pop star, and pop stars are supposed to be wealthy and extravagant: there is no need for them to feel guilty. In pop, wealth is fun; or rather, making money is an accepted part of the business. The British singer Toyah Wilcox represented a novel variant of pop's attitude to money. She invested some of her earnings in jewellery and make-up companies: 'I can talk about money because it's not sitting in my bank account for drugs or whatever . . . It's money to carry on. It means we can do other work.'[26] Wilcox, sitting between the worlds of pop and rock, experienced the conflicting pressures and opportunities of each – the need to justify the money; the opportunity to invest in cosmetics. Straight rock stars are more constrained. Their private behaviour can feature in public assessments of them. The means by which they are assessed may make little moral or political sense (they can waste a fortune on drugs – it is almost more acceptable to be a junkie than an entrepreneur), but the point is that the judgement is made; and one major concern is the extent to which money is the motive for the music. George Michael of Wham! was quite prepared to admit that it was the money that attracted him to pop. It is less easy for rock stars; they have, in Springsteen's words, to combine 'making a lot of dough' with 'chang[ing] the world a little bit'.[27]

Being a rock musician is, in many ways, just another job, but the money it pays is not meant to be too important. Musical inspiration is not supposed to come from the bank. Ian Dury once said: 'Money doesn't really enter into my motivation at all. I enjoy doing silly things with it, but only the silly things I could do without.'[28] Very few musicians would admit they were only working for the money. The exception is the session musician. Within rock, the idea that money may have inspired music is an obvious source of criticism – hence the Mothers of Invention's *We're Only in it for the Money*, a parody of the Beatles' *Sergeant Pepper* album; and hence the admiration for Jerry Dammers, who spent two years, and a small fortune, making the Specials Aka's *In the Studio*. If music is being made for money, then there has to be a good (musical) excuse or (political) cause. In pop, there are less inhibitions. Popularity and financial reward are expected to go together. Rock's puritanism owes more to appearance than reality. As UB40's Robin Campbell once explained, everyone, even rock musicians, has to make money to live. It is just that rock's ethos mixes ideas of artistic integrity with the idea of the 'suffering artist', creating a mistrust of money and its effects.

Myths about money give way to real political questions, however, when the issue is tax avoidance. This is an exclusively British phenomenon. Rock stars have chosen to leave the UK in order to avoid paying tax at the top rate (83 per cent from 1974 to 1979; 75 per cent since then). This was how David Coverdale of the heavy metal band, Whitesnake, explained his decision to become a tax exile:

> When the socialists moved in in '74 I moved out; there's no incentive to work. They wanted 90% of unearned income and 83% of earned income. I'd been on the dole earning £1.05 until then, so to be suddenly asked for that didn't seem fair, so I fucked off. I bust my bollocks for what I do, I get paid for it, incredibly well paid for it, but it's 24 hours a day, 52 weeks of the year non-stop.[29]

But this does not tell the whole story. All the departing stars have accountants who could ensure that no more than 50 per cent of their earnings go to the government. Furthermore, however brief their working life, and whatever they pay in tax, they are still going to be comfortably rich. Though their decision to leave may be dressed up in rhetoric about the rights of governments to tax their citizens, it is difficult not to see the underlying motive as greed. The fleeing stars leave behind those who earn as much but who choose to stay.

However, although some stars may have no higher reason than greed, there are other explanations. Some of the musicians who made their fortunes in the 1960s combined financial innocence with bad advice. By the time the tax officials caught up with them, they had huge, unpayable debts: the money was gone as was their fame. Leaving Britain was their only option. Other musicians have left because their market lies in the US; just as others (Status Quo, for example) stayed because their audience was almost exclusively British.

Money poses a whole series of practical and ethical problems which rock musicians have to resolve. How they decide and what they do are crucial components of the political world they inhabit, but money is not the only factor that forces choices upon musicians.

When Paul Morley interviewed Phil Oakey of the Human League, there was this exchange:

> Oakey: I was married and I was going out with another girl, and I
> told lies to my wife.
> Morley: That infected what you were doing with the group?
> Oakey: Absolutely.[30]

The moral dilemmas which are unavoidable in personal relations are, of course, a constant source of inspiration in popular music, where the dry language of morality is translated into more lively terms. There are, for example, hundreds of songs about the pains and pleasures of the unfaithfulness which Phil Oakey describes: Z.Z. Hill's 'Love is So Good when you're Stealing it', Betty Lavette's 'Tell me a Lie', Laura Lee's 'If I'm Good Enough to Love (I'm good enough to marry)', Dr John's 'Such a Night', Tammy Wynette's 'Almost Persuaded', and Robert Cray's 'Playing in the Dirt'. Yet while some of the moral concerns of musicians are familiar enough, there remains the fact that the moral worlds of the artist and the audience appear to be divided by a vast gulf. May Pang, John Lennon's friend and assistant, described the problems of making an appointment with Phil Spector:

> It was hard to get Spector; then it was hard to get him to make up his mind after you got him. It would take four or five phone calls to set up the first time. Then Spector would call to change the time, and there would be three or four more phone calls. Spector refused to go anywhere until the sun went down; he insisted on being home before the sun rose.[31]

Brian Jones, the Rolling Stone, fathered three children by three different mothers. He deserted them all in turn. On one occasion, an angry mother came to claim the financial support that Jones had failed to provide. A friend of Jones recalled the scene: 'Brian was upstairs, hissing, "Get rid of her, man!" Keith [Richards] just thought the whole thing was a laugh.'[32] Reflecting on the girls the Beatles slept with on tour, Paul McCartney said:

> It was definitely the biggest perk of touring – I can't deny that. It was only later I started thinking, 'Shit – I probably broke somebody's heart there.' You don't think about that at first, but a little later you realise . . . they are real people.[33]

Rock's indulgence of such behaviour is hidden beneath ideas of 'eccentricity', 'genius', 'freedom'. They are, in fact, signs of an absence of responsibility. Success in rock is represented by the fact that stars have other people to take responsibility for them: personal assistants, managers, maids, hotel staff.

This kind of morality is a part of the 'gypsy' image of rock'n'roll: the rootless artist, free to roam, free of responsibilities. It is also an essentially male ethos. Women serve as extras in the gypsy fantasy. Mick Jagger once said: 'There's really no reason to have women on tour unless they've got a job to do. The only other reason is to screw.'[34] Male freedom without male responsibility is more oppressive than liberating. It is the freedom to become addicted; it is the freedom to ignore the consequences of your actions. 'My responsibility', says Jagger, 'is only for myself.' In the cocooned world of the rock star, the only point of reference is the self; the only thing that matters is pleasure.

Very few musicians are ever rich or successful enough to actually experience this world. Nonetheless it remains a potent source for the imagery of rock. Heavy metal is rife with it. The political significance of the morality therefore emerges in the way the myth is perpetuated or altered or challenged. Some post-punk musicians have refused to live out rock's myths. As Lydia Lunch once said:

> I decided it was too ridiculous to go out and even attempt to have sex, because nobody's going to do it right. I can just stay at home and do it myself. Boys are so dull and stupid . . . [35]

Although there is no simple connection between matters of personal morality and popular music, the link exists as part of the lived mythology and the practical reality of being a pop musician. Although musical genres differ in their emphasis, the consumption and production of popular music assumes a link between personal experience and musical performance. The moral choices musicians face and the myths they live out (or reject) are part of personal experience and part of their music and its politics.

Musicians as Workers

It may be possible to ignore the bomb, not to vote, not to know the name of the Prime Minister, to disown responsibility for your children, but it is not possible – as a pop musician – to avoid the politics of work. All musicians are workers of some kind; they have contracts and bosses; they have conditions of work and pay. In their relations with their record company, they will differ in the degree to which they are exploited and the degree to which they can control their work. In this world there are decisions to make about how rewards should be distributed, about royalties and rights, and about how the music should be presented and marketed. All these issues are political: they all involve questions of how people should be treated, of what they deserve and what they need.

At all major stages in a musician's career there are choices – questions of which company to sign for or of whether to sign at all. Most musicians get little chance to choose, either because they only get the one opportunity or because no one ever offers. For the lucky few, the choice is never a simple matter of comparing money offered by the rival companies. There are questions of control and opportunity to be considered. Encompassing all these questions is the idea of 'selling out'.

To sell out is to be bought off by the Establishment and to desert those who once trusted you. In popular music, selling out may mean reneging on political principles or abandoning loyal followers or sacrificing artistic integrity to commercial success. Signing to a large corporation, as when the Gang of Four signed to EMI and the Clash signed to CBS, is the most commonly cited example of a sell out. But a sell out can be musical as well as contractual. When Scritti Politti rejected experimentation in favour of seductive pop tunes (albeit with radical chic titles – 'Jacques Derrida'), they were said to sell out. Sell outs are also about appearances. The Clash signed to CBS but refused to be seen on *Top of the Pops*.

The idea of 'selling out' has doubtful credentials. Not only is it impossible to avoid making some concessions to the music industry, it is difficult to imagine making popular music without engaging in some form of commercialism. Pop music is commercial music; and part of its pleasure lies in the tension it sets up between the delights and doubts of selling art. 'Selling out' is too crude and too easy an accusation, and yet it is a part of the political culture of pop music. But it does not apply universally.

Madonna or Duran Duran could not 'sell out'; the Clash or John Lennon (but not Paul McCartney) could do so in countless ways. The imperviousness of Madonna or Duran Duran has nothing to do with their determination to succeed or their integrity; it has everything to do with the kind of music they make. 'Selling out' only means something in the worlds of rock and folk; it makes little sense to pop and soul musicians.

ABBA were in many the archetypical pop group. Each single was crafted to reach as large a market as possible. For ABBA, the worry was not 'selling out'; the point was to sell. Or so it must have seemed to record buyers outside ABBA's native Sweden. However, at home the group was regarded rather differently. In Sweden, the band was deemed to have folk connections; their music drew on traditional, national music from Scandinavia and elsewhere. Because of these links, the issue of selling out applied to the group in Sweden; they were the target of those who objected to the commercialization of music. Concern was expressed over their vast wealth, which played an important part in Sweden's economy, and over the way their publishing company controlled 'a fair percentage of the heritage of the Swedish pop song'.[36] So while outside Sweden, ABBA's pop associations prevented the issue of selling out from arising, within Sweden their folk associations assured that it would.

Pop music is explicitly commercial music. Success is measured by sales. It is also primarily recorded music; live performances are advertisements, opportunities for the audience to look (not to participate) – when Frankie Goes to Hollywood and the Thompson Twins performed 'live' in Norwich for BBC TV, they all mimed. As the sound of daytime radio, pop accompanies other activities, it is not a substitute for them. There is little reason or desire to discover an alternative to commercialism. The musician's contact with the audience is indirect. Stardom is not something to be avoided; it is to be celebrated. There is no pressure to address political issues. What pop musicians think is not important; and what they do is judged only in terms of image and sound. 'Selling out' does not enter into it. Madonna fans are wholly indifferent to her wealth; if anything they enjoy it vicariously when they dress up like her or together sing 'I'm a material girl, living in a material world', and she is under no pressure to justify it. For pop musicians the politics of work resemble the politics of enterprise.

Within pop there may be no established tradition of songs that address social or political issues, and this may explain the absence of the idea of 'selling out', but the same explanation cannot work with soul. Soul rests comfortably with the razzamatazz of show business. Soul artists wear their sequins proudly. They recognize themselves as entertainers, and they put on a show. Showbiz style is not a compromise. Political argument is not threatened by sartorial extravagance. Commercial success is not regarded as extracting a high price in musical and political integrity. Such ideas seem to belong to white rock critics, or to black artists (Jimi Hendrix) who associate themselves with musical traditions in which the 'sell out' plays a part. Some white critics may see the 'authentic' character of black music being threatened by the commercialism of the industry, much in the same way that they preferred 'authentic' raw soul over 'synthetic' sweet soul. These judgements, however, misunderstand the sound and the style. The flamboyance of black stars is not necessarily a sign of capitulation to white values and money. Writing about the 'jazz star', Francis Newton explained:

> he was an enthusiastic and flamboyant dresser, regarding his dress
> as a symbol of wealth and social status . . . If he was a free spender
> it was for the same reason – casual earnings breed casual spending
> – and because his social standing in his world depended on
> behaving like a king . . . he had to live up to his part. For the star
> was what every slum child and drudge might become: the king or
> queen of the poor.[37]

A similar story can be told of another genre where the audience expects flamboyance: country and western music. Once again, a music born of a poor community delights in the extravagance of sequins and rhinestones as a way of elevating the fans as much as the performers. Artistic integrity is not threatened by wealth in country or soul, it is measured by other things (the voice and the performance). In rock and folk, however, wealth can undermine art.

Folk and rock have created an ethos of musical integrity which judges musicians both aesthetically and politically. Rock's idea of 'selling out' originates in the protest folk music of the 1950s and 1960s. Folk's particular use as a platform for social and political comment brought with it certain expectations for the form of the music. Musicians were supposed to combine social observation with musical honesty, authenticity and commitment. Insistence on authenticity, for example, meant that folk musicians were expected to concern themselves with live performances, and to remain loyal to traditional folk styles and instrumentation. Desertion on either count constituted 'selling out'. Bob Dylan was a folk music hero until 1965. But in that year, he appeared at the Newport Folk Festival with an electric guitar. For many folk fans, this was proof that Dylan had sold out to rock'n'roll. His performance was met with silence, until someone told him to throw away his guitar; then the audience applauded. Playing an electric guitar meant, to the fans at Newport, playing rock music. Rock music was commercial music; it was music whose origins lay not with people but with profit. Dylan's adoption of the electric guitar was also symbolic of another heresy. He was no longer singing protest songs. For those who stressed folk's political dimension, Dylan had been co-opted by the music business. His music was being electrified, commercialized and sanitized. In the words of *Broadside*, Dylan swapped 'meaning' for 'innocuousness', 'idealistic principle' for 'self-conscious egotism'.[38] Ironically, the twin standards of political commitment and authenticity – once used by folk to distinguish itself from rock – have become part of the world of rock music. This is most noticeable in the way that the musician's relationship with the audience is treated as central to the music.

Although the folk idea of a 'sell out' is similar to rock's version, they are not identical. Selling out only became a feature of rock in the 1960s, when folk and rock intermingled. Dylan was the key figure. Dylan provided pop artists with a new model of 'the star' and a new range of topics for songs. But in creating these opportunities, Dylan also brought with him some of folk's ethos. Some folk fans may have rejected Dylan, but Dylan had not completely deserted folk. Dylan clung to folk's belief in honesty, but he shifted its emphasis. He was not so much concerned with the political honesty of 'telling it like it is', but more with the personal honesty of 'saying how it feels'. The measure of good music was the genuiness of the emotions that inspired it and the effectiveness with which they were conveyed. Folk virtues like 'authenticity' and 'integrity' became attached to the artist's introspection. Self-expression was the guiding principle. To sell out was to lose touch with your real feelings.

Rock's idea of selling out was not wholly a creation of Dylan and folk. It owed much to the traditions which rock's art school students brought with them. John Lennon, Keith Richards, Pete Townshend and Ray Davies all spent time at art college. The idea of 'the artist' and of 'art' which they learned there added emphasis to the idea of music as self-expression. Rock was another, better way of painting; another way of talking about 'my generation'.[39]

Because musicians were artists, it mattered what they thought and said because that was what their art was about; because they were popular artists, they owed an allegiance to their audience. Together these ideas suggested a mistrust of 'commercialism' and a commitment to writing about how they and their audience lived. Musicians, like artists in garrets, were expected to 'pay their dues', to earn the right to talk – rock writers understood blues singers as 'suffering'. Pop stars operate under no such constraints; no one cares what they have done or seen. Though much of the rock ethos is myth (the commercialism is unavoidable), it had a powerful effect on the way rock musicians were judged and interpreted.

Punk went some way to overturning these rock myths. It challenged ideas of 'paying dues' and artistic skill, suggesting that anyone could play; but it kept ideas of self-expression and ideas of style (punk musicians had also been to art school). Punk also maintained the idea that musicians had a special relationship with their audience. It may have been expressed in insults and gobbing, but it still supposed the link between performer and listener was crucial. Commercialism and the industry remained enemies of 'true music'. The business, however, remained a necessary evil. Punk musicians, like their predecessors, had to balance the competing pressures of the industry and the music's ethos.

After signing for CBS, the Clash had to face hecklers who accused them of selling out. Joe Strummer, the band's singer, responded, 'Well, if we hadn't signed with CBS none of you lot would've heard of us.'[40] For the Clash there was no alternative: to reach a large audience, a deal with a major was essential. To Crass, such a decision was unacceptable. Crass run themselves on a self-sufficient basis, organizing their own tours, records, and distribution. Their sole concern is to make enough to live, not to have Top 40 hits or to play in large stadiums. Most bands, given the choice, sign for an established company: they want to be popular. For those concerned about 'selling out', the task is then one of resisting the pressures their record company applies. The Gang of Four tried to keep control of the studio master tapes, but in letting them do this EMI stood to make less money from the sale of their records so they in turn spent less on promoting the group. The Gang of Four also found commercial and political considerations in conflict when deciding on which song to release as a single: the more appealing 'Waiting for My Elevator' or the more radical 'At Home He's a Tourist'. They chose the second one, and it got no higher than No. 58 in the charts, partly because the band refused to remove the 'rubbers' from the song and were prevented from appearing on *Top of the Pops*.

The Clash, another band whose politics featured prominently in their lyrics and their image, seemed less anxious than the Gang of Four about joining a large corporation. Asked by Caroline Coon whether signing with CBS worried him, Joe Strummer said:

> I still come to this cafe for my beans on toast. I don't want anything else. But signing the contract did bother me a lot . . . but now I've come to terms with it. I've realised that all it boils down to is perhaps two year's security. We might have an argument with CBS and get thrown off! For me it has been a gift from heaven. Before, all I could think about was my stomach . . . Now I feel free to think – and free to write what I'm thinking about.[41]

As if to demonstrate their independence, the Clash insisted on using their sound engineer as the producer for their first album. For the most part, the Clash focused their politics on the music itself, and paid only limited attention to the industry. The Clash preferred to believe in the idea of a rock community, organized by the power of music. CBS was just a way of conveying the band's message. The US rock writer, Lester Bangs, writing about the Sex Pistols, expressed a similar conviction:

> If the Sex Pistols are so anti-establishmentarian, why should they even bother with bourgeois outfits like A&M and EMI – why don't they just do like half the other bands in the world today and put out their own records, completely uncensored, on some underground label?

Bangs answered his own question: 'The main thing is that I need more Sex Pistols singles so I can feed my rage; I don't give a damn if they're on Capitol or Ork or Binky's Backroom Bootlegs.'[42] Other writers were less sanguine, less convinced of either the power of the music or of the impotence of the industry. Julie Burchill and Tony Parsons, discussing punk's political impact, remarked that, 'The establisment never so much as trembled in its well-heeled shoes.'[43] Two years into their contract with CBS, the Clash's rhetoric remained, but the company seemed to be in charge. The band had had some well-publicized rows with CBS, and in their frustration, they released a single, 'Complete Control', about their disputes. CBS responded by declining to promote the single; and when the band wanted to make *London Calling* as a budget-priced double album, they were forced to pay for the recording costs themselves – 'otherwise CBS would've . . . sent us another list of debts when we asked them to put it out cheap.' In the end, Joe Strummer concluded that fighting the record company was 'a waste of time'.[44]

It is easy, of course, to be smug about radical posturing. The Clash did believe their own rhetoric; they saw their music as being beyond control. Compromise (just like age) is difficult for those whom it affects to detect, particularly when the isolation that fuels self-deception is an almost inescapable part of success in the music business; failure allows few opportunities for compromise because it allows few opportunities for a choice.

Musicians have attempted to retain musical control and their political integrity by establishing their own label, recording studio, or touring organization. But paradoxically, the only people who can afford to do this on a sufficiently large scale are those people who have spent several years contracted to a major company. And though such solutions may be obvious they are not easy. The Beatles, the Grateful Dead, the Who, UB40 have all attempted this route, in their different ways, for different reasons and with different degrees of success. Many less well-known bands have, since punk, produced and distributed their own singles. Some have done this in the name of necessity – there was no other way to get themselves heard; and others have done it in the name of their principles, transferring their own master copy onto the cassettes sent to them by their followers (there is no charge). These practices, whatever the enthusiasm or worthiness which inspires them, only constitute a very small proportion of record sales, and all of them make the inevitable trade-off between popularity and integrity.

One of the few sources of political strength open to workers are unions. The vulnerability of isolated individuals can be replaced by a collective power. Pop musicians, have, however, remained resistant to union organization, partly out of an individualist mistrust of organizations and partly because of the weakness of the Musicians' Union, which only appointed a rock organizer in 1977. Even with the necessary bureaucracy, the rock world is peculiarly difficult to organize. The MU's closed shop policy is of limited effectiveness in a world in which venues and bands flourish and fade overnight. The union's difficulties are exacerbated by rapid changes in technology. Every innovation appears to threaten jobs, and the MU has resisted each one in turn, first opposing multi-track recording, then mellotrons, and finally synthesizers and drum machines. While inspired by a desire to protect members, the MU's policy appears as merely reactionary to those musicians who want to use the new technology for cost (they are cheap) or musical reasons. The union's attempt to protect the craft status of musicians works against the ethos of spontaneity and of creative individualism which colour a pop musician's self-image. Nonetheless, musicians are also workers, and the union remains one of the few sources of systematic power available to them. It is a strange contradiction of the world of the popular musician that, while they resist union organisation for the bureaucratic constraints it imposes on them, they remain content to cooperate with the vast bureaucracies of the record industry. It is not as if musicians have developed alternative forms of control.

Few musicians reinvest in their industry, even fewer have managed to alter their working conditions, and none have done so without paying a considerable price in money, music or popularity. Most musicians are uninterested in such ventures. Only in rock, where political myths are built into the making and consumption of music, do questions of 'integrity' and 'commitment' arise. But these myths are less a basis of personal and political action, and more the object of musical games.

Punk, for example, took an ambivalent view of the 'sell out' and its attendant ideals. It made fun of the idea that music and money could be separated, but it continued to propagate ideas of political and musical honesty. The Clash represent the simplest response: to keep singing about politics. The Sex Pistols, though less 'politically aware' than the Clash, posed many more problems for EMI and A&M. Where CBS could compromise easily with the Clash, EMI found their artists more difficult to handle. It did not matter that these problems were partly engineered by the Pistols and their manager. They still succeeded in both exposing the politics of the record industry and in protecting the integrity (for what it's worth) of the group.

What the Sex Pistols did, and what the Gang of Four most eloquently articulated, was to portray popular music as business. Punk and new wave took delight in exposing the process of making music. The myths of artistic sensitivity and of indifference to money which had shielded many rock stars, were discarded; and although as many other myths were established in their place, it was no longer possible to see music making just as the work of a talented artist. Music was simple ('take three chords, any three') and it was organized as much according to business principles as musical ones. Where the 1960s had defined integrity in terms of musical expressionism and rural self-sufficiency – doing your own thing, not working for the Man, and so on; punk shifted the focus to musical self-sufficiency and urban survival. Where hippy musicians tried to avoid the business; punks confronted it. Initially, this was expressed in terms of independent production and a celebration of musical incompetence. But this could not last long. The independents lacked the resources to propagate the music; and once the three chords had been thrashed to death, there was little more to be said. A new musical and cultural language was needed. Integrity became an ironic celebration of the myths and truths of record production. This trend was most blatantly expounded by a group like Public Image Ltd (PIL). The record was presented as a product and the group as a company. It was also offered as a work of pure self-sufficiency; the sleeve note reported, 'Public Image Ltd would like to thank absolutely nobody.' On the cover of their single, 'We are all Prostitutes', the Pop Group announced, mixing pleasure, marketing and politics:

> Yes, any kind of entertainment in a capitalist society is made to rebuild the work force. So have fun. Then you're ready for 1000 years of exploitation. The function of entertainment is just that.

The Pop Group's intention was to make their audience 'question as much as possible. All the rules, conceptions everything'. The Gang of Four set themselves a similar goal: 'Going against the dominant musical practice, that's the way.'[45] Their challenge was to the business and the musical form. They followed a path marked by earlier travellers. Henry Cow, one of Virgin's earliest signings and a radical band in every sense, set out to play 'music which would make people think and criticise, and which would make them dissatisfied with . . . the hollow products of the music industry'. Their intention was to play against established industrial and musical structure. Chris Cutler, Henry Cow's drummer, explained, 'We had to make what amounted to political decisions about the organisation of the group and its relations to the commercial structures, and this was bound to be reflected in the music too.'[46] But Henry Cow, like the Pop Group, found not only that breaking established interests was almost impossible, but also that this limited their ability to find an audience. Their music never rose above cult status.

Most 'political' groups, unlike Henry Cow or the Pop Group, have confined their politics to those of style and ideas, rather than power and action. The terms which bind musicians to their companies are not questioned, and nor, despite the disruption caused by punk, is the organisation of the industry. Those changes which have occurred owe less to the musicians and their principles than to the conditions of the market. It takes more than a good conscience to change the industry or society: the beat and the bureaucracy have to be altered. Musicians compromised their politics in the name of pop's populism. Meanwhile, those musicians who saw themselves as challenging the system, found that they had to sacrifice pop's populism to their politics.

The choices are, of course, neither this stark nor this simple. The point simply is that these alternatives exist, and in every respect of a musician's life – as citizen, individual, or worker – they require a decision. They are part of the choices musicians face *as artists*. But as we have also seen, those choices are themselves structured by the music itself. There are the coventions of different musical forms which raise different issues for different kinds of musician. But there is an even more pervasive question, which underlies all these choices and which recognizes no boundaries: how to make music that is popular. Ultimately this is where all political issues in popular music reside. How are people moved by the music? What makes music popular? When does music successfully combine political ideas and musical popularity?

Part Three
Music and Messages

8

What's that Sound?

'Whatever any record's about you want it to sound good'
(Robert Wyatt)

Musicians play the music, companies manufacture it, radio stations broadcast it, governments censor it, and political movements use it, but ultimately all these activities depend on what the audience makes of it. It is only in listening and dancing to music that people bring it alive. Only then does it take on a meaning; only then are its politics fully apparent.

Giving sense to the sounds involves any number of factors, none of which are absolutely decisive. Neither the politics of the musicians, nor the marketing strategies of the industry, nor the programming of the radio producers, determines completely how a song is heard or what it means. Anyone who writes about pop has to be wary of giving a 'definitive' interpretation of a song. The complexities of production and consumption are enough to induce caution into even the most arrogant of analysts. Jerry Dammers recalled how his song, 'War Crimes', was composed: 'I actually wrote the rhythm a year ago and recorded the rhythm track nine months back, but the lyrics . . . only got written three months ago.'[1] In these circumstances, just talking about the composer's intentions becomes a confusing business. Much of what follows, therefore, is both speculative and contentious. My concern is to explore the ways in which meaning is taken from the music, to see how musical form and political ideology are linked. This chapter is about the general question of how sounds and ideas are related; subsequent chapters consider particular versions of the relationship.

The limits of our language, it is said, are also the limits of our world. Our experience of the world is shaped by our ability to describe it. We can know no more than we can express. Whatever the limitations of this theory as an account of the way we think and act, it provides a good way of exploring how popular music and political ideas combine. What can we say within pop; what are the limits and the reach of pop's language?

I am not concerned with the ideas and arguments that have been expressed in particular pop songs. This is not an opportunity to explore, for example, the way songs like Lennon's 'Sunday Bloody Sunday' or Stiff Little Fingers' 'Alternative Ulster' treat the issue of Northern Ireland. Instead, I want to ask whether pop poses any limits to the way Northern Ireland can be tackled in a pop song. Sometimes pop can speak lucidly of politics; at other times it is struck dumb. It depends on both the character of the politics and the character of the music. Some issues fit better – peace and freedom, rather than action and equality; some approaches are more successful – raising money rather than raising consciousness; and some musical styles are more adaptable – soul rather than pop. The effectiveness of the link between politics and music is not determined by the strength of the argument or the intensity of the singing. Because records are bought for their sound rather than their politics, the meaning will depend on the way it is communicated. Just as the rhetorical flourishes of *The Communist Manifesto* are crucial to the persuasiveness of its argument, so the political power of a song depends on the way its message is conveyed. A record, whatever its political sentiments, will be ignored if it sounds dull. The problem is, however, that in making music that is fun or exciting, its particular meaning becomes ambiguous as it is taken over and interpreted by the audience. As Robin Campbell of UB40 remarked ruefully, 'Our first big hit, "Food for Thought", was a political song, but you go and ask 99 out of a hundred people who bought it what the song's about and they won't be able to tell you'.[2] Reading the politics of popular music must involve more than a content analysis of the lyrics or a political biography of the performer or a sociological analysis of the audience. It has to begin with the musical form itself.

The Folk Connection

Why has folk had a long association with politics and political movements? Folk's emphasis on the words and on simple instrumentation make it both adaptable and hospitable to politics. The song is carried by the voice. In soul, where the voice is equally important, it conveys a sound; in folk, the voice serves the lyrics. With these priorities, folk's lyrics can perform a variety of politically useful tasks: they can argue, analyse, explain, describe and encourage. It does not follow, however, that folk allows manifestos to be set to music; there are folk conventions which shape the form and content of the song. The verse-chorus structure, the instrumentation, the performer's relationship with the audience, establish expectations and rules which define 'folk music'. Nonetheless, within these boundaries, folk remains relatively flexible in its choice of subject matter: its form imposes few, if any, limitations on the political content of its lyrics. However, the ability to discuss political issues is only one measure of a musical form's politics. Much more important is how ideas, lyrics and sounds are communicated. The politics of folk depend on how the music works as music, not as political analysis.

The emphasis on the informative role of the lyrics establishes a relationship with the audience in which it is difficult for the listener and singer to share the song's meaning. Particularly in the protest form of folk, the message is delivered, not discussed. Despite the audience participation (in the singing of the choruses) that characterizes a folk performance, this involvement does not change the song's literal meaning. Participation serves to confirm the song's sentiments, giving authority to its argument. The way folk addresses and reaches its audience limits its political impact, yet there are other features of folk which extend its political effect.

Folk forms of music can create a sense of certainty and community. They can express and embody a spirit of solidarity. The collective singing of nationalist songs, for example, can evoke the idea of community that is a component of nationalism; similarly, on picket lines, communal singing can strengthen resolve as the police charge, just as army songs have helped to comfort soldiers' fears. The singing gives assurance and unity; the song simultaneously provides a message and an experience, something which neither rhetoric nor manifestos can do. The power of this form of folk, however, depends on the context in which it is employed: in the republican club, on the picket line, in the trenches. Outside these settings the music loses its political effectiveness.

When Jon Landau compared Bob Dylan's early folk-protest songs with his later, oblique and introspective songs, he distinguished their impact in terms of the musical traditions upon which they drew. The early works borrowed from folk; the later ones from rock. Landau takes Dylan's 'Masters of War' as an example of the folk genre:

> You that build all the guns,
> You that build the death planes . . .

Landau attacks the crude dichotomies established by the song: it is 'a song of deep hatred' which exhibits 'Dylan's polarizing and dualistic tendencies':

> The Masters are on one side and he [Dylan] is on the other.
> Neither his own righteousness (as the first person of the song) nor

their wickedness is ever questioned. Not only does he end up wishing the death of his enemies but he wants to bury them himself and then stand over the grave until he's sure they are dead. What is jarring here is not Dylan's political judgements – they are unobjectionable by themselves – but the unreality of Dylan's responses to the situation. He is creating an abstraction, a stereotype, upon which he can justify his hatred, not the other way round ... The entire conception suffers from one-dimensionality.[3]

For Landau, the polemical character of the song works against its apparent intention. It insults, rather than involves, the listener – a listener whom Landau imagines is at a concert or at home, but not at a peace rally. Dylan creates illusory, disposable enemies, and because they have no substance, there is no point of access for the audience. There is no use for the listener's imagination and no explanation for the origins of 'them' and 'us'. The audience is given a portrait of an enemy that is no more real than the cardboard targets in a shooting gallery.

Implicit in Landau's argument is the idea that, for the music and the politics to work, the audience need to know more about the 'masters of war'. The listeners need to have their world painted in less stark colours, and to experience some sense of doubt about who the enemy are, about how different 'they' are from 'us', and about what is right and what wrong. The more the enemy is understood the less easy it is to condemn them outright. In comprehending them, they become more sympathetic characters; they become rational people taking rational actions. They cease to be cardboard cut-outs; they cannot be dismissed as mad or evil. Instead, they become more and more like the listeners themselves, and in resembling their audience their predicament and actions are made more complex and more comprehensible. This process of sympathetic involvement and understanding is what Landau takes as a defining feature of good music. 'Masters of War' fails by these standards because, however well-meaning its politics, it is unconvincing. It allows its listeners no alternative; it denies them the use of their imagination.

Musical and political criticism are inextricably tied in this argument. And importantly, the critique applies not just to a single song, but to a style. The faults of the song are less those of the writer than of the musical tradition. Using folk to make a protest is inevitably to embrace a format in which certainty takes a priority over doubt, and in which simple dichotomies are preferred over endless confusions. While such techniques may work on a demonstration, they are ineffective in the typical settings and mood – in private and for pleasure – in which people hear music.

Making Music, Making Sense

When Dylan moved from folk to rock, he changed more than the instruments. It meant the adoption of a new musical and political language. Adding a stack of speakers and some electric guitars would not turn 'Masters of War' into a rock song. Dylan's adoption of rock meant a change in how he wrote and what he wrote about. The meaning and the effect of his songs were altered. Dylan communicated with his audience in a different way and with new assumptions. When Greil Marcus, the rock writer, explains what Dylan's 'Memphis Blues Again' meant to him, he does not dwell on Dylan's literal meaning, whatever that is:

> Now the senator, he came down here
> Showing everyone his gun
> Handing out free tickets
> To the wedding of his son.

Marcus' understanding of the song emerges from his own circumstances, from his sense of political disillusionment and confusion:

> I didn't 'interpret' those words, they interpreted my situation. They existed to act on me, not for me to figure out 'what they mean'. They'll mean something else the next time I hear them. The music carries those words – I might never have heard them without the jangling of the guitar that caught my ears and made me jump. But the words don't exist as statements; they just exist as part of a song, as a moment on the journey that I was trying to get through.[4]

The song's meaning depends both on what the listener understands and on what the singer intends. A literary critic may be able to describe what the lyrics say, but the critic cannot determine what the song means. Where Dylan's protest song had an unambiguous message, his rock song had on ambiguous meaning. In this distinction lies the key to the two styles' different treatment of politics. Where protest-folk operates at the level of conventional political analysis, and has little to say about the participants, rock works in almost the opposite way: about politics it is silent, about human motivation it speaks volumes. Rock's politics are – at best – profound but imprecise, moving but inarticulate.

It is because a rock song's meaning lies in its sounds and its context, that it defies a definitive interpretation, and therefore contains ambiguous politics. As Greil Marcus wrote:

> If music is 'meaningful', its meaning must be free enough to
> depend on how one hears it. 'Shooby shooby doo wah', heard in
> the right mood, has more meaning than a flat-out protest song
> ever does, because by definition when you listen to a protest song
> absolutely nothing is in doubt; the listener is in a box.[5]

It is the indeterminacy of the song's meaning which forges the bond
between the audience and the performer. Popular songs depend on
their listeners. However determined a singer is to convey a particular
message or experience, success is never guaranteed. If singers say
exactly what they mean, the musical form will collapse beneath the
weight of their words. The price of accepting the constraints of the
musical form, however, is that the performers can never convey quite
what they mean. On *Nebraska*, using only a voice, a guitar, a
harmonica, and a lot of words, Bruce Springsteen gives a detailed
account of blue-collar life. But the record is impressive without ever
being moving; his honesty and accuracy are admirable, but the listener
is always at one remove from the experience. Its poor sales perhaps
reflect this. *Born in the USA*, the successor to *Nebraska*, has sold in
millions. It marks a return to a conventional rock format and a lyrical
sparseness. Its literal meaning is less clear, but its emotional impact is
far greater. When Springsteen performed in the north of England in
1985, 37,000 people raised their fists and sang 'Born in the USA'.
Whatever this meant it cannot have been what Springsteen himself
meant. Where the folk style of *Nebraska* allows control over the
music's meaning, it limits the music's power. However when songs
from *Nebraska* were performed live, with a band to accompany them
and an audience to interpret them, their character changed as their
meaning was fragmented. They gained rock's power and lost folk's
precision. Rock's effectiveness seems to be won at the cost of control
over its message.

Rock and Politics

Because of the way rock is enjoyed and understood, it is ill-suited to
the task of accompanying political manifestos. Rock cannot typically
work as oratory or as rhetoric; it cannot turn paying customers into
political activists. The political scientist and rock writer, Langdon
Winner, once asked:

> who could seriously believe that a person seeking the most incisive
> analyses of the world's current problems will find them on
> Columbia or Capitol LPs? Rock is not political theory and never
> will be.[6]

Putting political thought into song, Sting succinctly commented, is 'very hard'. Rock's emotional sensitivity works against political sophistication. It is almost as if rock's ability to express feelings prevents it from articulating explicit political ambitions. There is, however, a danger of being too dismissive of rock's political potential. It is certainly true that if politics is confined to the world of political theory, oratory, manifesto and action, then rock will seem an irrelevant distraction. If, however, politics' boundaries are drawn wider, then rock does not find itself out in the cold.

One of Landau's criticism of 'Masters of War' was that it was peopled by caricatures, who were, as a result, unbelievable. Its musical impact was diminished by this fact, and the implication was that for a song to work it needs to involve its listeners; the characters have to be recognizable. This reduces a song's ability to deal in generalisations or systems or social classes; it has to be concerned with specifics and with individuals. But it does not mean that the music has to be politically naive. It is just that class inequalities, for example, will be viewed through individual experience. Rock's politics will emerge in its understanding of private states in a public life; and as a result, its politics will have a distinct focus and style. They will be concerned with how the individual encounters the world; and they will be interested in comprehending and sympathizing with the individual, not in berating or lecturing them.

The political content and musical success of a song depend on more than the right intentions and a correct analysis. They rest on the way musical sounds and political sentiments are allied within the confines of a musical form. My argument can best be understood by comparing two songs, which share a subject matter but differ vastly in their musical treatment. The subject is homosexuality, and the two songs are Tom Robinson's 'Glad to be Gay' and Rod Stewart's 'The Killing of Georgie'. My claim is a simple one. Whatever the political sympathies of the two performers – Robinson's involvement in the gay movement, Stewart's right-wing pronouncements – it is Stewart's song that best exploits rock's ability to deal seriously with political issues. 'Georgie' actively involves a politically uninterested audience, where 'Glad to be Gay' speaks only to the converted. Stewart gives his audience an individual to latch on to; Robinson only provides a category and a cause. The argument is not about the politics of the singers; it is about the politics of song. Stewart may be a less acute social critic than Robinson, but in this instance, he is a better song-writer.

'Glad to be Gay'

The lyrics of 'Glad to be Gay' indict contemporary attitudes to homosexuality. Robinson begins with the announcement that 'the British police are the best in the world', and then proceeds to disbelieve mockingly all the stories told about the persecution of homosexuals. The chorus continues in a similarly ironic vein, mixing a challenge with a celebration: 'sing if you're glad to be gay'. Through the use of irony and heavy sarcasm, the lyrics recount the plight of the gay community. They make a strong case, but it is at some cost to their persuasiveness. What power they have depends on the listener already sharing their sentiments. To appreciate their message, it is necessary to understand that the British police are not the best in the world, that they do raid pubs and clubs, that they do search houses, and that they do kick gays. Such facts may well be commonplace to many people, but they will not be shared by the majority. However widely appreciated the facts, the songs are for those who are aware of them, and the song divides those in the know from those who live in ignorance. The song also brooks no argument. It simply documents the facts. The song's meaning and purpose, therefore, is largely established in terms of some preconceived or pre-existing audience. It reinforces what they already know. It makes no attempt to explain the injustices and their persistence. Writing lyrics which address a particular audience with particular causes, while perfectly legitimate in itself, inevitably redefines the idea of 'popularity' in the idea of popular song.

The song's inaccessability is also sustained by its use of categories rather than individuals. Were Robinson engaged in social science, this approach might be entirely appropriate, but because he is making music, it fails. Discrimination becomes an object 'out there' in the world. This is true whether the listener is a victim of persecution or not. The private experience of listening becomes a process by which knowledge is acquired, rather than feelings shared.

The exclusiveness of 'Glad to be Gay' is further emphasized by the sound. The song is sung with a bitter sneer which mixes passion, defiance and defeatism. The effect of this can best be detected in the chorus, where the claim that gays are glad to be gay is countered by the feeling that it is impossible to be happy and gay in present society. The anger in Robinson's voice expresses his feelings but somehow it also excludes his audience, whatever their sexuality. The voice's sneer defies sympathy and mocks political action. The lyrics' irony seem to embrace fatalism. Between them, the voice and the lyrics exclude gay and straight audiences by asking for no help and offering no solution and no explanation. It is the way of the world.

'Glad to be Gay' was an important political gesture, but it was not a good popular song – something to be admired but not enjoyed. Its sneer, its fatalism, its exclusiveness and its use of categories undermine its ability to communicate. Chris Kirk, writing of his own taste in gay records, said of 'Glad to be Gay':

> Though I'll readily admit that the record is a trail-blazer, hearing it always depresses me into the ground. And not only because of the often-ignored ironic lyrics. I can't bear it because it's so bloody butch, like a football chant for gays . . ..[7]

The idea of 'Glad to be Gay' as a football chant perfectly identifies its failure as a song. Football chants work precisely because they establish which side you're on. 'Glad to be Gay' is an emblem of membership, a musical lapel badge. Pop involves its audience in a quite different way to the way a chant unites its singers. Where the chant provides a public statement of the public existence of an identifiable group, pop gives public expression to the private feelings of a heterogeneous audience. Notions of 'them' and 'us', uses of sarcasm and irony, clear statements of right and wrong, all become anachronisms in the context of a pop song. 'Glad to be Gay', for all its faults, does nonetheless have an easy, sing-along chorus, and audiences, whatever their sexuality, have joined in the singing. The effect of the communal singing, however, is to deprive the song of its irony. It becomes, like communal singing generally, an assertion of community and certainty – we are glad to be gay. The singing reduces the song's political effectiveness yet further. The cheery singing undercuts, rather than underlines, the song's political astringency.

'The Killing of Georgie'

Where 'Glad to be Gay' fails musically and politically, Rod Stewart's 'The Killing of Georgie' seems to succeed – it is a better pop song. For all Stewart's self-absorption and macho posing, he has a better understanding of pop's conventions than Robinson, and this enables him to write a much more effective song about the plight of homosexuals. 'Georgie' may lack the polemical force or the political astuteness of 'Glad to be Gay', but it is a more powerful song.

'Georgie' conveys a sense of the injustice, avoids fatalism, and offers a glimmer of hope. It achieves all this by focusing on an individual; the group (the category) is there only by implication. The song is the story of a gay friend of Stewart who was kind and 'needed love like all the rest'. It tells of parental incomprehension, of leaving home, and of Georgie's success in the New York social scene. Then one night Georgie is murdered by a New Jersey gang, and the song ends with Stewart mourning his friend and celebrating Georgie's love of life. There is no point in denying the clichéd sentimentality of the lyrics – the gay with the heart of gold, all you need is love . . . But for all this, Stewart engages the listener's attention, tells them a story and elicits their sympathy. He can do this because he is not dealing in categories. Bronski Beat's 1984 hit, 'Smalltown Boy', did the same thing in dealing with a similar subject. Though the boy has no name, he is not anonymous – he is you/me; the song gives him/you a story and a motive. Like Georgie, the smalltown boy leaves because his parents neither accept nor understand his sexual preferences. The song speaks of the boy alone on a railway platform; he is escaping because

> the answers you seek will never be found at home
> The love that you need will never be found at home . . .

Bronski Beat's Jimmy Somerville explained:

> Obviously we talk about the things that affect our lives – what else am I going to write about? . . . We're not screaming, we're gay and oppressed. We're doing it in a way that puts us across to people.[8]

Both 'Georgie' and 'Smalltown Boy' draw the listener into the song's world. The moral or the message of the songs are not carried polemically but emotionally. Stewart's husky, world-weary delivery and the mournful tune set the tone of the song – there but for poor fortune, go you or I. Bronski Beat used Jimmy Somerville's falsetto to cry in defiance and in sadness ('And as hard as they would try they'd hurt to make you cry/But you'd never cry to them just to your soul').

Neither song is conventionally 'political', but both deal with political issues. It is true that because they operate at the level of the individual and at the level of personal sympathy, they ignore the wider causes of the individual's plight and they discourage organized political activity. For all these omissions, these songs have the ability to connect private experience to public political processes. Pop can capture what it is like to be oppressed; it cannot explain that oppression or remove it.

Media and Messages

So far the argument has tried to combine sweeping generalizations with specific examples. This has been necessary partly because of the subject matter and partly because I want to establish the broad outlines of an approach to the politics of popular music. Crude distinctions have been drawn between folk and rock, and pop and rock have been used interchangeably, but such vagueness can only take the argument a limited way and more discrimination is required.

Because the audience is a partner in the creation of popular music, it is important to distinguish between the ways it hears music. A song heard on the radio means something different when heard in concert. When Tom Robinson first performed 'Glad to be Gay' in concert, his sneering voice fitted with punk's tone of cynicism and anger. On the radio, the song was denied this context, and became instead a petulant stamp of the foot. Then, six years later, when the song was again performed in concert, it had a new context and a new meaning. Robinson's own political profile had changed, as had his audience's. Where, during punk, Robinson had united an audience in its anger, he now linked them in a kind of friendship. 'Glad to be Gay' was no longer a song of righteous anger, but rather a song of communal defiance. Its anger was used to link the audience, not to set them apart. Robinson's unassuming friendliness, his total lack of false sincerity, his new musical concerns, allowed him to change the song's meaning, while the words remained the same.

A song's context and its form affect its meaning. Music heard on the radio (pop) and in concert (rock) carry different meanings and work within different constraints. If the dominant political language of pop is individualism, rock adds the communalism of the concert to its vocabulary. How the medium affects the (political) message can best be appreciated by looking at how John Lennon tried to reconcile his political interests and his musical ideas.

'You Say You Want a Revolution . . .'

Lennon's least commercially and musically successful album, apart from his excursions into the electronic avant-garde, was *Sometime in New York City*, a joint venture with Yoko Ono. It was also their most explicitly political record. Every song, with the notable exception of the title track, referred to an important political issue and advocated political action in pursuit of a variety of ends. *Imagine*, by contrast, was Lennon's most successful album. It too was political, but somehow this did not affect its sales.

Critics of *Sometime . . .* had a number of explanations for its failure. Some people argued simply that its politics were uncongenial; they disagreed with its politics rather than disliked its tunes. Charles Shaar

Murray spoke of it as 'irritating, embarrassing and finally, just plain unpleasant'. The lyrics caused the offence. They were 'clumsy, didactic, enormously condescending, breathtakingly simplistic and almost devoid of poetry'.[9] 'Sunday Bloody Sunday', for example, was condemned for its sloganeering commemoration of the occasion when the British army opened fire on an unarmed crowd. Lennon was clear where the blame lay for the death of the 'thirteen martyrs'. It did not lie with the people of Derry. It was the army which was responsible:

> Not a soldier boy was bleeding
> When they nailed the coffin lids.

Critics were uncomfortable with the way Lennon and Ono referred to 'you' in the song. Who was being addressed? A similar question was asked of the 'they' who imprisoned John Sinclair for ten years for the possession of two joints ('They gave him ten for two/What more can the bastards do'). Or who was the 'we' in 'Woman is the Nigger of the World' – 'we make her paint her face and dance'? The critics were unhappy with Lennon and Ono's challenges and accusations, and with the assumptions they made about their listeners' beliefs and responsibilities. In their accusations they attacked their listeners' behaviour, in their polemics they insulted the audience's intelligence. Lennon and Ono were not entitled, the critics argued, to address their fans in the way they did.

Interestingly, it was precisely Lennon and Ono's politics and the way they were expressed that won over those who applauded the record. They too dwelt on the sentiments and ignored the sound. *Sometime. . .* was treated as a political challenge. Your response to it was determined by your political awareness. The record's virtue lay in its political correctness and Lennon and Ono's boldness. This defence of the record, however, is unconvincing.

In 'Attica State', Lennon and Ono demand: 'Free the prisoners, free the judges/Free all prisoners everywhere', adding 'Now's the time for revolution'. The chorus announces that 'we're all mates in Attica State'. In 'Born in a Prison', they explain, 'We're born in a prison, raised in a prison . . .'. The songs all propagate the view that society imposes itself on individuals' lives, and that the only answer is to fight oppression collectively. When Lennon wrote 'Come Together' for the Beatles' *Abbey Road*, he was thinking of sexual pleasure rather than political action. On *Sometime. . .*, 'come together' means 'join the movement'. It is this shift in meaning which sets up the tension between form and content in the music. The politics' emphasis on public political action sits awkwardly with pop's concern with private pleasure.

Few would dispute Lennon and Ono's right to their political views, but the right to be heard does not include the right to agreement. And if the aim is to persuade, then consideration has to be given to the feelings and experiences of others. As popular musicians, Lennon and Ono had to recognize the limits that the music imposed on what can be said and how it can be expressed. Being correct is not enough, the song has to be catchy too. The music has to be part of the argument. John Hoyland, who shared Lennon and Ono's politics and admired their music, was cautious in welcoming *Sometime. . .*: 'conventional heavy rock backing and wailing saxophones aren't necessarily the best vehicle for all these ideas'.[10]

Rock *and* the politics had to be adapted. In particular, Lennon and Ono's almost exclusive concern with public political activity conflicts with rock's concern with the individual. Even in concert, the audience becomes a community only when their private concerns are made public. Only on special occasions – at a benefit or a rally – can the political convictions of the audience be assumed, and even then nothing is certain (see chapter 4).

Imagine was a political and musical success because it avoided the traps which were later to ensnare Lennon and Ono on *Sometime. . .*. The title track itself best illustrates the record's achievement. 'Imagine' embraces neither the analysis nor the practices of socialism, and yet its socialist sympathies are obvious – 'Imagine no possessions . . . A brotherhood of man/Imagine all the people/Sharing all the world.' Its politics and its effectiveness depend not so much on what the song says, but how the listener is addressed and on what is expected of them. The certainty in Lennon's voice is not the same strident sound that was to berate his audience on 'Sunday Bloody Sunday'. Lennon does not tell them what to think, but to 'imagine'. The assuredness of his voice is not that of dogmatism but of a wish to share a vision and of a respect for the intelligence of those who listen. Elvis Costello once explained what it was he wanted from his songs: 'What you really want is not songs that tell you what to think but songs that teach you to think for yourself.'[11] This was exactly what Lennon did in 'Imagine'. He made explicit what all successful popular music depends on: the imaginative involvement of its audience. Where on *Sometime. . .* that audience was lectured, categorized and lost, on 'Imagine' they became, in their thousands, willing participants in Lennon's dream. And once again, this collaboration between audience and artist was also a compromise between politics and music.

The song's politics were limited by its musical constraints. Because this song worked through the imagination, its attention was not directly on the 'real' world of practical politics. When Lennon imagined a world without hunger or greed, he made no pretence at explaining why there is famine, why some starve and others grow fat. Moreover, by directing his audience's thoughts, rather than their actions, Lennon offers no guidance as to how his imagined world could be achieved. Such omissions are not Lennon's; they are a consequence of the medium itself and its use of fantasy as a means of connecting private and public worlds, individual and collective experiences. Antoine Hennion described popular music like this:

> Imaginary identities, sentimental adventures, a taste of what reality represses; pop songs open the doors to dream, lend a voice to what is left unmentioned by ordinary discourse.[12]

It is the ability to create possibilities out of existing realities that captures pop's – and 'Imagine' 's – musical and political strengths, and its failings.

This chapter began by asking what limits there were to pop's language and how these affected its politics. We are now a little closer to answering these questions. Although the form and context of popular music varies, these variations take place around a single theme: the relationship between the private and public world of the individual. It is this that shapes and limits pop's musical and political effectiveness. Not only is pop limited in the ideas it expresses, it is constrained too in the way it can treat an idea. Modestly, but perhaps accurately, Jerry Dammers explained his song-writing: 'most of the things I write about are more or less common sense, I wouldn't even call it political, it's just seeing something that's wrong and writing about it.'[13]

Pop's power lies in its ability to give form to common sense; it is also, of course, its weakness. 'Common sense' is how we cope with the present, it discourages any expectations for an improved future. What is true for pop is also true for rock.

Rock may be more adept than pop in creating a communal identity for its audience, but it is still required, as Tom Robinson showed, to forge that audience out of the private responses of isolated individuals. It cannot assume the existence of a self-conscious political community; it has, instead, to work with what is shared in a much less coherent and articulated form.

Popular music's interplay between everyday common sense and imagination makes it a wholly inappropriate vehicle for accompanying political manifestos or inspiring collective actions. It is not, however, politically inconsequential. Pop's inability to change the world is compensated for by its ability to articulate and alter our perceptions of that world, and perhaps more importantly, to give a glimpse of other, better worlds.

Robert Wyatt's version of 'Shipbuilding', a song inspired by Britain's Falklands war, eloquently demonstrates how private experiences and public events can be productively combined in popular song. 'Shipbuilding' explores the conflicting emotions which the war generated. It is about an individual's dilemma, but not the dilemma about who is right and who wrong. It is not a polemic. It is about what it means to come down on one side or the other. The song asks questions and raises doubts. Building ships for war brings work but it also brings loss:

> Within weeks they'll be re-opening the shipyard
> And notifying the next of kin

The lyrics keep posing the same doubt: 'is it worth it?' Wyatt's voice, a delicate, slightly strained tenor, mixes regret and confusion. But where other singers might imbue the song with a maudlin sentimentality, Wyatt maintains a clear-eyed, restrained view of the dilemma. The restraint in Wyatt's voice and the song's even-handedness manage to make the war's waste seem all the more intolerable. 'Shipbuilding' says nothing of events in the South Atlantic, or in Westminster, or in Buenos Aires. It says nothing about sovereignty or lease-back agreements. It condemns no country and names no politicians. Yet it eloquently evoked the experience of the war; it gave voice to the emotions which fuelled concern about the war. 'Shipbuilding' was, in this sense, a profoundly political song. And its politics lie as much in its sound as in its well-crafted lyrics. The singer's mimicry of the sounds of speech and of emotion carry the song's message.

When Aretha Franklin sings 'Respect' it is the sound of her voice that tells us what she means and what she wants. When the Silhouettes sing 'Sha da da da/Sha da da da' in 'Get a Job' we do not hear nonsense. Just because it is sound, not literature, a pop song is neither inarticulate nor apolitical. It simply means that its politics emerge from the way that sound acquires a shared understanding, from the way that personal emotion becomes a public experience. Such politics may not have the rigour of political theory nor the effect of political action, but they exist, nonetheless, amidst the complicated intermingling of artistic intention, audience response, musical convention, and social context.

Emerging from such confusion, a song's meaning and its politics can never be fixed, and yet there are constantly recurring themes. The next three chapters explore three of them. We begin where most pop begins – with the ideas of liberalism: 'I want to be me', 'I want to be free.'

9

Freedom's Just Another Word . . .

'I was me back then and now I'm *me*. You dig?' (Bob Dylan)

The definitive liberal song is 'My Way'. Everything, I did 'my way'; every problem, I solved 'my way'; every choice, I made 'my way'. It is a celebration of the idea that success is just a matter of effort. Anyone can be President; anyone can be a star. But such ideas are not the subject of a single song, they are embedded in almost all the ways in which popular music is heard and enjoyed. Pop's exploitation of the imagination enables it to propagate the liberal idea that everything is possible, that the world is what we choose to make it. But like liberalism, pop also meets with frustration, when either dreams of freedom turn into nightmares of isolation or when the imagination's wishes are confounded by reality. Pop's escapism can turn into just another way to keep everyone chained.

Liberalism is the faith of the individualist. Where socialism and conservatism emphasise 'us', liberalism stresses 'me'. For the liberal, the world is composed of lonely individuals who are distinguished by their differences rather than their similarities. The liberals mistrust socialism for its attempt to create unity out of disparity; they mistrust conservatism for its belief in a hierarchical, natural order. Liberalism extols the value of doing what you want and saying what you feel. It is sceptical of the idea of doing what is good for you or of doing what is good for the nation or the state. Liberals are wary of politics, because politics is the way people are organized and manipulated, the way their freedom is curtailed. The liberal mistrusts such intervention; instead it values individual initiative and individual effort, and gives priority to the private world over the public world. Everything becomes what you make it. As Geraldine Ferraro said on being acclaimed as Walter Mondale's Vice-Presidential candidate in 1984, 'We have shown there is no door we cannot open.' For the liberal, society is not ordained by

God, nature or class; the only limits are those of the imagination.

The ideas of liberalism dominate Western thought: they shape societies and they shape people's vision of themselves. And just as liberalism affects the social and political world, so it penetrates popular music and art. Not that the translation is a simple or straightforward one. For every version of 'My Way', there is a song that twists or modifies the liberal idea (Sid Vicious' irreverent interpretation of 'My Way' made this point most decisively). Nonetheless, liberalism is ever present, as target or ideal, throughout pop. It is there in the obvious things: in the lyrics and in the record industry's business practices, but it is also there in the way popular music explores the imaginings and fantasies of its audience.

Hedonism in the Clouds: Flower Power

In the late sixties, liberalism was given a new lease of life. It became a central part of youth culture and was celebrated in the ideas of 'doing your own thing', 'being yourself', and so on. The conservative philosopher Michael Oakeshott captured the ethos of the era when he described what he thought of as the follies of youth:

> Everybody's young days are a dream, a delightful insanity, a sweet solipsism. Nothing in them has a fixed shape; everything is a possibility, and we live on credit . . . Nothing is specified in advance; everything is what can be made of it.[1]

In the 1960s, youth's demand for freedom was directed against old, constricting moralities. The combined effects of music, affluence and drugs were deployed to open up new worlds and new ways of living. Drugs had a particular symbolic and practical importance. Drugs provided access to new insights and forms of expression; in 1967, Pete Townshend paid tribute to the jazz saxophonist, Charlie Parker: 'I think drugs brought out in him something, that little extra in him, that has made him go down in history.'[2] Psychedelic drugs provided a way of showing that the world was what you made it (with a little help from your friends). Reality became a matter of perception, and perceptions could be changed. The music reflected and reinforced these ideas. Like drugs, music could seem to create an alternative world. In live performance, the concert could become a 'total experience' – lights and sounds combined to create an environment at odds with that of the 'straight world'. One member of the San Francisco community said: 'We were held together by our own good vibrations . . . we'd moved to a life style directed by music and acid. Acid and bands became the loci of our lives.'[3] The vast music festivals, from Monterey to

Woodstock, were seen as the logical extension of these alternative environments. (Woodstock was the site of a display of the liberal conceit that everything can be controlled by individual will. As rain threatened, someone shouted from the stage, 'Hey, if you think real hard, maybe we can stop the rain!' A chant of 'No rain! No rain!' began. So did the rain.)

During the sixties music and musicians changed in keeping with the new musical ethos. White rock music came to be seen as 'art', and art took on the guise of 'self-expression'. The Grateful Dead were one of the leading exponents of this new rock art. Borrowing from the idea of free (improvised) jazz, their concerts were long jam sessions in which songs were loosely structured and contained lengthy solos. Though this use of improvisation was borrowed from black jazz, and though the language of freedom was attached to it, its political significance had a different source. For the white rock artist, 'freedom' meant release from parental and school control, and from materialism. For the jazz player, freedom meant freedom from racial oppression and from poverty. But both black and white musicians used their music to express a desire for freedom, however different the musical and political constraints from which they tried to escape. Jazz in the sixties challenged the formal structure of previous music, questioning ideas of harmony and time. Sixties rock had more modest ambitions. It reacted against the musical traditions of fifties rock'n'roll to give a new voice to the sound of complaint. Rock'n'roll had been no less a 'protest' music than sixties rock – Chuck Berry's 'School Days' or Eddie Cochran's 'Summertime Blues' were protest songs of a kind. What sixties white rock did was to give a new guise to the protest. It was more (self-consciously) serious, cerebral and introspective. But it was still the sound of the rebel – and never the revolutionary. (The same rebel was to appear later in punk and in the rock revival bands of the 1980s – Jason and the Scorchers and the Blasters.)

For the white US rock stars of the sixties, music became a means of expressing private frustrations and aspirations. No collective political action was implied because no collective, systematic oppression was experienced. Listening to and playing music owed more to religious rites than to political acts. Drawing on Eastern uses of music, rock became a kind of musak for the mind. It acted as a spur for inner thoughts and fantasies. The ethos of music making and music consumption echoed the liberal's celebration of the private individual. The songs championed the liberal idea of freedom – 'be what you are', 'do what you want'. This meant avoiding the outside world; it did not involve re-ordering it. Freedom was a sensation, not the exercise of a political right. Freedom was represented in the feelings induced by drugs 'I Can See for Miles', Purple Haze', ('White Rabbit', 'Eight Miles High'), or by time and place ('Summer in the City', 'The 59th Bridge Street Song (Feelin' Groovy')). While such things were enjoyed, politics itself was avoided. Politicians and political institutions were treated with disdain ('I feel-like-I'm-fixing-to-die-rag'). Insofar as political concern existed, it was personalised – and political action moved from institutions to emotions: 'All You Need Is Love'. Or as Lennon told an interviewer, 'It all comes down to changing your head'.[4]

It is, of course, easy to exaggerate the effect or the reach of these changes. For the British, pop music in 1967 was not dominated by the sounds of psychedelia, but by those of Englebert Humperdink who seemed to be in the charts for most of that year. It is easy, too, to overestimate the self-awareness that accompanied the changes. The radical–liberal rhetoric tended to dress a more mundane reality. William Kotzwinkle's creation, Horse Badorties, was perhaps the archetypical hippy. Badorties begins his day:

> Looking through the shambles wreckage busted chair old sardine can with a roach in it, empty pina-colada bottle, sweet gummy something on the wall, broken egg on the floor, some kind of coffee grounds sprinkled around. What's this under here, man? It's the sink, man. I have found the sink. I'd recognise it anywhere . . . wait a second, man . . . it is not the sink but my Horse Badorties big stuffed easychair piled with dirty dishes. I must sit down to rest, man, I'm so tired from getting out of bed.[5]

This was not the life of the political activist bent upon changing the world; it was the life of someone whose world was on the brink of collapse, whose only hope was to survive. Finally, it is easy to forget how quickly it was all over. By 1968 white youth came to recognize what black people had long known, that it took more than well-meant words and nice thoughts to change the world. But for all this, popular music altered considerably. Rock musicians started to be taken seriously as 'artists', as social commentators, and as representatives of youth opinion. Music came to be thought of as both a vehicle for social comment and the embodiment of a self-contained world. Music's use of the imagination was politicized, and the politics it adopted were those of a liberalism which holds that everything is a matter of choice, everything is relative. While the rhetoric spoke of cataclysmic social changes, the reality revealed something else. While 1960s rock musicians discovered that the freedom they sang about was almost meaningless when applied to society, it did affect the way people thought about themselves and their desires. This was where the music found its power.

For Your Pleasure: Glam-rock

Though the music of David Bowie, Roxy Music and the so-called glitter or glam-rock bands was very different to that inspired by flower power and love, the same theme recurred. Both eras were occupied with the transforming effect of ideas and images. Glitter replaced the rhetoric, sequins replaced beads, and decadence replaced politics. But underneath, much remained the same. The hedonism of nature and drugs became the hedonism of cocktails and clubs. The search for sensations continued, while the styles and the tastes changed.

Liberal mistrust of conventional politics was translated from disdain into indifference. Bryan Ferry sang Bob Dylan's 'A Hard Rain's Gonna Fall', and what was once a song of bleak foreboding became an ideal accompaniment to a tequilla sunrise. The idea of individual creativity that had been current in the sixties was replaced by a delight in plagiarism – everyone was free to steal. The market was the only authority to be obeyed, and there was no copyright on ideas and images. Slade and Gary Glitter borrowed showbusiness razzamatazz. Ferry took from night-clubs and the upper-class aloofness of Noel Coward. David Bowie combined bohemia and science-fiction.

Whatever their sources, the music and the associated style were an end and a world in themselves. Nothing else mattered. Commitments of all kinds – from the personal to the political – were treated warily. No one could really believe in love anymore. This was not just a reflection of post-hippy disillusionment. It was also part of the world of 'dressing-up'. Everyone was playing a part: one minute Bowie was 'Major Tom', the next he was 'The Man Who Sold The World', then he was 'Ziggy Stardust', then 'Aladin Sane', and then The Thin White Duke. Ferry too changed from zoot suit to tuxedo. If you could change appearance and, the logic went, personality so easily, then there was no possibility of making commitments or falling in love. Nobody would be the same in the morning.

Although the era of glam-rock avoided politics, and thereby set itself apart from the hippies, and although it elevated style to a new importance, a significant common ground remained. Both eras celebrated the individual and each person's ability to change their world; and both sought to do so by escaping from the established world through music.

The idea of human malleability was common to the music of both the hippies and the glitterati. In the sixties, it came, in the words of Jefferson Airplane, with the injunction to 'feed your head'. In the early seventies, the exhortation was to paint your face. On both occasions, the ability to change the experience of life was used to escape from a particular version of reality. The main differences lay in the means (fashion replaced pharmacology) and the focus (style replaced politics). The liberalism of individuality remained.

Importantly too, this liberalism had a political impact, despite – or rather because of – its scepticism about, and its inability to change, conventional politics. And perversely perhaps, it was glam-rock, for all its apparent indifference to politics, that had the greater political influence. Two features of hippy liberalism mitigated against it having any lasting significance. Firstly, drugs were the key to personal change, not individuals themselves. Change was measured in terms of the effect produced by the drugs. Taking drugs did not allow people better control over their world; it released them from it. Secondly, while drugs addressed a very self-centred, hedonistic world, the 'politics' of hippy liberalism focused on a much larger vista: war and peace, materialism and poverty. There was a clear contradiction between the two. You cannot put an end to war just by thinking good thoughts, just as you cannot stop the rain by chanting. The music reflected the tension. The politics often seemed unconvincing and empty compared to the enthusiasm with which personal 'highs' were celebrated.

The liberalism of glam-rock was different. Though it was as self-centred as the hippy version, it depended on make-up and clothes more than drugs. These were things the individual could control, albeit mediated by shifts in fashion and notions of (un)acceptability. Moreover, glam-rock made no attempt to address world problems. Instead, it focused on things that could be altered: images and forms of sexuality. Bowie and Ferry were not just 'camp'. The games they played with gender were genuine challenges to existing assumptions. Dick Hebdige said of David Bowie that he was 'responsible for opening up questions of sexual identity which had previously been repressed, ignored or merely hinted at in rock and youth culture'. What they stood for was much more shocking than being against war and for peace. Bowie and Ferry, wrote Hebdige, 'artfully confound[ed] the images of men and women through which the passage from childhood to maturity was traditionally accomplished'.[6]

There were limits to these challenges and to their success. The attack was on the images, rather than on the source of gender typing, and its success as an agent of change was clearly parasitic on its commercial success. Glitter rock emerged from a music industry which had managed to reassert itself after the 'radical' noises of the late sixties. Glitter rock was, in part, a self-conscious attempt by musicians and the industry to revive the old showbiz values, albeit with a touch of irony. The record industry was much more able to understand people who donned sequins and platform boots than it could people who wore beads and refused to trust anyone over thirty. But the fact that the business could sell glam-rock more easily should not necessarily detract from the music's subversive potential. Glitter rock may have expressed, as Taylor and Wall censoriously describe it, 'the emptiness and decadence of bourgeois society', but this did not mean that it extolled unambiguously the values of that society.[7]

That glam rock dealt in images and was a commercial product, that it failed to address the 'real' issues, is hardly the point. Such comments could be made about every era of popular music. Pop, whatever the sixties myth-makers believed, cannot change the world. It can, however, alter the ways in which people experience that world; it can upset old images and provide new ones. The 'political success' of a musical form cannot be judged in the same way that we judge a political movement or government. Its success is determined musically, visually and commercially. Its political impact is marked by the way the music is consumed. Music that works politically is not necessarily music that makes political change its self-consciously ascribed goal. Conventional politics, as we have seen, fit uncomfortably into popular music. It is the 'unconventional' politics that work. This was what glam-rock demonstrated. It suggested one way that pop's liberalism could be put to political effect. It showed that what pop can change depends on what individuals and audiences already control themselves. Glam-rock was one way of interpreting the limits and strengths of pop's liberalism. Later musical styles have shown that there are other ways for pop's liberalism to take political shape. Once again, as with Flower Power and glam-rock, much changed and much remained the same.

I Want a Riot of My Own: Punk

In punk, the self-conscious politics of the late sixties was revived while the musical indulgences were rejected; and in the post-punk emergence of artists like ABC, Boy George and Prince, the style and sexual concerns of glam-rock were reintroduced, but with new styles to plunder and new ideas to convey.

For all their radical rhetoric and posturing, punk's politics were not quite as their appearance suggested. Though the accounts of commentators and musicians used the language of socialism, they disguised the real importance of the music and the true nature of the politics. The public image of punk dwelt on the working-class character of the audience and the musicians; on the experience of unemployment and urban decay; on disillusionment with the existing political order and the desire for a new one. Taken together these features of punk suggested a musical socialism. Certainly, some of bands were working class, some of the musicians were socialists, and some of the songs dealt with radical politics. But it is also true that some of the musicians came from middle-class homes, albeit via art school; some of the bands were distinctly right wing; and many of the songs had only the vaguest relationship with politics of any kind.

If any political ideology could be applied to punk, then rather than socialism, it should be anarchism. Punk will be remembered for the Sex Pistols' 'Anarchy in the UK' and for Johnny Rotten's shout of disgust – 'And I wanna anarchy/Know what I mean?/And I wanna be anarchist/Get pissed/Destroy . . .'; or for the Clash's 'White Riot' – 'White riot! I wanna riot/White riot! I wanna riot of my own.' Punk celebrated chaos and a life lived only for the moment. Socialism is for those who anticipate a more certain future; for punks only the present mattered. They were not interested in promises – 'There is no future/ No future for you/No future for me, (Sex Pistols' 'God Save the Queen'). The cynical slogan was 'from chaos into cash'. Such phrases and sentiments owed little, however, to political theories; they were as much the product of musical and artistic theories.

The ideas behind punk were not developed in the seminar rooms of the LSE or in cadre meetings of the Workers' Revolutionary Party. They came, as many British pop ideas have come, from the art schools. The ideologues of punk, Malcolm McLaren and his friends, drew on what they had learnt about the French situationists. The situationists used the symbols and artefacts of everyday life to subvert that life and to expose its rules by disrupting the organizations which maintained them. 'The construction of situations', the situationists announced, 'begins on the ruins of the modern spectacle'.[8] But while the situationists saw themselves as revolutionaries working collectively to achieve the revolution, McLaren and his cohorts were only interested in the disruption of the existing order; they were not much concerned about 'the system' or capitalism. The point was not to create a new world, just to mess up the old one. Malcolm McLaren remarked once, 'I never vote . . . I simply refuse to do anything like that.'[9] For all its hatred of hippies, punk shared this attitude in common with the Flower Power era. Politics was part of the style; and liberalism was its particular cut. It was no coincidence that a number of the key figures in the punk era had been equally prominent in the late sixties - Caroline Coon moved from running Release, the alternative advice centre, to managing the Clash. It was all done in the spirit of individual freedom. Sounding like generations of musicians before him, Johnny Rotten explained, 'We're doing exactly what we want to do – what we've always done.'[10] The same spirit was expressed in punk's do-it-yourself philosophy: anyone can be a musician, anyone can make a record (anyone can be President). In celebrating individualism and chaos, punk's ideology owed as much to anarchic liberalism as socialism, but this did not mean it was politically inconsequential.

Like glam-rock, punk's version of liberalism had its radical effects. The proliferation of independent labels, inspired by the DIY ethos, disrupted the complacency of the majors who had got rich on glam-rock and superstardom. Less tangibly, punk exposed rock's rules. It poked fun at ideas of romantic love; it celebrated boredom and mocked the idea that being a teenager meant perpetual pleasure; it forced the pop business, its controllers and its motives, into the limelight. And although this was sometimes done in the name of socialism, its inspiration lay in an anarchic liberalism which was uninterested in party organisation, revolutionary strategies, or consciousness raising. The point was to have a good time. This meant causing havoc, not reading Marx; it meant celebrating the moment, not the future; it meant mocking the established order, not working for a new one. Those who thought they were changing the world when they were changing chords were wrong. The important changes happened away from the rhetoric, a point made yet more eloquently by post-punk liberalism. Just as glam-rock politically upstaged flower power, so punk's successors were more politically effective than its progenitors.

The Look of Love: Post-Punk

There is always a danger that punk's high-profile politics will obscure the less pronounced politics of what followed. Both eras were, in fact, similar in the way they mixed style and substance; it was just that punk's radicalism, with its political gestures and poses, attracted popular attention and encouraged the idea that politics was its only concern. After punk, politics was played down, but this did not mean that the music was without political significance. Popular music just shifted its attention from the public realm to the private one. Instead of disrupting the organizations and laws that ordered the public activities of business and politics, pop became more interested in the rules and fantasies that ordered private life. Following in the footsteps of glam-rock, post-punk liberal scepticism was turned towards established ideas of sexuality and romance.

Post-punk music, like glam-rock, came to terms with the limits of pop's reach and power. There was no point in pretending that pop was not part of showbusiness (with the emphasis on the business). Making pop music meant being aware of more than the creative process. There was little place for the innocence that characterized the songs of the early Beatles, the Everlys, and countless other sixties performers. Everyone knew that pop had a history, that everything had a precedent. Jon Savage has labelled the modern method of music making as 'the art of plunder'.[11] Singing was done with the tongue firmly lodged in the cheek. After all, it was difficult to believe in the ideas of romance that had fuelled earlier eras. Public Image Ltd captured the spirit with their song, 'This is not a love song'. The title was the lyric.

Musicians were recognizing that ideas of 'self-expression' had little meaning amidst the marketing departments and sales figures. Being a musician meant developing a strong sense of irony. The most interesting artists were those who explored the power of this new self-consciousness. Romance, love, passion – the traditional fare of popular music – were given a theatrical setting, in which everyone over-acted and in which the audience never quite suspended disbelief. But whatever the parodies and rewording of old myths, post-punk pop returned its attention to the thing punk had ignored: love. Love songs have always been at the core of pop; the music is used to declare love, to chronicle love, to complain about love. Pop takes the private desires and longings of love, and makes them public.

ABC's album, *The Lexicon of Love*, is a brilliant catalogue of post-punk love songs. The title of the record captures the spirit. Love is no longer something that happens; it is something you look up and categorize. The cover reinforces this impression: two young lovers, he with a gun, she dying from the bullet of an unknown assailant; love as a matter of life and death . . . except that the setting is a theatre stage, a bright red curtain forms a line between the dramatic action and the off-stage preparations: the flowers, the curtain operator etc. Love, the cover suggests, depends on a pretence. And then there are the songs. The promises of love are forever being undercut by the doubts; 'The Look of Love' is threatened by a 'Poison Arrow'. 'If I were to say to you "can you keep a secret"/would you know what to do or where to keep it?'; 'When I'm shaking a hand I'm clenching a fist.' These are the doubts of liberalism. As long as my happiness depends on others, then I am trapped in a permanent state of insecurity. For if everyone does what they want, I can no longer be certain that I shall have what I want. Liberalism celebrates the freedom of the market, and relationships are judged in terms of customer satisfaction. Love is no longer for ever; it is just for as long as it works for each of you. Love is a contract, and ABC know this: 'Everything is temporary, written on the sand, looking for a girl that meets supply with demand.' But ABC are not simple cynics. They couldn't make pop music if they were. Theirs is not the defiant, alienating irony of Tom Robinson. Their cynicism and their music depends on the idea that there is another kind of love. You cannot be disappointed by love if you do not believe in it. ABC are believers, and their music works off the tension between how the world seems and what they would like it to be. Unrelieved cynics do not become successful musicians, just complacently miserable people. Making music, and attracting an audience, depends on being able to undercut pessimism with hope and cynicism with faith.

What ABC succeeded in doing was to use pop's new self-consciousness to play with the conflict between the two things which pop has always celebrated: love and freedom – 'your reason for living is your reason for leaving.' They articulated the doubts that every liberal knows: 'you can't always get what you want', especially when you want somebody to love. ABC offered no answers, only the dilemmas. Pop's liberalism, just like political liberalism, rejects organized solutions or rules. It is only music built on conservatism (or socialism) that can do that. Tammy Wynette can offer advice: 'Stand by Your Man'; ABC can only ask 'What's it like to love and lose that much?' ABC, nonetheless, used pop's liberalism to good effect. They managed to work within (and to extend) the conventions of the music to explore real issues. Their ability to do so emerged from the new possibilities that punk had created, but they left behind the public, overtly political rhetoric, and concentrated instead on the private politics of personal relationships. Both punk and ABC succeeded in the way they used style as the medium and the message. Ideas and images were their weapons; private feelings about public realms were their focus. Just as punk was incapable of changing the world of conventional politics, so it would be wrong to see ABC as capitulating to the ethos of showbiz superficiality. They were more subversive than that.

Playing with Sex

Where ABC subverted traditional ideas of romance and love, so other artists have challenged the models of gender and sexuality that underpinned these ideas. They have followed the pattern set by glam-rock, filtered through the lessons of punk. ABC's questioning of old images of love inevitably raised doubts about how people were supposed to behave when they were in love – what roles were appropriate, what promises were meant to be kept. Where relationships look like contracts, the uncertainties are endless, and the anxiety is intense; but at least the contract recognises its signatories as equals. In this kind of world, women are less likely to be seen as 'dependent appendages' to men or men to be seen as 'tough-minded protectors' of women. This new awareness seeped through into ABC (in Martin Fry's melodramatically passionate singing, for example), but it is much more apparent in the sounds and styles of people like Culture Club, the Eurythmics, Marc Almond and Grace Jones.

Like David Bowie, to whom they all owe a great debt, these artists refused to accept orthodox personality and gender models. In a fragmented, confused and yet commercial way, they have managed, in Jon Savage's words, 'to inform and comment upon the relationship between the dominant – what we are *told* to feel – and the subconscious – what many of us are actually feeling – at the same time as shift[ing] units'.[12] They have accentuated the subversive element within the offer which liberalism makes to us: to choose who we are.

In accepting this challenge, pop musicians were not breaking into uncharted territory. Extravagant 'dressing-up' has always been a part of showbusiness (from Liberace to Elton John; from Danny La Rue to Boy George). Similarly there is a long history of songs which, more or less unambiguously, explore homosexual life and love: from Noel Coward's 'Mad About the Boy' to Tom Robinson's 'Glad to be Gay', from Soft Cell's 'Tainted Love' to David Bowie's 'Boys Keep Swinging', and from the Village People's 'YMCA' to Bronski Beat's 'Smalltown Boy'. Even the socially sanctioned assumptions of heterosexual relations have never been given an entirely easy time. Women singers have given voice to their dissatisfaction with their treatment by men. Black music, in particular, has been a rich source of such complaints: from Bessie Smith to Aretha Franklin ('Respect') to Gloria Gaynor ('I Will Survive'). The self-conscious dissection of relationships by Dory Previn and Joni Mitchell has been paralleled by the less literate, but equally articulate, passion of performers as diverse as Janis Joplin, Dusty Springfield and Dolly Parton.

Rather than breaking with these long traditions, post-punk styles opened new ways to voice dissent and explore alternatives. The euphemism, which once disguised what could not be spoken, has become the metaphor to explain what is felt. Grace Jones' 'Pull up to the Bumper' is neither purely an exercise in *double entendre*, nor an invitation; it is also a challenge or a demand. The cool, distanced observations and confessions of Previn and Mitchell have been supplemented by attempts to give a sound to women's experience, as in the work of, for example, the Raincoats, who refused to make music that conformed to traditional instrumental hierarchies; the instruments did not simply accompany the voice, and the music acknowledged no automatic priorities among the various sounds. The effect was to undermine the listener's expectations about how feelings are experienced and expressed.

Post-punk pop has also been used by women to question the stereotypes which have previously confined their images and their interests. Groups like the Raincoats, the Slits and the Mistakes have not allowed themselves to be sold as glamorous puppets, dancing to the strings of sexual and pop convention. Musical and social survival has become intertwined. And this has involved more than getting the lyrics right – 'People blow words out of all proportion', said Georgina of the feminist band, the Mistakes.[13] It also meant that the context and the form of the music mattered. (Eighty per cent of the Mistakes' gigs were benefits. They chose to play 'Women Only' concerts and to use – when they cound find one – a women-run PA system.)

The Au Pairs built their music around the relations between the women and men in the group, using group dynamics to express and explore sexual conflicts. Not that the Au Pairs were a post-punk version of Fleetwood Mac, who used their complicated romantic entanglements to fuel their *Rumours* album. The Au Pairs were more interested in politics than gossip. Lesley Wood of the Au Pairs described their songs as not 'just feminist songs . . . They're songs that just try to describe certain situations between men and women.'[14] In 'Love Song', they sang: 'Take out the ring – two fates sealed – negotiated a business deal – Is this true romance? Champagne bubbles – Going flat – gone flat.' The commercial analogy recalls ABC. But the differences between the two are more pronounced than the similarities. While ABC used the mythology of love and love songs to evoke new ideas and attitudes, the Au Pairs were more interested in a harsher reality. The music was a vehicle for their anger and frustration – it is deadly serious, it is sex as power; for ABC it was a source of fun and fantasy – it is all a game, it is sex as drama. While ABC are devising a new disguise for reality, new myths for love, the Au Pairs are singing about the politics of sex, about the gap between male fantasies and women's experiences ('Come Again', 'Set-Up'). There is another difference between the Au Pairs and ABC. This is measured by record sales. The Au Pairs' political honesty would not translate into songs with the popular appeal which ABC's enjoyed. This was not just a question of the subject invoked (though 'Come Again' was never likely to receive daytime airplay), it was also a question of the performance. The Au Pairs' passion offered confrontations with unpleasant realities; ABC's passion offered an escape from them.

Pop has also been used to identify new rhymes and roles for men. Although the image of the rock performer changed considerably from Elvis Presley's pelvis and tight trousers to Mick Jagger's long hair and white dress, their images were constructed around a fairly standard view of (hetero)sexual relations. For all its emphasis on sexual freedom, Flower Power's celebration of the idea of birth and the 'earth mother' reproduced conventional images of women's role as child-bearers. The freedom of 'free love' always suited men more than women, so that while the image of men in pop altered, it was firmly located within traditional male–female roles. Glam-rock and post-punk music presented an opportunity to break from these conventions.

Post-punk electronic technology, for example, has allowed for the emergence of a new type of performer. The posturing guitar hero, wrestling his guitar in phony sexual passion, was replaced by the computer operator, standing studiously over the keyboard. Howard Jones, surrounded by keyboards and computers, appeared as the lonely suburban boy, plucked unwillingly from his bedroom and his toys. Convention has been broken in other ways. Soft Cell gave voice to a darker side of lonely suburban youth than was suggested by Jones' teenage angst. This was not the Bacardi fantasies of Duran Duran – every travel agent's vision of an exotic 18–30 Club holiday. Instead they were the fantasies and exploration of sexual confusion, using ideas and images which the adult world describe as 'perverse' (in *The Face*, Soft Cell were pictured harnessed like huskies, being whipped forward by a leather-suited woman). The politics of playing games with traditional ideas of 'the pop star' emerge in the reaction they create. Marc Almond recalled his experiences with Soft Cell:

> Do you know the thing I feel really creepy about is when I read things like Sexy Super-Hunk Marc Almond! . . . anyone with an ounce of sense in their head would NEVER call me a hunk. I've looked in the mirror and I can't even say that I'm good looking. I'm rather an odd looking person if anything.[15]

Almond was able to make a small chink in the established view of the male star. Ugliness may be acceptable – even essential – within heavy metal, but pop has always been more selective. (It is noticeable how heavy metal bands feel the need to dress up for *Top of the Pops*.) Playing with sexuality is to engage in the politics of what it is acceptable to be or want. Paul Rutherford, one of Frankie Goes to Hollywood's two gay singers, once said:

> a stance about being on the dole is one thing. It might be radical to an extent, but I think we hit a far more radical stance by touching on sex, gay sex, or whatever it happened to be turned into by the media.[16]

The changes did not just involve images. The sound too allowed for a new kind of male vulnerability and confusion. Frankie Goes to Hollywood did not use the sound of the 'sensitive' singer-songwriter, seeking protection. Instead theirs was the sound of anxiety, expressed through ordinary, flat voices forced into a strained operatic style. Where the singer-songwriter James Taylor sang in a flat tone to indicate the sincerity and authenticity of his feelings, Marc Almond and others expressed their feelings by exaggerating, and almost parodying them. Their emotions were no less genuine than Taylor's, it was their character and the manner of their expression which differentiated them. By introducing a theatrical element into the performance, these post-punk singers could also explore a wider range of emotions and feelings than was allowed for in Taylor's autobiographical reportage.

Liberalism's Limitations

However sexual identity is explored in pop it remains constrained by the medium. Making popular music cannot be separated from the struggle to win popularity. The Mistakes' decision to concentrate on benefits and women-only audiences automatically ruled out a mass audience. The alternative was to accept the restrictions and conditions imposed by the musical form, the industry and the broadcasters. For the Mistakes, this was an unacceptable cost; for others it was worth paying. Marc Almond and Boy George wanted popular success and mass exposure; this was what being a pop musician meant. As Jon Savage explained:

> they still play the traditional pop game – and it's hard not to: their refusal to commit themselves on matters of specific sexual activity is partly born out of self-protection . . . but it is also down to an understanding of the way pop works – not by specific or slogans, but by hints and inferences loose enough for the imagination to leap in and resonate.[17]

The price of popular success is a liberal politics. The politics of sexual identity are turned into questions of individual choice. The solutions are ideological and individual – not practical and collective.

Pop's liberalism is an inescapable part of the music. It is not just a matter of the political beliefs of the musicians or of the beliefs held by society at large. Pop, like any mass medium, does not act as a blank blackboard on which ideas are simply chalked; there are too many intervening factors. It is a long and tortuous journey from artist to listener, but this does not mean that the values of the industry and the broadcaster are the only ones to shape the music's meaning. It is, of course, important that record companies operate in a market economy which values the 'free competition' of liberalism. It matters too that record executives pay little attention to the actual content of a record and are only concerned that it sells. It is of even greater significance that radio and TV exposure is organized around chart performance, itself a crude reflection of market decisions.

It is not surprising that the music's organization and content reflects liberal ideas. But it is too easy to argue that the meaning of the music is forged by these factors alone. Not only are there clear tensions between the liberalism of, say, the record executive and the musician, there are also contradictions within liberalism itself. But even if everyone involved in making music shared the same, consistent version of liberalism, this would not give us a complete picture of the music, because that depends on what is heard as well as what goes into the making of it.

Most popular music is caught from the radio or TV. It is listened to – casually – by isolated individuals. Popularity depends on how successfully pop blends with or heightens the private thoughts and experience of these individuals. This reproduces the typical liberal distinction between the public and private world. Events are channelled and understood through the perceptions of the individual. Things seem to 'happen'; their cause and explanation lie 'out there' beyond the reach of the individual. Further, pop is entertainment. It is part of the world of leisure. Almost by definition this sets it apart from conventional politics, and thereby reinforces the typical liberal scepticism of politics. By being located in the world of leisure and in the experiences of the individual, pop's 'politics' are those of the intimate worlds of desire and relationships. It finds its resonance in the ambiguities and confusions that are characteristic of liberalism. In celebrating the idea that we can do or become what we like, pop raises questions about what limits our present actions and aspirations. Even in offering escapism, pop implicitly points to what is being escaped from.

Rock's politics use a similar ambiguity. They play off the dilemma between the desire to rebel and the fear of what lies beyond the rebellion. Simon Frith explains rock's power in its ability to capture the confusion between freedom and loneliness, between liberation and alienation.[18] And for Greil Marcus, this ambiguity was embodied in Elvis Presley, and echoes through all who have come after him: the country boy who became a king, but who always looked back to what he had left behind.[19] In rock and pop, the promise and disappointment of freedom both inspires and limits the politics.

Popular music celebrates the hopes and miseries of love – 'you are my everything', 'there will never be another you'. It is much less interested in the institutions of marriage, family, status and class, which may frustrate the hope and cause the misery. Pop reflects; it does not reform. In its images and experiments, pop reveals possibilities, but it can only hint at their realization on stage, on celluloid and on vinyl. Pop can allude to the thoughts and fantasies which defy other forms of expression, but it can do little to change the institutions which keep them repressed.

Not that pop's brilliance is always evident. There is much mud to cover the odd diamond. Nonetheless, these are the terms in which success is achieved, and therefore the way in which the political boundaries are set. For pop, these limits are those of liberalism. Judging pop's political significance depends on first recognizing these limits. The choices that musicians face cannot be spread out on a simple political spectrum, extending from left to right, with liberalism somewhere in the middle. The political impact of pop is measured by the way that the tensions within liberalism are exposed and explored. To ignore those tensions is to offer entertainment but not enlightenment. To offer solutions to those tensions is to enlighten but not to entertain. At its best, pop music simultaneously embraces and questions the liberal ideal by demonstrating both the limits and the reach of the imagination. Then it is the voice of the rebel. Then it understands that hedonism is an act of desperation, born of having to live alone; immediate gratification is grasped in default of some more distant collective solution; then pop understands that having fun is a serious business. But great pop also knows that the expression and exploration of desires and pleasures is as potentially disruptive as any demonstration or political tract. It is only when pop is at its worst that it presents liberal utopias or dour realities, when it either pretends that 'I did it my way' or that there was no other way. Then it is the voice of the conservative, not the rebel.

10

Ragged But Right?

'Please don't ever change/I like you the way you are' (Goffin/King)

For all pop's delight in freedom and rebellion, it is also conscious of their double-edged qualities: knowledge of the proximity of freedom to loneliness, the understanding that being born to run means never having any place to call home. The freedom of the rebel is the absence of security and certainty, but without such things it becomes very hard to establish an identity. Without an identity, freedom itself loses its appeal. There is no point to freedom if you do not know who you are and what you want. Only by belonging to a community, by enjoying the trust of others, is it possible to take on an identity. The trouble is, of course, that the community necessarily stifles freedom, and inspires the wish to escape. And so the cycle goes on. The frustrations of the community create the need for freedom, just as the frustrations of freedom establish the need for the community.

Some pop simply pretends that change and certainty can be combined: 'it's getting better all the time.' Some pop promises an escape from having to choose: 'Let me take you down 'cause I'm going to Strawberry Fields/ Nothing is real, and nothing to get hung about.' Some pop celebrates the pleasures of change and uncertainty: Culture Club sang cheerfully, 'When we cling our love is strong/ When you go you're gone for ever.' Some pop dwells on continuity, on the way things stay the same; this is often the message of country music. And among all these types of song there are those for which the choice between change and certainty is an endless source of anxiety: 'will you still love me tomorrow?' Each form of pop song takes a different attitude to the alternatives of freedom and continuity, of independence and security, of the individual and the community. A pop song which chooses the second of these possibilities often appears as conservative. The urge to remain, to let things be, is a conservative response, so too, though in a different way, is the pretence that there is an escape from reality or that the world is a matter of what you make it. This chapter is about how these different kinds of conservatism are expressed in pop, and how sometimes they can enhance the music and at other times destroy it.

Community Singing

In one important sense, simply to extol the virtue of the community is to ally with traditional conservative thought. Unlike liberalism, conservatism places great emphasis on the ideas of belonging and permanence. The conservative community is based on a hierarchy in which everything is in its place, and there is a place for everything. Such a community is believed to have emerged gradually, through history's complex forces; its form, therefore, gives the appearance of a divine or fatal order. It is a history in which the common people have loyally borne their role in the great tide of events. From such a perspective, the value of the community lies in the idea that the whole is greater than the parts; that people are happier together in the security of their common identity than they would be as 'free' individuals. In emphasizing the community, conservatism also underlies the need for a common culture.

A community has to have an identity, only then can its members know who they are and what they belong to. Culture is one means by which such identities are established and maintained. Whatever view is taken of conservatism, it is difficult not to see popular music as part of this process of cultural production and, therefore, as part of the business of creating a sense of community, even when the music's delight in rebellion and freedom seems itself to challenge or deny the existence of any community.

Pop music, by this argument, works precisely because of its ability to show us that we belong. The very fact of a pop song's popularity is a kind of reassurance; it lets people know that their intuitive responses and feelings are shared. Without this knowledge, the sense of loneliness and self-doubt might be unbearable. Greil Marcus once wrote:

> We fight our way through the massed and levelled collective safe taste of Top 40, just looking for a little something we can call our own. But when we find it and jam the radio to hear it again it isn't just ours – it is a link to thousands of others who are sharing it with us. As a matter of a single song this might mean very little; as culture, as a way of life, you can't beat it.[1]

Marcus argues that the best pop works because of the way it plays off the tension between liberal freedom and conservative certainty. For him, it is a tension which goes to the heart of the North American way of life and the American dream. Elvis Presley was the incarnation of the dilemma. 'What I hear, most of the time,' says Marcus,

> is the affection and respect Elvis felt for the limits and conventions of his family life, of his community, and ultimately of American life, captured in his country sides; and his refusal of those limits, of any limits, played out in his blues. This is a rhythm of acceptance and rebellion, lust and quietude, triviality and distinction. It can dramatize the rhythm of our own lives well enough.[2]

Presley's phenomenal success was due to his ability to express the conflict between wanting to belong and wanting to be free, between being part of the community and being an individual, between security and liberty. For the liberal, these tensions are resolved in favour of the individual; for the conservative, in favour of the community. Neither solution can work alone. Elvis' music, in recognizing that neither answer was adequate, allowed his audience to share in their doubts: it let them see that their dilemmas were other people's too – that their confusions were part of what it meant to live in the USA.

Elvis was a particular American, of course. He was a Southerner. The South was poor and depended on the collective effort of the community to cope. Everyone suffered and survived together. The North was richer; and as a consequence, the people were freer – and suffered on their own. (In his song 'Rednecks', Randy Newman paints an ironic portrait of the North's sense of superiority over their Southern cousins: 'Down here we're too ignorant to realize/That the north has set the Nigger free/Yes he's free to be put in a cage/in Harlem in New York City . . .'). In the South, according to Marcus, music served two vital functions. It 'helped hold the community together, and carried the traditions and shared values that dramatized a sense of place. Music gave pleasure, wisdom, and shelter.' But music could also offer 'an escape from community'; it could give voice to the idea that there was a world beyond the community, a world inhabited by 'tramps, whores, rounders, idiots, criminals'. Musicians 'bridged the gap between the community's sentimentalized idea of itself, and the outside world and the forbidden'. A musician's talent was measured by their ability to 'take the commuity beyond itself': to show what was possible as well as reflecting what already existed.[3]

Rarely, however, does popular music manage to combine the realities of the community with the possibilities beyond. Because most popular music concentrates on the imagination of individuals, it dwells on those possibilities which we cannot – or choose not to – actually realize: our fantasies. It evokes a world without firm foundations, without a history or a future. The promise it makes, that we can be who we like, that we can escape what we dislike, is a commitment that cannot be honoured. Pop's pleasures, therefore, are confined to those happy moments before the truth is recognized or those melancholic moments after reality has imposed itself. The recognition and the acceptance of these harsh facts is at the heart of conservatism; it taps the realization that most people are tied down in place and time, that the prospects of change are small compared to the certainties of continuity. Country music is one of the most effective evocations of this knowledge.

Country Conservatism

The sweet moan of the pedal-steel guitar seems to be the sound of resignation, and country music seems sometimes to speak only of disappointment. The playwright and actor Sam Shepherd was once asked why he thought country was such sad music: 'Because, more than any other art form I know of in America, country music speaks of the true relationship between the American female and the American male . . . Terrible and impossible.'[4] But country is not the sound of self-pity; it has a dignity and a sense of security which owe their existence to the part played by 'the community' and fate in country's mythology. Dismay is mellowed by a strong sense of the inevitable. While Tammy Wynette knows that 'Sometimes its hard to be a woman', she also knows that there is a solution, 'Stand by Your Man'.

Crude interpretations of country music miss this sense of 'making do', seeing it only as a conservative manifesto set to music. In *Spare Rib*, Sue Tyrrell once decribed Tammy Wynette like this:

> She is . . . the figurehead of the counter-revolution, a glittering peroxide testament to White Womanhood and the homely virtues of the nuclear family. She is both a symbol and defender of the traditionally conservative Middle American way of life, spear-heading the inevitable backlash to the Women's Movement.[5]

Not only do these claims exaggerate Wynette's power, they also misunderstand her music. Tammy Wynette's voice does not ring with strident certainty nor with dogmatic assertiveness. Instead it is tinged with both a doubt and a dignity born of the knowledge that 'it is hard to be a woman'. 'The only image I want', Tammy Wynette once said, 'is that of the average woman in the audience.'[6] Country music tries to give voice to the realities of life, eschewing the easy, but impossible, escape routes offered by pop. Simon Frith and Angela McRobbie make this point in their comparison of 'Stand by Your Man' with Helen Reddy's pop song, 'I am Woman'. Wynette's voice and its setting, they argued, express 'a knowledge of the world' as women experience it collectively. While the lyrics of Helen Reddy's song may offer a more progressive sentiment, the sound undercuts it: 'what you hear is the voice of the idealised consumer, even if the commodity for consumption in this instance is a packaged version of women's liberation.'[7]

Country music is conservative in its emphasis on community, tradition and resignation. But it is not propagandist – at least, not if the music is any good. The mood of disappointment and fatalism that it evokes depends on the knowledge that there are possibilities which cannot or will not be explored. You cannot miss what you have never had; you cannot be sad for what you have never known. *Spare Rib*'s interpretation sees country as offering a single, self-contained vision of the world – 'the John Wayne ethic set to music'. But this misses the tension between the voice and the sentiments: they are not saying the same thing. The message of the lyrics may be 'stand by your man', but the voice speaks of the frustrations which make standing by your man the only possible solution. 'If I was back home in Mississippi, being a Mississippi farmer's wife,' said Tammy Wynette, 'you'd stand by a man regardless of what happened because you wouldn't have any reason or hope to do anything better.'[8] The song is not offering escapism: the problems still remain. It is offering a sympathetic understanding. Country music's political conservatism stems from the way it resolves the conflict between what is and what might be in favour of the status quo, but its resonance and its emotional power stem from its refusal to ignore that conflict.

Not all country music is like this. Country music has been used for straightforwardly right-wing propaganda, from racist chants to 'The Battle Hymn of Lieutenant Calley' (see chapter 3). However, these no more typify country than the Archies or the Wombles typified pop. Similarly, it would be wrong to define country by reference to the mundane and inoffensive songs which populate the country charts (who uses Men At Work to describe rock, when they could refer to the Rolling Stones or ZZ Top?). Though the ordinary features of country are illustrative of a certain kind of conservatism, it is the conservatism of certain record companies, radio stations, audiences and musicians. It is not necessarily the conservatism of the musical form. We can only judge that in country's best moments, when its limits are reached and its boundaries shifted. Country music may rework the same formulae more often and more doggedly than, say, pop, but the conservatism of musical change is not the same as the conservatism of the music itself.

A 'Progressive' Conservatism

The same distinction can be applied to all forms of music. All styles recycle their predecessors, and all pop music is based on established formulae. This kind of conservatism cannot be attributed simply to the dead hand of commercial interests. Folk, a relatively uncommercialized area, is as capable of being unimaginatively repetitive, despite the lack of business pressure to keep delivering the same product. A reluctance to change may owe as much to the conservatism of the musicians and their audience as to the business. All are tempted by the easy life in which expectations are met and successes repeated. Much rock is a result of this process of mutual reassurance. Appropriately, Status Quo made a career out of what seemed like a single riff and a single rhythm.

There is a less obvious conservatism in the 'progressive' music of the late sixties and early seventies which, despite its label, was deeply traditional. Exponents of this style – Yes, the Nice, the Moody Blues and Pink Floyd – deployed the newest technology (mellotrons, synthesizers, quadrophonic sound systems) to make music which seemed to boast of its technical and musical sophistication. The word 'progressive' was used to imply that the music and the musicians had taken a step up the aesthetic ladder. But 'progressive' had two distinct and, apparently contrary meanings. One referred to music's use of technical and scientific advances; the other referred back to past musical achievements. Either way it was conservative.

Although 'progressive' music was presented as an 'improvement' on its popular predecessors (rock'n'roll or 'commercial' pop), it allied itself with classical music or with the avant-garde. The Nice, for example, having rearranged Bernstein's 'America', revamped Sibelius' *Karelia Suite*, and later went on to perform their own pseudo-symphonic piece, 'The Five Bridges Suite', with a full orchestra. These pretensions were encouraged by members of the cultural establishment who seemed to bestow their blessing on pop's new guise. The Beatles received favourable reviews from *The Times'* music critic, William Mann; Tony Palmer compared them to Brahms, and Wilfred Mellers, a serious musicologist, wrote respectfully of their innovative musical style. Instead of pop being subjected to the 'I know what I like' school of criticism, it was now being compared – and more importantly, comparing itself – to the standards of classical music and 'Art'.

In borrowing these aesthetic criteria, musicians attempted, with the industry's blessing, to change the meaning of popular music. The very idea of popularity was itself called into question. The music acquired an aura of elitism, which was expressed primarily in a disdain for 'commercial' music. Progressive music was serious; pop was trivial. Its seriousness was demonstrated by the length of the songs (because the music had something important to say, it took a long time saying it) and by the use of 'concept' albums in which a single theme was pursued (the idea of the symphony provided the model). The audience was expected to listen and nod. The music's complex structuring and barrage of sounds denied any opportunity for popular involvement. It was to be admired. In trying to transform popular music into an electronic classical music, progressive music was, in fact, regressive; it sought to establish aesthetic criteria and patterns of consumption which were both elitist and traditionalist.

Progressive music also borrowed from modern jazz; and despite the avant-garde connotations of the source, the result was a further boost for the cultural status quo. The use of the extended, improvised instrumental solo had been featured in late 1960s music as a form of self-expression (guitarists always grimaced as they dragged another painful truth from their Fender Stratocaster); in progressive music, the solo took on the guise of artistic exploration. The experimental sides of Pink Floyd's *Ummagumma* and Soft Machine's *3* (both were double albums, a sign of the music's seriousness) used the techniques and sounds of modern jazz and the avant-garde to make a 'pure' music which had none of pop's typical concern with feelings and circumstances. On *Ummagumma*, the track titles gave an indication of the spirit: 'Sysyphus', 'Several Species of Small Furry Animals Gathered Together in a Cave and Grooving with a Pict'. The result was a music which tried to impress, which called for serious attention. Pink Floyd premiered their use of quadrophonic sounds in one of London's classical music concert halls. This combination of modern technology and traditional music captured the virtues and vices of progressive music. It explored the new possibilities which the studio and musical technology made available, but it measured these experiments against the elitist standards of the artistic establishment.

Progressive music's use of modern technology, in fact, did little to mitigate its conservatism. The technology of 'progressive' music, whether in the studio or on the stage, was very costly. The increase in financial commitment (by record companies and musicians) increased the cost of failure. Not only did this encourage a conservative caution in business decision-making, it also sustained a musical conservatism. With expensive, complex equipment, it was necessary to use highly skilled players. Such conditions created a bias in favour of those with money and musical training.

In 'progressive' music, the technology served to shore up conventional aesthetic standards. The technology represented 'complexity'. It allowed people to make 'difficult' music. But while the technology sustained traditional musical values, it also drew on the aesthetics of science. The technology came to represent some form of absolute control. Just as science is seen to furnish humankind with the means to control its environment, so the musical technology gave complete control over the form of the music. Nothing was left to chance. This, like the use of classical musical aesthetics, had the effect of excluding the audience. They became pure consumers of musical perfection. For all its disdain for commercial music and mass consumption, progressive music encouraged even more passivity from its audience than the much-derided pop, where it was expected that audiences would dance or listen with only half an ear. Progressive music wanted their full attention, and their almost complete passivity. In this, as in all else, it was profoundly conservative. It was also short-lived, but its legacy persists in ideas of technical 'perfection'.

Perfectly Conservative

Just as technology is seen to embody 'progress', it also represents 'perfection'. Practical changes in studio techniques and hi-fi equipment have established new standards for recording and reproducing sounds. Compact Disc systems, for example, turn master-tape hiss into an unwarranted intrusion; and detecting the hiss becomes part of the business of listening to the music. Musical quality becomes confused with technical quality; artistic judgements become transmuted into technical ones. With the developments of new computer-based musical instruments, musicians are able to *choose* sounds rather than make them. The music is programmed, not created. This can appear to standardize the creative process, and therefore enhance the industry's conservative tendencies and weaken the power of an organization like the Musicians Union. It can further encourage the confusion between technical and aesthetic quality.

A 'good sound' may mean one that has met certain clinical criteria: the purity of the sound, the absence of mistakes, the lack of extraneous noises. Radio programming follows similar priorities. There should be consistency of sound and mood; no disruptions, no awkward noises. A 'professional' broadcaster, therefore, is someone who can switch smoothly between records, cartridges and introductions. The quality of a broadcast is measured by the number of errors. Records are expected to meet these kind of technical standards. These are the values of the sound engineer, not the musician. It is the engineers who are important: who else understands the equipment; who else can provide the 'perfect' sound? The fact that sound engineers often go on to become producers is not just a feature of the career structure of the industry; it is also indicative of a particular ideology that matches technical with artistic perfection.

Music recorded or played in a world in which the sound engineer is monarch, is conservative in its resistance to change and innovation, except insofar as they improve the quality of the sound. The technical skills of musicians, the ability to avoid mistakes, come to be valued more highly than their imaginative skills. And as consumers at the upper end of the market improve their record players, so the industry adapts to provide music which meets the new technical standards. Technical and commercial conservatism combine to reinforce a market and musical conservatism. Like country's conservatism, it works by allowing its listeners a sense of community and of security. They know where they belong and what to expect. But unlike country, the conservatism of technical perfection allows for none of the frustrations of communal security. It offers the sound of complacency, not resignation. Music which offers unquestioning certainty, like music which offers pure escapism, ignores the tensions and ambiguities that give popular music its potency.

There is a sociological explanation for this technological conservatism. The music's values suit its audience. Known as adult-oriented-rock (AOR), it is music for the adolescents of the sixties to grow old to. It recalls a youthful past, without inducing a sense of unease or embarassment. It eradicates the tensions which inspired rock's original message. It sounds good on expensive hi-fi's; it is pleasant, inoffensive, tuneful and slick. It is the sound of Fleetwood Mac and Foreigner. But not all music intended for this market embraces complacency so completely.

Creative Conservatism

Sometimes, in recognizing the music's form and its audience, pleasure can be made out of the very unease that underlies mortgaged security and which the music is intended to gloss over. Roxy Music's *Avalon*, for example, manages to give voice to the sense of lost opportunity and disappointment that adulthood brings. *Avalon* succeeds in soothing and disturbing simultaneously. The album's opening song (and hit single, 'More Than This', uses a haunting, vaguely celtic melody to accompany Ferry's weary voice. He sings of the disenchantment that follows the pursuit of pleasure – 'it was fun for a while'; and of the disillusionment that comes with age and experience. The lyrics use images of fallen leaves and sea tides to capture a sense of inevitability. There is no bitterness to evoke guilt or frustration, but neither does it offer simple, unqualified comfort. There is no more than this. There is no more than *this*? The conservatism of a mortgaged life is simultaneously asserted and questioned. And as in good contry music, it works because it recognises problems but offers no escape. It is not simply the conservatisms of 'progress', 'perfection' and profit, which serve to turn aesthetic criteria into matters for engineers and accountants. Though all these are at play in the making of the music, they do not exhaust the content and the meaning of the song. What remains is to be found in the resonance between Roxy Music's wistful sound and their listener's melancholic experience: the hope that there is 'more than this' and the realization that there isn't. The music's power lies in the life it brings to this conservative conclusion; the music is no less potent for doing this.

The same wistful melancholy has come to pervade Madness's crafted pop songs. Madness began as 'nutty boys', playing a rollicking, ska-influenced pop; they wrote funny songs about having fun. But as they have grown older, they have written songs, which, while still witty, paint a bleaker picture. Their concerns are with age and with politics. Where before they looked forward, they now look back to 'One Better Day', and confront a 'Grey Day' (The world outside is wet and grey/ and so begins another weary day'); they look forward to 'Tomorrow's Dream', but wonder 'will it get better in the long run/will we be here in the long run?' ('Yesterday's Men'). Out of these melancholic concerns, Madness create clever pop songs with captivating choruses and understated verses. They use pop's pleasures to evoke a sense of sadness and to satirize their political enemies ('Uncle Sam'). Instead of composing maudlin tunes to underline maudlin sentiments, they express their disappointment by setting it against almost defiantly cheerful or elegant melodies. Madness, like Roxy Music, use their skills to comprehend the disappointments of age, not to remove them.

Whatever it pretends to the contrary much of the best of rock displays a similar virtue and a similar conservatism. Bruce Springsteen, once fêted as rock and roll's future, has come to exemplify all that is most conservative and all that is best in rock music. Springsteen's success, however, owes more to what he says about the past than the future; he offers comfort in the face of a bleak prospect. Where he once boasted 'this is a town full of losers, and I'm pulling out of here to win', he talks of the disappointments of those who stayed behind, the losers. The open road of rock's mythology, the dream of adolescent escape from impending commitments, was replaced by the harsh – yet typical – reality of marriage, work and unemployment. *Born to Run*(1975) has become *Born in the USA*(1984); the empty freedom of escape became the inescapable burden of belonging. Springsteen, for all his romanticism, never pretends that either is easy. Neither the escape:

> The highways jammed with broken heroes
> On a last chance power drive ('Born to Run').

Nor the belonging:

> Now those memories come back to haunt me
> They haunt me like a curse ('The River').

Springsteen's later songs have been sympathetic accounts of blue-collar life. He seems to be writing specifically for the generation that grew up with rock'n'roll. Where once they revelled in teenage dreams, and maybe believed in true love, they now struggle to adapt to a crueller world. Instead of the pleasures and thrills and fears of 'Thunder Road', 'Tenth Avenue Freeze-Out', 'Backstreets' and 'Jungleland', there are the traps and constraints and commitments of 'Factory', 'The Ties that Bind', 'Jackson Cage', and 'The Price You Pay'. In 'Born to Run' life was lived 'out in the streets of a runaway American dream'. Five years later, on *The River*, the streets are a place to escape to after a day's work; they are a place where the worker regains his pride: 'I walk the way I wanna walk' ('Out in the Streets'). Springsteen's workers are usually male. On *Born To Run*, Springsteen's bids for freedom seem always to be accompanied by the girl of his dreams; love is taken for granted. On the later albums, love has turned into marriage and into disappointment.

But as Springsteen charts the disillusionments of age, he holds firmly to his romanticism. All that happens is given a grandly melodramatic sound, captured in Springsteen's voice, Clarence Clemons' rough-edged saxophone, and Roy Bittan's cascading piano runs. These sounds play with and against each other to give rock's answer to country's mournful voices and sighing pedal steel guitars. The fatalist resignation is evident but not overpowering – the defeatism of the lyrics is always undercut by the defiant voice and the resolute rock beat. Springsteen may sentimentalize, but he also sympathizes, and in doing so gives some force to the idea that there is more than this. His is not the nihilism of someone like Leonard Cohen or early Jackson Browne, who add doom to the gloom of post-adolescence. Rather, Springsteen allows people to remember what they once were and once wanted. He recognizes the need to accept second best, but he does not pretend that life just 'happens' this way. The sounds and myths of rock rebellion act as a counterpoint to the subsequent realities. Like a photograph album, the music helps its audience to recall what they wanted and to acknowledge what they have become. Springsteen avoids the dishonesty of people like Rod Stewart, who recycle the old myths without qualification, pretending that nothing has changed. Their conservatism is that of adolescent escapism, made all the more pathetic by its hypocritical deceit.

Defiant Conservatism

Stewart and others play out rock's fantasies in a Peter Pan world, pretending to a life of easy hedonism, and as they do so, they become increasingly irrelevant. Only the Rolling Stones refuse to fade away. They manage, against all the odds, to remain half-convincing rock adolescents. With the very occasional exception, their songs continue to recycle the same rock'n'roll clichés. In their repertoire, there is a noticeable absence of songs about, in Springsteen's words, 'the ties that bind'. They seem to make no concessions to the disappointments and frustrations of age. Even as Jagger works harder and harder to get fit for each successive tour, even as Charlie Watts and Bill Wyman withdraw further and further from the world of rock, even as Keith Richards beats his drug habit and settles into (relatively) conventional domesticity, the Stones continue to make a success of rock's traditional mythology. It cannot just be a matter of nostalgia – their audience spreads too widely for that. Somehow the Stones survive, even as their music diminishes in its vitality. Simon Frith's answer to this apparent paradox is that the Stones have never been anything other than they are now. They have always shunned any commitment, any involvement in society. Their concerns have always and only been pleasure:

> The importance of the Stones is that they take pleasure completely seriously. Their commitment to it is total and the result is neither hedonism nor outrage but an awesome self-sufficiency.[9]

They are not concerned with age, obligations and work. Their music builds on the tension between promise and practice in the pursuit of pleasure. Taking rock's ability to express private fantasies and public realities, they give voice to the frustration of not getting what you want, not getting any satisfaction.

The Stones' politics, for all their social detachment, may be more telling than Springsteen's simply because pleasure is rock's only consistent subject. Where other rock stars simply celebrate it, the Stones know the costs and limits of pleasure, they know where our ideas of fun and desire fall apart. The conservatism is there: they make no attempt to change anything, but they use rock to express defiance in the face of 'the secret melancholy of life in the consumer collective'.[10] (In this sense, the Stones are the progenitors of the ABC of *The Lexicon of Love* and the Roxy Music of *Avalon*).

The Stones' political success lies in their distance from the world of conventional politics. Rock mythology is turned on itself to expose pleasure's double-edge, just as Springsteen uses rock'n'roll memories to expose the experience of growing up, or as Madness use pop's brightness to highlight their disappointment. The defiance the Stones evoke in their romantic imagery may be conservative, just like the defiance of the small community evoked by country music. But defiance is always in the face of something. Dull or escapist rock simply pretends there is no world to be contended with – it creates an enclosed, self-sufficient world to comfort the ego. It offers, in other words, the false promises of liberal capitalism: anyone can win, and losers only have themselves to blame. Great rock takes those promises apart. Literally, it makes fun of them. This is the strength of rock's conservatism: it's ability to provide temporary defiance in the face of the inevitable.

From Defiance to Self-indulgence: The Singer-Songwriters

Rock's defiance, however conservative, is in marked contrast to the maudlin conservatism of the singer-songwriters (Leonard Cohen, Jackson Browne, James Taylor, Dan Fogelberg) who embrace the inevitable without resistance. Rock's fun, its pleasure, is lost in chronic self-analysis and fatalistic social observation. The crucial tension between promise and fulfilment is ignored because nothing is expected. Instead, everything is just reported; it just happens. Greil Marcus analysed the singer-songwriter phenomenon like this:

> The imagination has fallen upon sorry times in post-Beatles rock'n'roll. Audiences are no longer used to the idea that someone might make something up, create a persona and effectively act it out, the way Chuck Berry and Bob Dylan used to.[11]

Marcus argues that the confessional style embodies a new form of conservatism, which has replaced the old conservatism of the community. The new conservatism is expressed in the intimacy of singer and listener. The audience is reduced to a single individual; and the artist, now no longer addressing a common predicament, speaks only of how he or she feels about their own private circumstances. For

Marcus, it is music for a time 'when pop culture and politics have lost their grander mythic dimensions, when there are no artists and no politics to create a community, and every fan is thrown back on himself.' Singer-songwriters were sold on the strength of their honesty; but it was an honesty which looked inwards to what the individual felt, not outwards to what society demanded or imposed. Where rock was concerned with a public life (even when dealing with personal concerns), the singer-songwriters made music for an audience that either finds itself, or feels itself, alone in the isolation of the nuclear family or the bed-sitting room.

In embracing the experience of privacy, this style of music took on a conservative character. It encouraged the feeling that there was nothing to be done; and that what happened in the world was a result of forces which could not be controlled and which operated far beyond the front door. In working from the enclosed world of their own feelings and experiences, the singer-songwriters sustained conservatism in the name of 'honesty' and 'truth'. They simply reported things as they were, giving no sense of how they might be. While borrowing folk's intimacy with its audience, the singer-songwriters turned folk's outward vision onto the individual. Folk's sense of collectivity, and its audience's sense of power, was inevitably lost. These modifications to folk gave sustenance to a conservative outlook. Writing in *The Fall of Public Man*, Richard Sennett argued:

> The reigning myth today is that the evils of society can all be understood as evils of impersonality, alienation and coldness. The sum of these three is the ideology of intimacy: social relationships of all kinds are real, believable and authentic the closer they approach the inner psychological concerns of each person. This ideology transmutes political categories into psychological categories.[12]

By celebrating personal experience, the singer-songwriters gave the world a hostile, uncontrollable character; it perpetually threatened to overwhelm the individual. Other people take on the guise of predators. There can be no trust, no community, no solidarity – just a constant struggle for pleasure and an endless anxiety about whether you are being short-changed.

Singer-songwriters were also conservative in their mistrust of imagination. In reporting experience, singer-songwriters become rock's journalists, not its novelists. Alternative, fictional worlds are buried by the dead weight of existing, immediate reality. There is no place for speculation, and no questions about how the world is for other people. Other people are only encountered in the way they impinge on the singer's world. Relationships exist in a world that is isolated from all other people, institutions, or obligations. Like the records themselves, they are shrink-wrapped. Rock's defiance is replaced by resignation, its sympathy by selfishness and its communalism by individualism. Rock's creative conservatism is replaced by a more defensive, self-centred individualism. None of which alters the fact of the singer-songwriters' popularity. The experiences they related and the moods they evoked clearly matched those of their fans. Robert Christgau explained James Taylor's success by the skill with which 'he vaunts his sensitivity'.[13] His audience borrow his vulnerability, taking part in his suffering and acquiring a style for their own anxieties. The singer-songwriters provide a lapel badge for the emotions – 'I am sensitive, love me.'

Imaginative Individualism: from Randy Newman to Billy Bragg

Not all singer-songwriters have sustained conservatism by their individualism. There are performers for whom truth is not just a matter of how you feel, and for whom musical integrity does not require an obsessive scrutiny of private thoughts. For them, truth is not confined to personal experience, nor is its communication confined to reporting personal feelings. Truth has to be created.

Songs become a stage on which both common and foreign experiences are acted out. Richard Thompson uses British folk to people his story-telling; Joe Ely draws on the music of Texan bars and ballrooms for his characters; and Randy Newman uses the traditions of American popular music to conjure up a gallery of misfits and forgotten people. None of these singers are committed to playing all the parts, or to confining themselves to their own experiences. When these singers say 'I', they are not pretending to the false confessional intimacy of Crosby, Stills and Nash or Dan Fogelberg.

In the course of Randy Newman's *Sail Away* album, 'I' refers to a slave-ship captain, a Sinatra-like star, an owner of a dancing bear, a son addressing his dying father, a father addressing his son, a citizen of Cleveland and of Dayton, Ohio, and God. All of them are brought to life by Newman, and all of them speak through his voice, but none of them could be mistaken for Newman himself. His songs are works of imagination.

Ray Davies of the Kinks explores a similar vein. His songs too tell a story and create characters, drawing on both the past and the present, the fashionable and the unpopular. Mixing humour with affection, Davies sings of Queen Victoria, Willesden Green, dedicated followers of fashion, dead end streets, sunny afternoons, and Waterloo sunsets.

In his affection for the quaint and the eccentric, and in his mistrust of change, Davies appears to be a conservative; but his music conveys a different impression. He does not sneer, he gently teases – 'The taxman's taken all my dough and left me in my stately home' ('Sunny Afternoon'). He borrows Cockney tunes to portray poverty – 'Out of work and got no money' ('Dead End Street'). On his finest song, 'Waterloo Sunset', Davies demonstrates an exquisite sense of time and place, capturing precisely a London sunset over the Thames and a crowded city. Although Davies leaves the world as he finds it, he somehow manages to dig beneath the surface of the mundane and the everyday, to comment on fashion and change, without deriding them, to evoke a world of his imagination, not his ego.

Where Newman and Davies create characters to disguise themselves, Richard Thompson uses his own experiences, and then hides behind them. Thompson mixes folk and rock sounds to create a community built on common experiences. His own feelings are excuses for songs, they are not their sole content. When Dan Fogelberg or Billy Joel offer their confessions, they are simply presented, albeit lavishly decorated, to their audience; the listeners have to take the performers' word for what happened. The music underlies the sentiments in the lyrics; it is mood music. There are no alternative perspectives and no ambiguity which allows entry to the audience. Richard Thompson's songs, on the other hand, use the music to involve his listeners, drawing them into a more confused world. The lyrics act more as clues than instructions. Though what he writes may be born of his own experience, its meaning does not depend on his audience knowing the details. It does not even depend on them sharing Thompson's reactions. All that matters is whether they find Thompson convincing. This does not turn on what Thompson actually felt and experienced, but on how feelings and experiences are transformed into songs. Thompson's voice conveys a public anxiousness which is quite different from Taylor's confidential certainty or Fogelberg's self-pity. Thompson's 'truth' is the truth of doubt and dilemmas. When he performed with Linda Thompson their two voices gave physical form both to the song's confusion and to the comfort of sharing. When he sings alone, he mixes a gravelly certainty with an anxious yodel. The music re-inforces the confusion. The seemingly sad 'Tear Stained Letter' – 'And just when I thought I could learn to forget her/Right through the door came a tear-stained letter' – has a jaunty rock accompaniment. The song refuses to confirm any impression; it thrives on its ambiguities.

Thompson's ability to give public form to private emotions depends on the musical conventions upon which he draws. When Joe Ely uses the sounds of Texas he relies on established responses and expectations. The singer and the listener already know the images and conventions in advance of the song. When Ely sings it is already understood that the characters in the song are not his exclusive property. When he sings: 'Spanish is a loving tongue/and she never spoke Spanish to me', we can share his disappointment, however remote the experience is from our own. Everything hangs on the musical form. Where the confessional singer-songwriters distorted folk to accommodate their individualism, Ely and others exploit the communal character of traditional styles to generalize their feelings.

The British singer Billy Bragg sings his songs alone, accompanied only by his electric guitar. But however personal his songs, their concerns are public property. It is almost as if they are public because he uses an electric guitar – 'That electric guitar', said Bragg, 'is the one thing that make me different to all other solo performers.'[14] Rock is public music, whatever its private inspiration. And in being public, its meaning cannot be determined or controlled by the perfomer. Thus, though James Taylor's lyrics may suggest a man more sensitive to the needs of women, and though Mick Jagger may, on the same account, seem brutally insensitive, the Stones' music can be more widely shared simply because whatever the lyrics say, they are only part of what is heard and felt. There is a conservative tyranny to the sounds of the confessional. It is just you and the singer. And the sounds, however complicated the arrangement or however sophisticated the production, are intended simply as embellishment to the message. The privacy of the confession excludes the possibility of dissenting voices. The music is prevented from taking on a new life out in the public world of rock.

Bragg, Ely, Newman and Thompson all recognize that an interesting experience does not automatically make a good song, and that a good song does not depend on real experience. (Randy Newman has never actually been any of the characters he plays or sings about.) The measure of a song is not its literal accuracy, but its effect on the listener's imagination. It does not matter whether Thompson has 'A Poisoned Heart and A Twisted Memory', as long as his audience shares the feeling; for the confessional singer-songwriters nothing else matters – and because it applies only to them, the song has nothing to say to the audience. Breaking with the conservatism of the confessional school of singer-songwriters depends on the writer's ability to link sentiments with imagination; on the singer's ability to speak for their audience; and on the music's ability to sustain both.

It is clear that conservatism runs through the heart of popular music, in the way it takes people and life as they seem. But what is important is that musical forms differ in the way this conservatism is expressed; there are endless variations of the conservative theme. There is the conservatism of the community; there is the conservatism of individualism. There are the very different conservatisms of rock, of country, and of the singer-songwriters. Even within each genre, there are alternatives to be explored. Sometimes rock's conservatism is used simply to reinforce its audience's prejudices and expectations; sometimes it is used to explore the tensions and doubts within those preconceptions. There are choices to be made, and the innovative artist is the one who rejects the easy options, and who finds a way of exposing the delights and the costs of our inclination not to change. For the rest, the stakes are less high, the conservatism more pervasive, and the music more comforting.

11
People Get Ready

'The first rule of subversive pop is: Don't say its subversive'
(Elvis Costello)

For all pop's natural affinity with liberalism and conservatism, and for all its complacency and escapism, it is also the sound of protest. To ignore pop's rebellious spirit would be to miss a vital feature of its potency. One of the most obvious guises for its rebelliousness has been in its link with socialism. Folk music has produced many songs which advocate social change, celebrate trade union achievements, and support left-wing causes – in 1967, *Melody Maker* carried an advert headed 'Folksingers for Freedom in Vietnam' which was signed by more than 100 perfomers. Blues, reggae and soul, too, have a long established reputation for songs which chronicle the evils of racial oppression and the struggle for black liberation. And even rock has had its moments of socialist commitment, although this is typically associated with individual artists (John Lennon, Paul Weller, Steve Van Zandt, Bruce Cockburn), rather than any consistent aspect of the music itself. Listing the occasions on which popular music and socialism have been linked would, however, only touch on the relationship. When the Crystals sang 'He's a rebel', they did not mean he was a revolutionary socialist, but neither was the description without its political connotations. The sound of socialism is not necessarily the same as socialism set to music. Pop's socialism owes as much to the medium as the message, and the important question is how socialism fits with different sounds. One way of finding an answer is to look at the way popular music deals with the particular socialist concerns of work and the working life.

'Welcome to the Working Week'

Work is a central concern of socialists and socialism. Workplace organization, it is argued, is crucial to creating social change;

unemployment diminishes human self-respect; capitalist work severs the individual from his true nature; and socialist work allows for the flowering of people's full potential. Whatever version of socialism is advocated, work features prominently in its analysis, its organization and its vision of the future. We might expect, therefore, that pop's socialism would be represented in a concern for work and the plight of workers. Certainly, there are a good number of famous songs about work: Eddie Cochran's 'Summertime Blues', Fats Domino's 'Blue Monday', Lee Dorsey's 'Working in the Coal Mine', Sam Cooke's 'Chain Gang', Roy Orbison's 'Working for the Man', the Silhouettes' 'Get a Job', the Easybeats' 'Friday on my Mind', Elvis Costello's 'Welcome to the Working Week', Dolly Parton's '9 to 5', Bruce Springsteen's 'Factory', and Chelsea's 'Right to Work'. It is true, too, that each of these songs involves an implicit or explicit criticism of work and its constraints. But what is also distinctive about this fairly random selection of songs is that most of them deal with the prospect of leisure, rather than the tedium of work.

Only in folk, and occasionally in blues, is it common to find work addressed directly. In pop and rock, it is pleasure, not work, that occupies performers and audiences. 'Work' appears only as a contrast to pleasure or as euphemism for it; as in the Midnighters' 'Work with me Annie':

> Work with me Annie
> Let's get it while the getting is good.

The use of the word 'work' is almost wholly coincidental. The follow-up record by Etta James changed the euphemism to 'roll' ('Roll with Me Henry'). The point was the sex, not the euphemism. The traditional topics of popular music are usually those activities which occupy people after work. Pop songs are about the vagaries of love, not the speed of the production line, for the simple reason that pop is part of leisure, itself defined *against* work. The expectations of audiences are compounded by the experiences of performers. 'Work' for a musician means touring, recording, rehearsing; it also means playing and creating. For their audience, 'work' often means monotony, discipline and a total lack of creativity. Pop, therefore, seems unrelated to the world of work and the concerns of socialists.

It might be, of course, that pop, in acting as a counterpoint to work and in concentrating on leisure, highlights the work's dull, routine and alienating features. The pleasure of pop could be tied to the discomfort of work. But this argument begs awkward questions: how exactly does work's frustrations find expression in pop? Why should pop not be about love, just as the words suggest? Why should it be supposed that pop is *really* about work? After all, pop's audience may have more to be frustrated with than just work, so it is not clear which songs refer to work and which to parents or whatever. It may be that work does inspire the pleasure taken in pop, but without closer examination, it remains only a hypothesis.

Bosses and the Blues

Both country and blues music have a long tradition of songs about work. Writers on music have traced the blues back to the worksong sung by slaves in the fields of the American south. The call-and-response pattern of the blues was a response to the work patterns of the slaves. Paul Oliver has written:

> Within the blues are to be heard the compelling rhythms of work song and spiritual that embrace the listener and draw him into the inevitable participation, much as the exhortations of the gang-leader or the preacher exert their influence on workers or congregation.[1]

It was not only the structure of the blues song that evolved from slave work. The music took on political overtones by the same process. Eugene Genovese describes how slaves exercised a form of job control through their singing:

> The slaves expressed their attitude in song. The masters encouraged quick-time singing among their field slaves, but the slaves proved themselves masters of slowing down the songs and the work.[2]

This spirit of subversion is also demonstrated in the use of euphemisms which excluded the white establishment; white people had no idea of the sexual connotations of 'jelly roll' or the voodoo origins of 'black cat bone'. Because a euphemism depends on people being 'in the know', the meaning of songs could be the exclusive possession of performers and their audience. By creating its own musical language, the blues provided a small bulwark against white attempts to control every aspect of black life.

But although the blues can be traced back to the experience of work and the politics of its organization, it does not follow that the blues was exclusively a political music concerned with work struggles. The blues, writes Oliver, was 'primarily the creation of men at leisure'. The blues' main purpose was to express a more private, but less specific, frustration than that engendered by work alone. Oliver explains the music's development like this:

> As the blues crystallised as an extemporized song performed with
> improvised instrumental accompaniment, its practical function as
> an aid to work virtually ceased. On commercial records the blues
> is not sung in the process of work, and labour figures in the blues
> in retrospect, the singer reflecting upon employment and still
> more on the lack of it.[3]

Rather than the blues providing a home in which work has a natural
place, the music, like the pop that followed it, responded to the
experiences and expectations of the non-work hours. Work appears
only as the backdrop to leisure. The songs dwell on the private world
of pleasure, and not the collective activity of work. Even in the slave
fields, writes Genovese, the songs referred 'beyond a direct concern
with labour to a concern with the most personal expressions of life's
travail'.[4] The blues idiom became a medium for evoking private
suffering and private feelings. The blues summoned up the loneliness
of social life as much as the alienation and oppression of work. The
wails and shouts and hollering of the blues singer speak of an agony
that inhabits the soul, not the factory. Writing about the blues singer
Robert Johnson, Greil Marcus said:

> He sang about the price he had to pay for promises he tried, and
> failed to keep; I think the power of his music comes in part from
> Johnson's ability to shape the loneliness and chaos of his betrayal
> or ours.[5]

Marcus' interpretation of Johnson derives from the assumption that
popular music acts as a bridge between the public and private world.
All pop songs work through their ability to give public expression to
private feelings, or to convert public values into private experiences. A
song's meaning, whatever lyrical device is used, lies in the language of
personal sensations and feelings. Work, therefore, features in popular
music as a metaphor for a private emotion, and not as a description of a
particular social arrangement.

Because popular music is rooted in the emotional and personal life of
the individual, it sits uneasily with the considerations of socialists who
emphasize the importance of work to socialism. For them, socialism is
primarily concerned with the way in which workers can organize
collectively to restructure their work-lives. This attention to work and
workers is not shared by the blues. Its interest is both wider and
narrower. Wider because it is not just concerned with work, but with
life in general; narrower because it is not interested in workers as such,
but in the individual.

Though the experience of work can be read into the music, and
though it can be used to explain the form of the music, work itself is

not what the music is about. The production, consumption and structure of the music limits its ability to discuss institutions (like work) *as institutions*. In the same way, the music's meaning and its message cannot be discovered simply by sociological analysis of its audience or its origins. What is true for work and the blues is also true for school and pop or rock.

There are no more songs about the iniquities of the educational system than there are about the division of labour. Many of the songs that mention school do so to poke fun at it, or to juxtapose it to pleasure. Chuck Berry's 'School Days' is no musical *Blackboard Jungle*. It is a cheerful song which gleefully recounts everyday school life: lessons, teachers and exams:

> Working your fingers right down to the bone,
> The guy behind you won't leave you alone.

Like another school song, Alice Cooper's 'School's Out', Berry's song is mostly about what the pupils do after classes are over. The song is about pleasure not school. For the same reason that blues songs do not focus on work, pop songs ignore school, except as a way of highlighting pleasure. Attempts to capture the misery and unpleasantness of school are rare – Pink Floyd's *The Wall* and Jethro Tull's *Thick as a Brick*. Both these exceptions present school as part of a 'system' which crushes life out of individuals. Almost inevitably the music takes on the same deadening effect of school; the beat becomes a monotonous hammer because the music is about education not fun – 'School's Out' is about fun, not education. Pop and the blues live in the shadows cast by school and work, but they do not work well when they try to throw light on the institutions themselves. This does not mean, however, that popular music is indifferent to the miseries of work, just that its treatment of them is shaped by the medium.

The Sound of Work

'Uptown' was a hit for the 1960s girl group, the Crystals. The song was written by Barry Mann and Cynthia Weil, and was produced by Phil Spector, who gave it a typically brilliant arrangement. The indignities of work are detailed as the song begins. It tells of a man going downtown to work 'where everyone's his boss' and where he is made to feel alone and insignificant. The worker's humiliation is evoked by the solo voice and spanish guitar which picks out the melody. But just as the verse ends, the voice and guitar are joined by strings, castanets and the backing vocals. The mood shifts from melancholy to relief; the setting moves from downtown to uptown; and the worker is transformed into a king. Uptown, in the poorer part of the city, the man is reunited with his woman and his dignity:

> Then he's tall,
> He don't crawl,
> He's a king.

As a piece of socialist analysis this may seem unimpressive; as a piece of pop music, it is unsurpassable. What gives it its power as pop are precisely those qualities that seem to weaken its claim to be 'socialist'.

The problem identified by the song is one of self-respect; the worker's pride is undermined by his role as a servant to numerous masters. Two thing are important: firstly, the loss of dignity is suffered by an individual worker and not by a class; secondly, the worker's servitude is a consequence of his relations with other individuals – the bosses – and seems to owe nothing to the operation of a particular social system. These points matter to a socialist who is intent upon criticising the song; they are of little consequence either to the songwriters or to those who are moved by the song, whatever their politics happen to be. Indeed the effectiveness of the song depends on the worker's problems being identified in terms of 'pride'. To fix the problem any other way would be to deny it a solution.

'Uptown' provides an answer to misery which is immediate and available to everyone. In this sense, it works like Tammy Wynette's 'Stand By Your Man', providing a possible solution to a real problem. The songs are similar, too, in the way they offer individualist answers to collective problems. Because socialism rejects individualist solutions, and because pop celebrates them, once again it seems as if the two are incompatible. And yet without an answer, the song would lack a structure and a purpose; there would be no release, no escape. There is, after all, nothing to celebrate if there is nothing anyone can do. By describing the problem as one of individual respect, and by providing a solution that is attainable, the song can move from self-doubt to elation, and in the transition, expressed both musically and lyrically, lift its listener. If the worker's oppression could not be removed by love, then 'Uptown' would sound like something written by one of the more maudlin singer-songwriters, whose songs dwell on the idea of love as doomed, on the fatalism of romance's decline into habit and worse. Where they offer a lush musical accompaniment to disappointment, 'Uptown' defies experience and offers hope. The melancholy of the singer-songwriter may represent observable experience more accurately, but it is no better or more true as a song for that.

Experience is not the same as truth. The hope offered by 'Uptown' may be false, but it fits both the conventions of popular music and the hopes of socialists. It asserts that there is a better world. This argument can best be demonstrated by comparing 'Uptown' with Bruce Springsteen's 'Factory', which, while being a more accurate document about work, is a less effective song. It fails popular music and socialism by its fatalism.

'Factory' is a mournful song, sung by Springsteen in a weary, almost slurred voice over a muted backing of drums, organ, guitar and bass (there is no soaring saxophone to relieve the mood). The lyrics evoke feelings of gloom, as Springsteen sings of workers leaving a factory in the rain 'with death in their eyes'. Their lives have been taken by the factory and by the dull, repetitive routine of 'the working, the working, just the working life'. Unlike 'Uptown', 'Factory' offers no solutions. The problem – the working life – is too pervasive for that. Instead the song evokes a mood of fatalism through its dour, almost funereal accompaniment. Where 'Uptown' juxtaposes humiliation with hope, 'Factory' underlines its gloom with despondency. While 'Factory', like 'Uptown', focuses on an individual (man/daddy), it differs in the way it identifies the problem of work and its solution. 'Factory' views work's character as deep-seated and intractable. *Working life*, an entire existence, deprives the worker of his faculties and his will to live. There are no feasible changes to be made, only temporary relief to be had – 'somebody's gonna get hurt tonight.' The working life is a fact of life; it is not caused, it just envelops those who work.

Treated as a piece of social science, 'Factory' shares some of the features of socialist analysis of capitalism. The experience of work is not determined by the isolated decisions of individual bosses; it is the consequence of the system's structure. But there is an important difference. Springsteen offers no escape or hope. Both as a piece of music and as a piece of socialist analysis or propaganda it fails because it portrays the working life as inevitable, as beyond all control. No one is responsible and there is nothing for anyone to do.

'Factory' ends up as a profoundly conservative song – not conservative because of its sympathies or its portrait of factory life, but conservative because of its fatalism and defeatism, conveyed in sounds and words. 'Uptown's' defiance and hope may be naive, but they place it closer to socialism than is 'Factory'. 'Factory's' desire to reflect the reality of the worker's life, paradoxically, serves to maintain the status quo. In describing the world, Springsteen fails to change it. He gives dignity to defeat, and no hope to victory. Simon Frith identified the same problem in Paul Weller's songs for the Jam:

> Paul Weller made graphic images out of the ideology implicit in
> working class youth pop from Slade to Oi. This music is about
> making the best of a bad situation; it is not about changing it. It is
> structured by class consciousness – a brooding sense of 'us' and
> 'them' – but it is, for all its angry petulance, oddly complacent.[6]

Where Weller's musical heroes, the Who, made rebellion a matter of
style – 'they' put 'us' down because 'we get around' – the Jam were
obliged to make their rebellion a matter of sociology. Weller and
Springsteen's commitment to realism is also a mistrust of imagination.
Fantasy is discarded in the search for documentary accuracy. But in
overlooking imagination, the performers deny access to the means that
allows people to see how things might be, that lets them believe in a
better world and their ability to create it.

Socialism depends on this capacity to transcend the present and to
plot the future. A song like 'Factory' is so firmly rooted in the present
that it eradicates any other possible world. In fixing the listeners and
the song's characters in the reality of the moment, 'Factory' is both
more conservative and less musically potent than it might be, because
much of pop's power lies in its ability to stir the imagination. 'Uptown'
uses the imagination; it creates, in sounds and words, two worlds: the
existing one and an alternative better one. What 'Uptown' lacks in
realism and political acuity, it makes up for in promise and pleasure.
We may disagree with the way 'Uptown' identifies 'the problem' and
'the solution'; we have to admire the way it exploits the language of
popular music.

Even punk, which seemed to be able to distil rebellious anger into a
single powerful burst of musical energy, was not able to break with the
limits under which pop communicates. Not all punk's frustration was
expressed with Weller's eye to sociological detail. The Sex Pistols and
the Clash seemed more interested in integrating their politics into their
use of sound. Theirs was the noise of anger, not of observation and
explanation. They were, in this sense, less conservative than the Jam,
but they could not go beyond their gestures of frustration. Punk's
anger all too easily sounded either merely petulant or banal; and even
at its most inspiring, its power lay in its ability to disrupt rather than to
transform dominant assumptions. The same is true of US hard-core
rock (Husker Du, for example). Here raucous, untreated guitars
thrash out the sound of suburban frustration with the same energy that
fuelled urban punk in Britain. The voice curses and shouts; the beat
stomps; and the lyrics speak of boredom, frustration and depression:

> Trying to find an unknown something I consider best,
> I don't know if I'll find it, but until then I'll be depressed
> ('Somewhere' from *Zen Arcade*)

The music and the lyrics capture the spirit and feel of suburban teenage angst; and, turned up loud, the sound's manic rush carries the listener along in its wake. But the momentary relief is where the effect ends; everything in the sound – voice, guitar, drums – is directed to a single sensation: a release of pent-up confusion and frustration. There is no attempt to explain or explore these feelings; the point is just to mimic them in sound, drawing on rock's expressive conventions. Any attempt to be more musically or lyrically specific would destroy the sounds momentum. Writing of one of Husker Du's progenitors, the MC5, the prototype punk band whose *Kick Out the Jams* seemed (in 1969) to be as raw and raucous as rock could be, Dave Marsh explained rock's musical and political strengths and weaknesses:

> the Five's politics were an outgrowth of their very unsophistica-
> tion, their teenage frenzy and their musical approach, which
> encompassed both. They carried these values and qualities into
> each successive battle like a tattered flag, doing macho duels with
> the forces of Good Vibes and Capital M Music as well as the
> partisans of the correct line.[7]

The MC5's 'socialism' was forged by the band's music and its concerns; in this respect, their politics were like the Crystals': the style shaped the socialism.

Pop seems either to offer the conservative realism of 'Factory' and the Jam, or the naive promises of 'Uptown', or the unfocused anger of punk. Either there is the documentary, the escapism, or the surly relief. It seems impossible to combine them or go beyond them. While popular music may accord with conservatism and liberalism, it seems to sit awkwardly with socialism. This incompatibility stems from pop's apparent inability to offer anything other than individual escape or complacent comfort. It cannot, it seems, give a sound to collective responses to present problems. One way of testing this claim is to look at pop's treatment of the union, the embodiment of the attempt to find a collective solution to work's indignities.

'You Can't Touch Me, I'm Part of the Union'

In *Mystery Train*, Greil Marcus pays special tribute to the Band's 'King Harvest (Has Surely Come)'. The song uses the popular imagination, drawing on references to the United States' past and employing them to create a sense of community. This is the backdrop against which a story of working life and union organization is told. 'King Harvest' offers no easy solutions, but neither is it fatalistic; it offers hope in the shape of the union, which is addressed in the language of love – as Marcus says, the song is optimistic precisely 'because it is so full of desire':[8]

> I work for the union,
> Cause she's so good to me.

The indignities of work are counterposed by the power of the union. Instead of going 'uptown', the worker in 'King Harvest' turns to his union leader:

> And then, if they don't give us what we like,
> He said, 'Men, that's when you gotta go on strike'.
> (© 1969 Robbie Robertson, Canaan Music/Warner Bros. Music)

'King Harvest', therefore, suggests the possibility of combining popular music and socialism. It observes the conventions of pop, through its use of popular imagination, and the cannons of socialism, through the focus on the union; but 'King Harvest' is not without its limitations.

'King Harvest' depends on a set of cultural and historical references by which to create its effect. The particular commitment to the union is part of a wider sense of common experience and identity. The Band use their own history to bring together the music of their native Canada and their adopted North America. They combine the sounds and images of rock'n'roll, folk and the blues. These diverse sources have one thing in common: they all exploit the idea of community. The Band use their audience to (re)create the set of shared ideas and understandings that characterize a communal life. The Band's audience-community is linked by the historical myths it shares. For Marcus, the Band's music gives to Americans a sense of their country's history and of their own identity:

> The songs were made to bring to life the fragments of experience, legend, and artifact that every American has inherited as the legacy of a mythical past. The songs have little to do with chronology; most describe events that could be taking place right now, but most of those events had taken on their colour before any of us was born.[9]

Marcus' interpretation needs to be qualified. His claims for the Band's ability to capture American culture has to be set beside their relative lack of populist acclaim. While the group had many devoted fans, and enjoyed the admiration of critics and fellow musicians, they never won massive popularity. They were victim to a paradox: their success in creating a sense of community and in evoking past images to forge contemporary links also led to their failure in the mass market. The community they helped to forge identified itself *against* the rest of the people, not as part of them. The rock community is built on the division between people; it depends on setting 'them' apart from 'us'. In these distinctions is contained rock's excitement and the limits of its popularity.

The problems of creating a community, and the tensions inherent in such attempts, are central to the degree to which popular music can create the collective identity to which socialism aspires. The Band were not alone in facing the problem. In the mid-1980s, it could be seen in the revival of traditional US rock sounds from bands like the Blasters, Jason and the Scorchers, Los Lobos, and Rank and File. They used country, blues and local ethnic music, each with their own sense of community, to create a setting for their collective concerns. Just as Creedence Clearwater Revival used southern country and swamp rock to give voice to their tributes to blue collar feelings and populist uncertainties ('Who'll Stop the Rain?', 'Fortunate Son'), so the Blasters paid tribute to the 'Common Man'. Rank and File too have drawn on a range of traditional musical idioms to give expression to their collectivist concerns:

> You wake up every morning still got the sleep in your eyes,
> Working for the boss, you never stop to wonder why,
> So join the rank, this is the rank, we are the rank and file.
> ('Rank and File' from *Sundown*)

Jason and the Scorchers mix country and rock, using the sounds of rebellion and disappointment to query the values of patriotism and materialism. Los Lobos, part of a long tradition of Chicano musicians who have evolved their own brand of rock'n'roll, made their first record with support from the United Farm Workers union. The UFW saw in Los Lobos the opportunity to reach Chicanos caught between two cultures; the band's music combined rock and Mexican music, making pleasure out of the tension between isolation and community.

All these bands, like the Band, used traditional music to convey contemporary feelings. The music's populism was directed against the failures of a populist democracy. Their success depends on how the sounds and conventions of popular music can be adapted to fit the politics. The community created by the music threatens to undermine its populism, just as populist politics cannot provide the basis for a musical community.

Rock and Pop Communities

The attempt to use history, to summon up communities, does not fit easily into the language and consumption of contemporary popular music. It is not just that records and performers have brief lives. The whole medium seems to live only for the moment. 'King Harvest' has the political and musical advantage over 'Factory' because its world is that of myths and imagination, and not the social documentary; both are at a disadvantage next to the hope and delight offered by 'Uptown'. Rarely can pop and rock artists depend on or find the communities, histories or contexts that allow them to inhabit a world of collective certainties. For pop, the only community is that of two people in love; the only history is that of romance. For rock, the only community is the audience; the only common history, adolescence. Despite the recent fashion for political rock events (Artists United Against Apartheid, Farm Aid etc.), they form rare and brief opportunities for music to link directly with a wider political community. Typically, songs like 'King Harvest' gain their meaning from the experience of belonging to an audience for whom unions feature as symbols rather than solutions. Yet more typically, unions appear rarely or in an unfavourable light.

To sing about unions as a source of strength and solidarity depends on the idiom as much as the composer. 'King Harvest' only works because of its rock setting, where collectivities have some meaning, if only as a means of enjoying music. Folk too works through its audience's sense of itself as more than customers. In folk, performers sometimes occupy the role of representatives, and speak for the audience. This relationship allows for songs which celebrate the union and castigate the scab. Dave Harker cites 'The Blackleg Miner':

> So join the union while ye may,
> Don't wait till yer dying day,
> 'Cause that may not be far away,
> Ye dirty blackleg miner![10]

Pop's natural sympathies, in contrast, are with the scab.

In pop, there is not the bond between audience, singer and song, and as a consequence unions, if they appear at all, come as tyrants not saviours. Though pop audiences have much in common with each other, and though the consumption of pop brings them together, their identity remains that of isolated customers united by their wish to consume. Rock audiences are also made up of consumers, but the experience of consumption is mediated by a sense of community which the rock artist assumes or tries to create. Pop works with our experiences *as individuals*. Where folk's conventions can give sense to the idea of one for all and all for one, pop's conventions tend to emphasise the experience of one against all. A British folk group, the Strawbs had a hit with the song 'Union Man', which had begun life as an anti-union song but whose message was reversed by union pickets to support their cause. The Strawbs version turned it into a pop song, and in the process, it reverted to its anti-union form; not because the words changed, but because their meaning altered. 'You can't get me, I'm part of the union', sung on a picket line, is the sound of defiance in the face of an identifiable enemy; as the Strawbs sung it on daytime radio, it was the sound of cowardice, of someone who dared not stand alone, someone who was afraid to do it 'their way'. The listener's attention was shifted from the strength of the collective to its threat, from the reassurance of solidarity to the freedom of individualism. As 'Uptown' made clear, pop looks to personal solutions to what are seen as personal problems. The union inevitably appears as an alien force, just like the bosses in 'Uptown' or 'the working life' in 'Factory'.

The Kinks' 'Get Back in Line' is an example of how pop's natural sympathies work against unionization. Its sensitivity makes it an excellent song – and an anti-union one. It begins with an individual on the corner of the street, reflecting on life:

> Facing the world ain't easy,
> When there isn't anything going . . .

These reflections are cut short by the appearance of the union man:

> . . . he walks right past,
> And I know I have to get right back into line,
> 'Cause that Union man's got such a hold over me,
> He's the man who decides whether I live or die, if I starve or eat.
>   (© 1970 Ray Davies, Davray Music Ltd)

The tune is elegantly sad; it is a gentle song. Its descending bass line draws the listener into sharing the sentiments of the first verse. The uncertainty in Ray Davies' voice reinforces our identification with the person stranded on the kerb, we see the union man through their eyes. The union man's appearance is accompanied by a more strident rhythm – the gentle tap which takes the beat in the first verse turns into a thud in the chorus. There is no escaping the impression that the union man is a source of fear, not help. In this sense, 'Get Back in Line' is clearly a conservative song, but its conservatism cannot simply be attributed to Davies' political sympathies. The song's politics owe as much to the world view with which pop works.

Deliberate attempts to promote unions in pop, however intense the political commitment of the performers, are undercut by the genre. The Redskins' 'Unionize' is a pure statement of socialist principle, a persistent cry to 'unionize, unionize . . .' But it is unpersuasive. Heard on radio or even in concert, it is not clear who is to unionize and as what (rock fans? adolescents?). The singer's specific passion only makes sense to him; he may be thinking of mass working class organization, but his audience is not. The song works at a rally, but in an ordinary concert it sounds anachronistic. The song needs an audience with a sense of collective identity, and the band needs a music that expresses and uses the conventions of the collective. It is this thought which inspires the Redskins' admiration for black music, in which the community, not the individual, is the natural constituency. Their choice of a basic rock three-piece band, and a punk-influenced vocal style, prevents them from using black music's sense of community.

Soul and Socialism

In music, as in politics, socialism depends on an image of community, of common identity. Rock and pop are limited in their ability to generate, sympathetically, the collective spirit. Reggae and soul do not labour under quite the same constraints. Both their forms and their audiences are importantly different from those of pop and rock. It is not just that reggae and soul audiences are not defined so specifically by their age; they are also linked by more than the delights and doubts of adolescence. Reggae and soul artists can draw on the wider, adult concerns of the audience, as well as the conventions, the language and images of community. Soul is more than a way of singing. Criticizing Janis Joplin's pretensions as a soul singer, Julie Burchill remarked that Joplin 'mistook shrieking for soul, sentiment for soul, tantrums for soul'.[11]

Soul's politics, and its differences with rock and pop, can be detected in its use of the word 'we'. In soul, 'we' refers to more than a group of isolated individuals gathered around radio sets, listening to personal stereos, or brought together as an audience. The music's conventions imply a permanent community. The call-and-response format, for example, creates an impression of collective participation in the making of music; each call building on the previous response, each line being repeated and extended so that the whole is made up from, while being greater than, the parts (the analogy with unionism is obvious). The origins of this style lie in Africa where music is integrated into social life and where there is no simple division of labour between musicians and non-musicians. It can be heard in the music of the South African Hugh Masekela. His songs pay little attention to personal feelings; his music lacks the obvious signs of anger. Instead of the rebellious shout of rock'n'roll or punk,

Masekela's sounds express, in their restraint, the certainty of solidarity. The same certainties are embodied in gospel, where the collective 'we' has been a constant part of the musical language, which itself rests on the convictions of religious faith. In gospel, the audience is united through its beliefs which are both expressed and sustained by the communal activity of making music. Preacher and congregation work together in the worship of the Lord. The blues too, argues Harriet Ottenheimer, expressed more than mere sadness, it included a sense of a common plight beyond the control of the lone individual.[12]

It is not, however, just the sense of community which gospel and blues express; they also call upon the language of liberation: the rivers to be crossed, the promised land to be reached, the trains to ride, the sweet release to be enjoyed, the babylons to escape. The spiritual emancipation of gospel is paralleled by the more secular escape of the blues – feeling good. Images of liberation are not imported into the music, as happened with rock in the 1960s, but are part of its standard lyrical repertoire. Soul added a political dimension to the sexual and spiritual liberation of blues and gospel. Soul's musical traditions allowed it to both comment on society and contemplate changes to it – blues and gospel expressed a wish to communicate and share experiences of this world and to celebrate release from it.

The careers of Aretha Franklin and Curtis Mayfield (and the Impressions) exemplified this development. Franklin's 'Respect' combined a gospel voice and a rhythm'n'blues accompaniment to demand equality as a woman and a black person. The equality before God of gospel becomes equality in the home and, in the context of the civil rights campaign of the late sixties, equality at the ballot box:

> All I'm asking for is
> A little respect, baby . . .

Curtis Mayfield also used the gospel sounds of his musical experiences to voice a plea for freedom and equality. Years later, Mayfield recalled his grandmother's gospel preaching: 'I came up in the church, and heard her words of inspiration and her ability to speak to the people of matters that would make them think and inspire or motivate them.'[13] Where Franklin personalized her collective demands, Mayfield generalized his in 'People Get Ready': 'There's a train a-coming . . . All you need is faith/Don't need no ticket/Just thank the Lord.' A decade later Mayfield's music was harsher, reflecting perhaps the loss of earlier hopes, but the language and the longings were the same. The voice too still retained its sweet, high tone. It is not the certain shout of the street orator. Mayfield does not harangue his audience, he seduces them by sharing their worries:

Well! Fallin' in – out on the streets again,
Unemployment lines – a lot of people standing,
News is bad on every TV show,
So I tune in my radio – talkin, 'bout
Love to the people . . .
                    (© 1975 Curtis Mayfield, Warner Bros Music)

Unlike pop's focus on a private, intimate world through which the wider world is understood or avoided, soul inhabits a more public stage. When Mayfield sings 'People Get Ready' or 'Love to the People', there is no doubt about whom he is referring to; it is anybody who is listening. Audiences may create different communities – men and women may not hear Sister Sledge's 'We Are Family' the same way – but they will all imagine communities of some kind. Soul can use words like 'people' and 'we' without embarrassment. In pop, such expressions have little meaning. In rock, they either refer to the exclusive community of the audience, or they are confusingly unspecific. When John Lennon sang 'power to the people' or 'free the people', it was not clear who he meant. The 'people' often seemed to refer to persons other than the listener. This is not just a facet of Lennon's politics, but of his medium. Politically, the 'people' are part of the world outside the relationship between artist and listener. Musically, the 'people' are his immediate audience, but his relationship with them is lived in terms of 'I' and 'me'; his politics, on the other hand, addresses an anonymous 'them' and 'us'. In soul, the 'people' are the listeners, and the politics are those of populism. The 'people' are subjects, not objects, in the music and its politics.

While soul's musical and lyrical conventions fit it more easily than pop for socialist ideology, this does not automatically make it the sound of socialism or of political rebellion. Soul, like pop, works at the level of feelings; and even though it celebrates the spirit of community, it cannot mobilise that community. And, as with all popular music, the subjects and the solutions available to soul are limited. Work, school, capitalism are not typically the subjects of soul songs. Its populist politics tend to be vague and utopian. Mayfield sings, 'But when cupboards are bare/our love we can share'; and in 'Wake Up Everybody', Harold Melvin suggests, 'Wake up all the doctors, make the old people well.' Rapping, for all its radical, street sounds, has not extended the range and form of the music's politics; all it changed was the tone of its politics. In 1982, Grandmaster Flash and the Furious Five had a hit with 'The Message'. It was a clever mixture of anger and wit, but it gave voice to defiance rather than to action. The 'message' took the form of a letter from the ghetto; it was not a call to arms. Instead, it described the city as a jungle which constantly threatened to crush the life out of its inhabitants. The song simply warned 'don't push me 'cause I'm close to the edge'. Only rarely are solutions offered, as when Brother D and Collective Effort announced, 'We gotta educate, agitate and organize'.

Roots Rebels

Soul is not the only popular music to have attracted attention for its politics. Reggae too has been associated with radicalism and its sense of community. Reggae is now a part of the international music scene. The musical freedoms allowed by its rhythm and its seemingly loose structure have been borrowed by white rock stars (the Police, the Clash, and Men at Work); its political anger has been appropriated by the victims of racism in Southern Africa, Australia and Britain. Reggae, like soul, has made available to these performers a language and set of conventions which accommodate radical political images and ideas.

Reggae has used the millenarian vision of rastafarianism for the same purpose that soul used religious salvation: as a metaphor for political liberation. Both soul and reggae employed the prospect of a promised land to give hope of future release. Where soul seems to take discrimination for granted but does not try to explain it, reggae uses actual historical references to make sense of present oppression.

Reggae employs history and the bible to establish a feeling of community among those who hear it, using biblical language and historical references to provide the images for describing past and present reality, and to conjure up future prospects. For every straightforward political statement – 'Them belly full but we hungry/A hungry mob is a angry mob' or 'Never make a politician grant you a favour/They will always want to control you forever' – there are countless other less explicit references which convey a similar message. Biblical language is as common as political rhetoric. At a concert promoted by Belgian socialists, Misty in Roots, a British reggae band, sang of 'Oh Wicked Man', 'Judas Iscariot' and 'Sodom and Gomorrah'. Historical references, too, function to make sense of a present predicament. Burning Spear's 'Slavery Days', both establishes a common past and a present analogy, just as their 'Marcus Garvey' pays tribute to a political hero and directs attention to future action. However, unlike the Band's use of history, where past rural poverty is intended to establish a sense of past certainties and present anxieties, reggae draws no apparent distinction between past and present; the two merge into each other to create an almost mythical time removed from existing reality. Where the Band employ their music to observe the past, in the light of present experiences, reggae involves its audience in the past and present. The same spirit of total involvement is apparent in the making of the music itself. As Misty in Roots say in their performance at the Counter Eurovision concert:

> When we travel this land we work for one reason, the reason is to help another man to think for himself. The music of our art is roots music, music which records history, because without the knowledge of the history you cannot control your destiny . . . Music which tells about the future and the judgement that is to come.

The coalescence of past and present in the lyrics is reinforced by the music's form.

The music does not simply sanctify the sentiments by using church-like organ sounds and militant rhythms; the music almost replaces the lyrics. The sound of reggae is the throb of the bass and drums. It is a sound which seems to envelop the listener, creating a world of its own in which time is measured by the beat. 'It didn't express something else, some prior reality', wrote Simon Frith of reggae, 'but *was* the structure of experience, for musician and audience alike.'[14] Reggae's community is partly established in the physical effects of its sound. It is also formed in the audience's participation in the music. Paul Gilroy has argued that it is the dub version of reggae, in which the music is taken apart and reassembled at the sound desk, that is reggae's essence.[15] The dub artist reconstructs a song, and then the audience/dancers hear it against their memory of the original. Out of these two versions, a third is built by all those involved. Dub accentuates what is apparent in reggae's unmodified form: the sound is not arranged hierarchically, no one instrument acts as the focus of attention. Where rock gives priority to the voice or the guitar, which between them carry a single message, reggae gives no single focus and no one meaning – both depend on the intentions and contributions of the participants. This does not mean, however, that the music is simply an exercise in democratic pleasure, devoid of political meaning. Its politics lie as much in its collective character as in its radical lyrics and apocalyptic visions. Even without the words, the sounds are those of collective resistance, of people making – albeit briefly – a world of their own. It is not, of course, a substitute for politics. Reggae is no different from other forms of popular music; it is a way of having fun. Its politics are shaped by how and why that fun is had. What is important about reggae, like soul, is the collective, democratic character of the way pleasure is taken from the music.

Pop is no more the sound of socialism than it is exclusively the sound of conservatism or liberalism. Its language is too ambiguous and too vague to be deposited in any particular ideological receptacle. And artists or socialist activists who think pop can become the voice of socialism – through its lyrical correctness or its political associations – are mistaken. Neither the words nor the performance can determine how an audience will interpret a song. Almost perversely, this lack of any fixed meaning is precisely where pop's socialism lies. By not saying what it means, the music allows others to decide that for themselves. The music can excite the individual imagination or create a public community; this is where its socialism resides. Different forms of music display these talents in different ways, and some are more effective than others, but where they succeed in giving people a shared sense of a better world or a private sense of present oppression, then they capture the essence of socialism. It is not a socialism of vanguard parties or common ownership or five-year plans; it is a socialism built of sensations and images, inspired by pleasure and personal desires.

Conclusion
...*Thank You and Good Night*

> Love songs cover the waterfront, of course, from the time you are
> looking at each other through rose-tinted contact lenses to the
> time you are talking to each other through solicitors.[1]

This was how Tony Parsons ended his singles column in *NME* one
week in 1984. Normally the singles column is an excuse for a random
selection of thoughts on a random selection of records. Parsons made
an exception. His piece used the week's singles to reflect his feelings
about the end of his marriage to Julie Burchill. The records he chose
were not about his experience in any direct sense; instead they focused
and emphasized that experience. It was touching, and strangely out of
keeping with the paper's political pre-occupations. It reminded me
why I enjoy pop so much and why, in a rash moment, I decided to
write this book.

What Parsons brought home was the realization that though pop's
pleasures are fleeting, they form part of the way we live and interpret
our lives. When pop affects us, it temporarily changes the way the
world seems or we feel; it may not change the world, but each time a
song seeps into our daily life, it becomes part of who we are. Greil
Marcus once wrote:

> Who knows if 'Eight days a week is not enough to show I love you'
> is a deep idea, or a trivial one, or any kind of idea at all? And who
> cares? The joy of pop is that it can deliver you from such questions
> by its immediacy and provoke them by its impact.[2]

Pop's pleasures, though brief, are real and important. While some of
the music's politics may lie in the hypes and crude commercialism, in
the industry's attempt to manipulate its customers, and in the
broadcaster's cloth-eared attempts to produce innocuous programmes,
there are times – those fleeting moments – when we, the consumers,

make the music our own, when it becomes truly popular, when it becomes, in Lester Bang's words, 'the ultimate populist art form, democracy in action'. When pop relieves people from tedium or unites them in fun, then it is really popular music, then it is part of the culture through which people identify themselves and each other.

Pop's power is the power to delight: the ability to draw people together and to find a common resonance in their private feelings. There is an aura of mystery about how music, any music, does this. As the Lovin' Spoonful once sung:

> Do you believe in magic in a young girl's heart,
> How the music can free her whenever it starts.
> And it's magic, if the music is groovy,
> It makes you feel happy like an old-time movie.
> I'd tell you about the magic that will free your soul,
> But it's like trying to tell a stranger about rock and roll.
> ('Do You Believe in Magic?' © 1965 John Sebastian/Hudson Bay
> Music/Robbins Music)

The magic depends, in part at least, on the conjurer, on the musician's ability to create an audience and identify a feeling. Some performers try to tell us something new, but in ways we do not care for; others confirm our prejudices and secure our affection; and just a few manage to combine innovation with popularity. These are the ones who tread a fine line between reassuring us and unnerving us; these are the ones who use pop's power to its fullest extent. They are the ones who understand what the politics of pop are really about. They may have no manifestos, they may never have demonstrated, but their music has managed to discover the ability to set us free and to tie us together – for a moment.

In the end, this book is an attempt to pay tribute to those occasions when pop's power captures us. The moments I recall – Al Green at the Albert Hall, Paul Young and Q-Tips turning a bleak, half-empty hall into a party, Elvis Costello everywhere – are part of a very personal collection, but understanding what they meant and how they worked underpins much of what has gone before. It is perhaps time to come clean.

A number of ghosts have presided over this book, some more conspicuous than others. The most obvious guiding spirit is John Lennon. Without Lennon's attempts to mix music and politics, punk and Rock Against Racism would have had no model to follow. But Lennon matters in more personal ways. He has given a sound and a shape to all sorts of private feelings. Lennon could be the rebel that I sometimes imagined that I was. He could speak for me; he could be defiant. He could give a dignity to my angst and self-consciousness. He could be witty and passionate, talented and concerned. I thought of him as a friend, and I was proud to know him. Paul McCartney was just too wholesome; and Mick Jagger too dirty. It had to be John. Like any fan, I created my own private vision of Lennon, filled out by the interviews and the songs. What was most important, however, was the voice. For me, it is the most potent sound rock has ever produced. Its grainy tunefulness was able to evoke all those feelings of vulnerability and frustration which are familiar to any teenager; later it came to represent other emotions: doubt, anguish and pleasure.

Whether he was singing 'Please, Please Me' or 'Mother', Lennon was able to turn his desires and faults, his certainties and anxieties, into the subject of songs which fitted into my life, whatever the distance between my world and his world. Lennon's confusions over fame and over life with Yoko were hardly my problems, but Lennon (and his voice) was able to find ways of giving those worries a public form which touched a whole range of other, different private worlds. I don't really know how he did it, and reading the 'biographies' that followed his death has done little to enlighten me. The books make depressing reading, and try as I might, it is hard not to find Lennon diminished by the stories the books tell. He wasn't who I supposed him to be; and I don't think I would have liked him. And yet every time I hear him sing, these doubts become irrelevant.

Other voices, other performers, have never been able to have quite the same effect, but they have mattered none the less. Bruce Springsteen mixes American populism and rock mythology to give a passionate voice to our sense of injustice. What I get from his songs, particularly on the later albums, is a way of expressing the outrage that unfairness inspires, but accompanied by dignity and defiance. For those who still hold rock in some kind of affection, Springsteen manages to revive its sense of rebelliousness and to reconstruct its fantasies. He gives an unashamedly grand setting for romantic hopes and disappointments. My view of Springsteen may be as misty-eyed as my feelings about Lennon, but I am convinced by how much he seems to care: about his audience, about the world outside his mansion, about his responsibilities. Where Lennon took his rock second-hand, and filtered it through English art school sensibilities, Springsteen has taken and celebrated rock's myths, and used them to bring out the darker sides of the American dream. Neither Lennon's nor Springsteen's music is more 'real' or more 'authentic' than the other's. The point is the way they drew on the images and sounds which their music allowed. People say 'Born to Run' is a mess, its production overblown, and its sound terrible; but to me, it seemed in 1975 the most exciting rock record I'd heard in ages. And as he and I have grown older, he has continued to turn rock's youthful obsessions towards new concerns, mixing the experience of everyday disappointment to a wider politics, finding new ways to exploit rock's styles and sentiments.

Pop's pleasures are not confined to single artists or genres. A song often takes us by surprise and defies our assumptions. Suddenly a tune gets stuck in your head, and it won't go away. Pop's magic works in peculiar ways. I would hesitate to explain why I'm moved by ABBA's 'Fernando' and Tammy Wynette's 'Almost Persuaded' (she decides against an affair when she sees her would-be lover's face reflected in her wedding ring). All I know is that the sounds of these records evoke times and places and feelings in ways which other records simply failed. They do it too in oblique and subtle ways. They defy any definitive interpretation; they are always ambiguous.

Smokey Robinson may be, as Dylan once said, 'America's greatest living poet', but what I hear on 'Tracks of My Tears' are the voices, not the words. Robinson does not imitate sobbing, but his high pure voice inspires a sense of elation which mixes with his melancholy, and makes the sadness more complete. When Robert Wyatt sang 'Shipbuilding' it was the very lack of passion and certainty about the Falklands war that made the song so moving. When Hugh Masekela sings of the train ('Coal Train') that brings workers to suffer in the mines of South Africa, his voice is gruffly informative, and the song's rhythm almost languid; and yet in their dignity, the voices and the music put apartheid beyond contempt. And when later a choir joins Masekela in an African chant, the song adds hope to its disdain for an iniquitous regime.

Towards the end of 'Midnight Train to Georgia', Gladys Knight and the Pips complement each other to extraordinary effect. The Pips' sing 'All aboard, the midnight train to go, all aboard . . .' while Gladys Knight sings 'my world, his world, my man, his girl, I've got to go, I've got to go'. Separately, they would have sounded ordinary or repetitious. Together, they are exhilarating; the timing of the two vocal lines, the juxtaposition of the restrained, regular backing voices and Gladys Knight's assertive interjections, are exciting in themselves, but their effect is all the greater for the way they mix the pleasure and anxiety of love. The Pips' chant begins to sound like the train pulling out of the station, and Gladys Knight keeps on singing. Her determination – 'I've got to go' – mixes the promise of love's release with its anxieties. Sometimes she catches the train; sometimes she doesn't. It depends on how you hear it.

'Midnight Train' embodied pop's virtues and its politics. It mixed the sound of the crowd with that of the individual; it found ways of articulating what we can only barely express; it gave a public sound to private feelings; and it was popular. It captured a moment, a glance, a feeling and then it was gone. Pop's ability to do this is both the weakness and the strength of its politics. It cannot change the world, it cannot turn audiences into movements or musicians into politicians; but popular music is one of the ways that we come to know who we are and what we want. Pop both unites and differentiates us in the pleasure it gives us. In taking pleasure, we grasp what is ours alone, and we deny the right of the greedy and the powerful to some part of ourselves.

Notes

Abbreviations

CDSP   Current Digest of the Soviet Press
IASPM   International Association for the Study of Popular Music
MM   Melody Maker
NME   New Musical Express

Introduction

1 S. Chapple and R. Garofalo, *Rock'n'roll is Here to Pay*, Nelson-Hall, Chicago, 1977; D. Harker, *One for the Money*, Hutchinson, London, 1980; S. Denisoff, *Solid Gold*, Transaction, New Brunswick, 1975. For the figures, see P. Hardy, *The British Record Industry*, IASPM UK Working Paper 3; P. Rutten and H. Bouwman, *Popular Music in the Netherlands*, IASPM UK Working Paper 4.
2 C. MacInnes, *Absolute Beginners*, Allison & Busby, London, 1980, p. 14.

Chapter 1

1 *Daily Express*, 31 May 1985.
2 J. Orman, *The Politics of Popular Music*, Nelson-Hall, Chicago, 1984, p. 3.
3 P. Norman, *Shout*, Elm Tree Books, London, 1981, p. 259.
4 See, P. Oliver, *The Story of the Blues*, Penguin, London, 1972, p. 167.
5 S. Agnew, 'Talking Brainwashing Blues', in R. Denisoff and R. Peterson (eds), *The Sounds of Social Change*, Rand McNally, Chicago, 1972, pp. 308–9.
6 J. Wiener, *Come Together: John Lennon in His Time*, Random House, New York, 1984, p. xvi.
7 *Report of the Broadcasting Committee*, 1949, Cmd. 8117, Appendix H, p. 315.
8 *NME*, 6 November 1982.
9 Quoted by R. Coleman, *John Lennon*, Futura, London, 1985, p. 246.
10 M. Clarke, *The Politics of Pop Festivals*, Junction Books, London, 1982, p. 187.

11 Quoted by G. Martin, *NME*, 24 August 1985.
12 Quoted by J. Marre and H. Charlton, *Beats of the Heart*, Pluto, London, p. 44.
13 M. Andersson, *Music in the Mix*, Ravan, Johannesburg, p. 111.
14 Andersson, *Music in the Mix*, p. 56.
15 Quoted by Lynn Hanna, *NME*, 18 September 1982.
16 *International Herald Tribune*, 30–31 October 1982.
17 A. Perris, 'Music as Propaganda', *Ethnomusicology*, vol. 27, no. 1, 1983; *NME*, 20 April 1982 and 8 January 1983; and D. Holm, 'The difficulty of "walking on two legs",' *Index on Censorship*, February 1983.
18 Quoted by V. Goldman, *NME*, 16 January 1982. For Hungary, see *NME*, 17 January 1981, and A. Szemere, 'Some institutional aspects of pop and rock in Hungary', *Popular Music 3*, 1983.
19 Quoted in V. Goldman, *NME*, 23 January 1982.
20 *NME*, 1 September 1984.
21 J. Skvorecky, 'Hipness at Noon', *New Republic*, 17 December 1984.
22 *Index on Censorship*, February 1983, p. 31.
23 Quoted by C. Bohn, *NME*, 25 June 1983; see also M. Garzetcki, *NME*, 9 January 1982.
24 'East Side Story', *The Observer Magazine*, 28 August 1983; also C. Bohn, *MM*, 6 October 1979.
25 Skvorecky, 'Hipness at Noon', p. 33; also *NME*, 21 January 1984.
26 Quoted by Chris May, 'Loose in the Bush', *Black Music*, April 1984.
27 C. Bohn, *NME*, 23 June 1983.
28 *Index on Censorship*, February 1983, p. 31; also *NME*, 3 April 1982.
29 Translated by R. Pring-Mill; see his 'Convirtiendo La Oscurana En Claridad', paper to IASPM conference, Montreal, 1985.

Chapter 2

1 Quoted by Paul Rambali, *NME*, 18 December 1982.
2 'Hipness at Noon', *New Republic*, 17 December 1984, p. 27.
3 S. F. Starr, *Red and Hot: The Fate of Jazz in the Soviet Union*, Oxford University Press, Oxford, 1983, p. 40.
4 Quoted by Starr, *Red and Hot*, p. 91.
5 Quoted by Starr, *Red and Hot*, p. 270.
6 *CDSP*, Vol. 28, No. 36, p. 14.
7 H. Smith, *The Russians*, Sphere, London, 1976, p. 219.
8 *CDSP*, Vol. 30, No. 6, 1978, pp. 18 and 27; see also J. Bennett, *Melodiya: A Soviet Russian LP Discography*, Greenwood, Conn., 1981.
9 *CDSP*, Vol. 35, No. 9, pp. 2–3.
10 *CDSP*, Vol. 38, No. 5, p. 16.
11 *CDSP*, Vol. 35, No. 24, pp. 6–7.
12 *The Times*, 9 August 1983; *CDSP*, Vol. 35, No. 44, 1985, pp. 27–8; *CDSP*, Vol. 35, No. 27, pp. 7–8.
13 *CDSP*, Vol. 35, No. 34, pp. 4–6; also Vol. 34, No. 38, p. 5.

14 *CDSP*, Vol. 35, No. 24, p. 6.

15 *CDSP*, Vol. 33, No. 37, p. 19; also Vol. 34, No. 16, pp. 8–9.

16 *CDSP*, Vol. 28, No. 39, p. 12.

17 *CDSP*, Vol. 35, No. 34, pp. 6–8; and Vol. 35, No. 15, pp. 6 and 18.

18 *CDSP*, Vol. 30, No. 34, p. 14; and Vol. 29, No. 1, pp. 11 and 20.

19 *CDSP*, Vol. 32, No. 9, p. 20; and Vol. 34, No. 9, p. 11.

20 Smith, *The Russians*, p. 217; for reports of the Elton John concert, see *CDSP*, Vol. 31, No. 22, pp. 12–13.

21 *CDSP*, Vol. 28, No. 36, p. 14.

22 Starr, *Red and Hot*, p. 293.

Chapter 3

1 Quoted by Stuart Cosgrove, *City Limits*, 16–22 August 1985.

2 *NME*, 23 February 1985.

3 J. Klein and D. Marsh, 'Rock and Politics', *Rolling Stone*, 9 September 1976.

4 Quoted by N. Polsby, *Consequences of Party Reform*, Oxford University Press, Oxford, 1983, p. 206.

5 Quoted in L. Sabato, *The Rise of Political Consultants*, Basic Books, New York, p. 159.

6 Quoted by Sabato, *The Rise of Political Consultants*, p. 161.

7 M. Kohn, 'The New Bohemians', *The Leveller*, No. 50, 1980.

8 Advert for *The Boot Goes In* cassette.

9 *Spearhead*, No. 162, April 1982; also No. 159, January 1982.

10 *Spearhead*, No. 147, January 1981; No. 143, September 1980; No. 148, February 1981; No. 138, April 1980.

11 *Spearhead*, No. 150, April 1981; No. 151, May 1981.

12 *Bulldog*, No. 27, April/May 1982; No. 24, September 1981.

13 Quoted by D. Hebdige, *Subculture: The Meaning of Style*, Methuen, London, 1979, p. 61; also *Bulldog*, No. 25, Nov./Dec. 1981; No. 29, September 1982.

14 D. Noebel, *Communism, Hypnotism and the Beatles*, Christian Crusade, Tulsa, 1965, p. 10.

15 N. Tosches, *Country: The Biggest Music in America*, Delta, New York, 1977, pp. 225–8; also J. Lund, 'Fundamentalism, Racism, and Political Reaction in Country Music', in Denisoff and Peterson (eds), *The Sounds of Social Change*.

16 *The End of Music*, PO Box V2, 488 Great Western Road, Glasgow.

17 Quoted by *Bulldog*, No. 18, n.d.

18 K. McDonnell, 'Music for Socialism', *Wedge*, No. 1, 1977, p. 26.

19 *Socialist Worker*, 6 March 1982.

20 *Socialist Worker*, 9 November 1982; and 21 November 1981.

21 N. Halifax, *Socialist Review*, No. 5, March 1983; M. Wohrle, *Socialist Review*, No. 49, December 1982; D. Widgery, *New Socialist*, Nov./Dec. 1981; N. Halifax, *Socialist Review*, No. 57, September 1983.

22 MacInnes, *Absolute Beginners*, p. 124.
23 Halifax, *Socialist Review*, No. 52, March 1983.
24 Wohrle, *Socialist Review*, No. 49, December 1982.
25 Widgery, *New Socialist*, Nov./Dec. 1981.
26 Widgery, *New Socialist*, Nov./Dec. 1981.
27 Quoted by Graham Lock, *NME*, 31 July 1982.
28 J. Boyd, 'Trends in Youth Culture', *Marxism Today*, Vol. 17, No. 12, December 1973.
29 L. Rosselson, *New Socialist*, No. 5, May/June 1982.
30 Rosselson, *New Socialist*, May/June 1982; also L. Rosselson, 'Pop Music: Mobiliser or Opiate?', in C. Gardner (ed.), *Media, Politics and Culture*, Macmillan, London, 1979, pp. 40–50.
31 G. Marcus, *Rock and Roll Will Stand*, Beacon, Boston, 1969, p. 90.
32 C. Schuler, *The Leveller*, No. 47, 1980.
33 S. Steward and S. Garratt, *Signed, Sealed and Delivered*, Pluto, London, 1984, p. 123.
34 Quoted by Ray Lowry, *NME*, 6 August 1983.
35 A. Thrills, *NME*, 3 November 1984; and X. Moore (Chris Dean) and T. Parsons, *NME*, 10 March 1984.
36 Thrills, *NME*, 3 November 1984.
37 S. Frith, *Sunday Times Review*, 9 December 1984.
38 Quoted by R. Denselow, *The Guardian*, 28 December 1984.
39 Quoted by P. Du Noyer, *NME*, 6 October 1984.
40 Du Noyer, *NME*, 6 October 1984.
41 Quoted by R. Edwards, *Jamming*, No. 25, February 1985.

Chapter 4

1 M. Dubofsky, *We Shall Be All*, Quadrangle, Chicago, 1969, p. 137.
2 R. Chaplin, *Wobbly*, University of Chicago, Chicago, 1948, pp. 167–8.
3 E. Southern, *The Music of Black Americans*, 2nd edn W. W. Norton, New York, 1983, p. 446.
4 S. Frith, 'Try to dig what we all say', *The Listener*, 26 June 1980.
5 J. Raban, *Old Glory*, Flamingo, London, 1983, p. 426.
6 V. Broughton, *Black Gospel*, Blandford, Poole, 1985, p. 157.
7 R. Taylor, *The Death and Resurrection Show*, Blond, London, 1985, chapter 15.
8 S. Kessler, 'Dancing in the Street', in Marcus (ed.), *Rock and Roll Will Stand*, pp. 64–5.
9 Quoted in R. Spitz, *Barefoot in Babylon*, Viking, New York, 1979, p. 76.
10 Coleman, *John Lennon*, p. 363 and pp. 370–71.
11 Wiener, *Come Together*, p. 180.
12 Quoted by A. Fawcett, *John Lennon: One Day at a Time*, New English Library, London, 1976, p. 54.
13 P. Bradshaw, 'Carnivals and Confrontations', *Comment*, 14 October 1978; J. Hoyland and M. Flood Page, *Socialist Review*, No. 3, June 1978; P. Du Noyer, *NME*, 11 July 1981; V. Goldman, *MM*, 5 May 1979.

14 R. Christgau, *Village Voice*, 7 May 1985; S. Frith, *Village Voice*, 12 February 1985.

15 Quoted by R. Cook, *NME*, 2 February 1985.

16 Quoted by D. Hill, *City Limits*, 2–8 September 1983.

17 I. Walker, *The Observer Magazine*, 28 August 1983; V. Grasnow, 'Political Culture and Popular Music in the GDR', unpublished paper, 1984.

18 *Index on Censorship*, February 1983, pp. 30–34.

19 Quoted by C. S. Murray, *NME*, 19 November 1983.

20 M. Garztecki, *NME*, 9 January 1982.

21 Quoted by R. Duncan, *The Noise*, Ticknor & Fields, New York, 1984, p. 15.

22 Mark P., *Time Out*, 17–23 December 1976.

23 *The Observer*, 5 December 1976.

24 T. Parsons, *NME*, 29 October 1977.

25 C. S. Murray, 'Brown Shoes Don't Make It', *School Kids Oz*, No. 28, n.d.

26 J. Burchill and T. Parsons, *The Boy Looked at Johnny*, Pluto, London, 1978, pp. 38 and 88.

27 J. Savage, 'The Punk Process', *The Face*, No. 19, November 1981.

28 S. Frith, *Sound Effects*, Constable, London, 1983, pp. 176–7.

29 J. Stratton, 'Between two worlds: art and commercialism in the record industry', *Sociological Review*, Vol. 30, No. 2, pp. 267–85.

Chapter 5

1 J. Sinclair, 'And then along came Jones', *Oz*, No. 36.

2 P. Hardy, *Time Out*, 26 March–1 April 1976.

3 Quoted by J. Orme, *MM*, 30 September 1979.

4 J. Smith, *The Day the Music Died*, Grove, New York, 1981, p. 241.

5 Quoted by D. Elliott, 'The rock music industry', in *Science, Technology and Popular Culture*, Open University, 1982, p. 35.

6 *NME*, 28 October 1978.

7 Hardy, *The British Record Industry*; and A. Tyler, *NME*, 17 July 1982.

8 Quoted by I. Birch and M. Ellen, *Time Out*, 11–17 June 1982.

9 Quoted by J. Orme, *MM*, 30 June 1979.

10 P. Morley, *NME*, 18 February 1984.

11 *The Times*, 5 December 1983; also *The Observer*, 10 April 1983; *The Sunday Times*, 8 May 1977 and 10 July 1983; A. Thorneycroft, *NME*, 17 November 1979; S. Frith, *MM*, 21 July 1979; D. Laing, *Marxism Today*, July 1981; and P. Hardy, *The Listener*, 24 May 1984.

12 Orme, *MM*, 30 June 1979.

13 *MM*, 28 June 1975.

14 Sir John Read, quoted by F. and J. Vermorel, *The Sex Pistols*, Star, London, 1981, p. 50.

15 Quoted in Vermorel, *The Sex Pistols*, p. 142.

16 M. Brown, *The Sunday Times*, 18 September 1983.

17 Quoted by V. Goldman, *MM*, 7 April 1979.

18 D. Laing, *One Chord Wonders*, Open University, Milton Keynes, 1985, p. 9.
19 N. Halifax, *Socialist Review*, Nov./Dec. 1981; for the pay of rock musicians, see D. Sinclair, '8 Days a Week', *One Two Testing*, April 1984.
20 Quoted by T. Parsons, *NME*, 14 October 1978; *The Sunday Times*, 20 February 1983; Chapple and Garofalo, *Rock'n'roll is Here to Pay*, p. 240.
21 P. Norman, *The Stones*, Elm Tree Books, London, 1984, p. 75.
22 *NME*, 25 August 1984; see also, Norman, *The Stones*, p. 310.
23 G. Stokes, *Star-Making Machinery*, Vintage, New York, 1977, p. 219 and p. 98; *NME*, 7 August 1982.
24 Quoted by C. Rose, *NME*, 8 September 1984.
25 *MM*, 28 June 1975; and P. Hardy and D. Laing, *Time Out*, 26 Oct.–1 Nov. 1979.
26 H. Stith Bennett, *On Becoming a Rock Musician*, University of Massachusetts, Mass., 1980, p. 126.
27 *NME*, 25 February 1978.
28 *The Guardian*, 28 August 1985.
29 V. Wilmer, *Time Out*, 29 Aug.–4 Sept., 1982.
30 *NME*, 14 April 1984.
31 Quoted by C. Bohn, *NME*, 18 February 1984.
32 *The Sunday Times*, 10 February 1980.
33 *NME*, 18 February 1984.
34 M. Harron, *New Statesman*, 28 January 1983.

Chapter 6

1 Quoted in R. Wallis and K. Malm, *Big Sounds from Small Peoples*, Constable, London, 1984, p. 242.
2 *NME*, 20 October 1984.
3 Harker, *One for the Money*, p. 38.
4 C. Gillett, *Sound of the City*, Sphere, London, 1971, pp. 24–5.
5 Quoted by M. Harron, *The Guardian*, 27 January 1984.
6 Quoted by S. Beresford, 'Invisible Hits – Orbitone Records', *Collusion*, No. 4, 1983. For chart-rigging, see A. Thrills, *NME*, 4 March 1978; P. Hardy, *Time Out*, 24–30 October 1980; H. Fielder, *Sounds*, 4 March 1978.
7 Quoted by N. Kimberley, *City Limits*, 28 Sept.–4 Oct., 1974; also, Harker, *One for the Money*, pp. 95–9.
8 *The Guardian*, 29 October 1983.
9 K. Barnes, 'Democratic Radio', in D. Marsh et al., *The First Rock & Roll Confidential Report*, Pantheon, New York, 1985, p. 49.
10 Wallis and Malm, *Big Sounds from Small Peoples*, p. 244.
11 Local Radio Workshop, *Capital: Local Radio and Private Profit*, Comedia, London, 1983, p. 47.
12 C. Belz, *The Story of Rock*, Oxford University Press, Oxford, 1972, pp. 29–30; also Chapple and Garofalo, *Rock'n'roll is Here to Pay*, pp. 239–40.
13 S. Frith, 'The despair of the record industry', *Music Business*, n.d., p. 19.

14 Barnes, 'Democratic Radio'; and Denisoff, *Solid Gold*, chapter 5.
15 S. Frith, 'The Pleasures of the Hearth: The making of BBC light entertainment', in *Formations on Pleasure*, Routledge & Kegan Paul, 1983, pp. 101–23.
16 Local Radio Workshop, *Capital*, p. 48.
17 Wallis and Malm, *Big Sounds from Small Peoples*, p. 247.
18 *NME*, 22 June 1974.

Chapter 7

1 Quoted in D. Marsh, *Before I Get Old: The Story of The Who*, Plexus, London, p. 350.
2 Faber & Faber, London, 1975.
3 *NME*, 11 June 1983.
4 See A. Goldman, *Elvis*, Penguin, Harmondsworth, 1982, chapter 30.
5 *NME*, 1 June 1983.
6 *Rolling Stone*, No. 145, 11 October 1973.
7 *The Guardian*, 15 June 1985.
8 Quoted by Mary Harron, *MM*, 3 February 1979.
9 *NME*, 7 January 1978.
10 Quoted by F. R. Powell, *The Face*, No. 39, July 1983.
11 Quoted by F. R. Powell, *The Face*, No. 46, February 1984.
12 Quoted in S. Booth, 'The True Adventures of the Rolling Stones', *Granta* No. 12, 1984, p. 42.
13 Quoted by F. R. Powell, *The Face*, No. 44, December 1983.
14 Quoted by M. Bell, *The Face*, No. 50, June 1984.
15 C. Cutler, *File Under Popular*, November Books, London, 1985, p. 156.
16 Miles, *Mick Jagger In His Own Words*, Omnibus, London, 1982, p. 112.
17 T. Sanchez, *Up and Down with the Rolling Stones*, New American Library, New York, 1979, p. 250.
18 R. Barnes, *The Who – Maximum R&B*, Eel Pie, London, 1982, p. 101.
19 Quoted in Spitz, *Barefoot in Babylon*, p. 460.
20 Quoted by C. Salewicz, *Time Out*, 4–10 June 1982.
21 Sting once said that The Police's records were very close to the original demos; other performers 'compose' in the studio – see the Beatles in the film, *Let It Be*.
22 *Time Out*, 6–12 August 1972.
23 B. Edmands, 'Have Pity for the Rich', in C. Gillett and S. Frith (eds), *Rock File No. 3*, Panther, London, 1975, p. 51.
24 Quoted in Barnes, *The Who – Maximum R&B*, p. 148.
25 Miles, *Mick Jagger In His Own Words*, p. 127.
26 *Time Out*, 11–17 June 1982.
27 *Rolling Stone*, 6 December 1984.
28 Quoted by P. Morley, *NME*, 2 June 1979.
29 Quoted by G. Martin, *NME*, 3 March 1984; see also, J. Black, *NME*, 15 August 1981; and S. Frith, *Village Voice*, 28 March 1977.

30 *NME*, 8 January 1983.

31 M. Pang and Henry Edwards, *Loving John*, Corgi, London, 1983, p. 101.

32 P. Norman, *The Stones*, p. 149.

33 *Jamming*, No. 14, 1983.

34 Miles, *Mick Jagger In His Own Words*, pp. 111–2.

35 Quoted by M. Harron, *MM*, 28 July 1979.

36 Wallis and Malm, *Big Sounds from Small Peoples*, p. 80.

37 F. Newton, *The Jazz Scene*, Penguin, Harmondsworth, 1961, pp. 199–200.

38 Quoted in Denisoff, *Great Day Coming*, pp. 190–2.

39 See S. Frith and H. Horne, *Welcome to Bohemia*, Warwick Working Papers in Sociology; and S. Frith, 'The Punk Bohemians', *New Society*, 9 March 1978.

40 G. Burn, 'Good Clean Punk', *The Sunday Times Magazine*, n.d.

41 C. Coon, *1988: The New Wave Punk Explosion,*, Omnibus, London, 1982, pp. 79–80; also C. Bohn, *MM*, 29 November 1979, and T. Parsons, *NME*, 2 April 1977. For the Gang of Four, see C. Schuler, *The Leveller*, No. 52, March/April 1980; and M. Harron, *MM*, 26 May 1979.

42 *NME*, 25 May 1977.

43 *The Boy Looked at Johnny*, Pluto, London, 1978, p. 55.

44 Quoted in Bohn, *MM*, 29 December 1979.

45 Quoted by J. Howlett, *NME*, 5 August 1978; and P. Rambali, *NME*, 30 September 1978.

46 C. Cutler, 'Technology, politics and contemporary music', *Popular Music 4*, 1984, p. 294.

Chapter 8

1 Quoted by N. Spencer, *NME*, 8 January 1983.

2 Quoted by M. Snow, *NME*, 3 September 1983.

3 J. Landau, *It's Too Late To Stop Now*, Straight Arrow, San Francisco, 1972, pp. 44–5.

4 Marcus, *Rock and Roll Will Stand*, pp. 92–3.

5 Marcus, *Rock and Roll Will Stand*, p. 93.

6 L. Winner, 'The Strange Death of Rock and Roll', in Marcus, *Rock and Roll Will Stand*, p. 53.

7 C. Kirk, 'What a difference a gay makes', *Collusion*, No. 4, 1983.

8 Quoted by D. Watson, *NME*, 19 May 1984.

9 C. S. Murray, 'Dear John', *Cream*, No. 18, November 1972.

10 J. Hoyland, 'Dear John', *Cream*, No. 18. November 1972.

11 *NME*, 8 October 1983.

12 A. Hennion, 'The Production of Success', *Popular Music 3*, 1983, p. 192.

13 Quoted by G. Martin, 18 August 1984.

Chapter 9

1 M. Oakeshott, *Rationalism in Politics*, Methuen, London, 1962, p. 195.
2 *MM*, 14 January 1967.
3 S. Kessler, 'Dancing in the street', in Marcus, *Rock and Roll Will Stand*, p. 64.
4 Quoted in J. Cott, 'No Real Sense', *Student*, Vol. 2, No. 1, Spring 1968.
5 W. Kotzwinkle, *The Fan Man*, Penguin, Harmondsworth, 1977, p. 8.
6 Hebdige, *Subculture*, p. 62.
7 I. Taylor and D. Wall, 'Beyond The Skinheads', in G. Pearson and G. Mungham, *Working-class Youth Culture*, Routledge & Kegan Paul, 1976, p. 112.
8 K. Knabb (ed.), 'Report on the Construction of Situations', *Situationist International Anthology*, Bureau of Public Secrets, Berkeley, 1981, p. 43.
9 *The Face*, No. 38, June 1983.
10 Coon, *1988*, p. 47.
11 *The Face*, No. 33, January 1983.
12 'Androgyny', *The Face*, No. 38, June 1983.
13 Quoted by A. Thompson, *The Leveller*, No. 45, 17 April–1 May 1981; see also articles by K. Benson and J. Ash, *ZG*, No. 1, 1981.
14 Quoted by M. Parker, *The Leveller*, No. 62, 7–20 August 1981.
15 Quoted by J. Savage, *The Face*, No. 21, January 1982.
16 Quoted by M. Kohn, *The Face*, No. 47, March 1984.
17 *The Face*, No. 38, June 1983.
18 S. Frith, 'The magic that can set you free': the ideology of folk and the myth of the rock community', *Popular Music 1*, 1981, p. 165.
19 G. Marcus, 'Elvis: Presliad', *Mystery Train*, E. P. Dutton, New York, 1975.

Chapter 10

1 Marcus, *Mystery Train*, p. 115.
2 Marcus, *Mystery Train*, p. 169.
3 Marcus, *Mystery Train*, p. 148.
4 Quoted by S. Fay, *The Sunday Times Magazine*, 26 August 1984.
5 S. Tyrrell, 'Tammy Wynette: Peroxide politics and the counter-revolution', *Spare Rib*, No. 42, December 1975.
6 Quoted by R. Carr, *NME*, 19 April 1975.
7 S. Frith and A. McRobbie, 'Rock and Sexuality', *Screen Education*, No. 29, Winter 1978/79, p. 31.
8 Quoted in Marsh, *The First Rock & Roll Confidential Report*, p. 166.
9 S. Frith, 'Beggars Banquet', in G. Marcus (ed.), *Stranded: Rock and Roll for a Desert Island*, Knopf, New York, 1979, p. 38.
10 Frith, 'Beggars Banquet', p. 39.
11 Marcus, *Mystery Train*, p. 122.

12 R. Sennett, *The Fall of Public Man*, Cambridge University Press, Cambridge, 1977, p. 25.
13 *Rock Albums of the 70s*, Vermillion, London, 1982, p. 389.
14 Quoted by P. Du Noyer, *NME*, 6 October 1984.

Chapter 11

1 P. Oliver, *The Meaning of the Blues*, Collier, New York, 1963, p. 317.
2 E. Genovese, *Roll, Jordan, Roll*, Vintage, New York, 1976, p. 324.
3 Oliver, *The Meaning of the Blues*, p. 324.
4 Genovese, *Roll, Jordan, Roll*, p. 324.
5 Marcus, *Mystery Train*, p. 23.
6 S. Frith, 'Post-punk Blues', *Marxism Today*, March 1983.
7 D. Marsh, *Fortunate Son*, Random House, New York, 1985, p. 208.
8 Marcus, *Mystery Train*, p. 63.
9 Marcus, *Mystery Train*, p. 62.
10 Harker, *One for the Money*, p. 72.
11 *The Face*, No. 39, July 1983.
12 H. Ottenheimer, 'Catharsis, Communication and Evocation', *Ethnomusicology*, January 1979, p. 79.
13 Quoted by C. Salewicz, *The Face*, No. 40, August 1983.
14 Frith, *Sound Effects*, p. 163.
15 P. Gilroy, 'Steppin' Out of Babylon' – race, class and autonomy', in Centre for Contemporary Cultural Studies, *The Empire Strikes Back*, Hutchinson, London, p. 300.

Conclusion

1 *NME*, 25 August 1984.
2 *Mystery Train*, p. 114.

Bibliography
and Discography

Most people, I suspect, have better things to do than wade through the references on the previous pages. This brief section, therefore, is a guide to some of the books I found most helpful and to some of the records that best illustrate my argument.

The two books to which I referred most constantly were Simon Frith's *Sound Effects* (Constable) and Greil Marcus' *Mystery Train* (E. P. Dutton). They are both superb. For a history of rock, Charlie Gillett's *Sound of the City* (Sphere) is still the best for the period from the 1950s to the 1970s; Iain Chambers' *Urban Rhythms* (Macmillan) begins in the same place but continues into the 1980s, filtering the story through his post-modernist sense of style. For intelligent, infuriating and stimulating criticisms of rock's pretentions, Robert Christgau's *Rock Albums of the 70s* (Vermillion) and *Any Old Way You Choose It* (US Penguin). Dave Marsh is a different kind of critic to the intellectual Christgau. Marsh is committed to rock as the authentic voice of working-class defiance (see his *Fortunate Son* (Random House) or *Born to Run* (Dolphin Books), the best biography of Bruce Springsteen, or his magazine *Rock & Roll Confidential*, which chronicles the politics of US rock).

The best work on the music industry is Geoffrey Stokes' *The Star-Making Machinery* (Vintage). Roger Wallis and Krister Malm's *Big Sounds from Small Peoples* (Constable) is a fascinating and comprehensive account of the music industry all around the globe. Dave Harker's *One for the Money* (Hutchinson) and Reebee Garofalo and Steve Chapple's *Rock and Roll is Here to Pay* (Nelson-Hall) make powerful cases for seeing the industry as ruthlessly expoitative and unremittingly cynical. George Martin's edited volume, *Making Music* (Pan), provides a good guide to the technicalities of making music: writing, recording and performing.

Anyone interested in the treatment of popular music in the Soviet Union should read S. Frederick Starr's *Red and Hot* (Oxford University Press); he seems to have an encyclopaedic knowledge about both Soviet politics and jazz. Josef Skvorecky's novel, *The Bass Saxophone* (Paladin), gives a fascinating insight into the significance of music to Czechs. Muff Andersson's *Music in the Mix* is a good account of the South African pop industry and its politics. Jeremy Marre and Hannah Charlton's *Beats of the Heart* (Pluto) provide a good accompaniment to Marre's films about music in South Africa, China, Jamaica, Brazil and elsewhere.

The politics of musicians have received little attention, but two books distinguish themselves: Jon Wiener's *Come Together: John Lennon in his Time*, a biography that dwells on Lennon's politics as much as his music; and Chris Cutler's *File Under Popular* (November Books, 583 Wandsworth Road, London SW8), in which a practising musician and articulate political theorist struggles with the question of how to make a new kind of popular music.

Each musical genre has many books devoted to it. Here is a sample of those that best convey the music's power. Soul: Ian Hoare, Clive Anderson, Tony Hoare, and Simon Frith, *The Soul Book* (Methuen); Gerri Hirshey, *Nowhere to Run* (Macmillan). Blues and Jazz: Peter Guralnick, *Feel Like Going Home* (Omnibus); Le Roi Jones, *Blues People* (Morrow). Gospel: Viv Broughton, *Black Gospel* (Blandford Press). Country: Nick Tosches, *Country: The Biggest Music in America* (Delta); Peter Guralnick, *Lost Highway* (Omnibus). Rap: David Toop, *The Rap Attack* (Pluto). Rock: Greil Marcus (ed.) *Stranded: Rock and roll for a desert island* (Knopf); and Nik Cohn, *AWopBopaLooBop ALop Bam Boom* (Paladin). Punk: Caroline Coon, *1988: The New Wave Punk and Rock Explosion* (Omnibus); Dave Laing, *One Chord Wonders* (Open University) and Julie Burchill and Tony Parsons, *The Boy Looked at Johnny* (Pluto). Reggae: Timothy White, *Catch a Fire: The life of Bob Marley* (Elm Tree). Flower Power: Greil Marcus (ed.), *Rock and roll will stand* (Beacon); Robert Spitz, *Barefoot in Babylon* (Viking).

Sue Steward and Sheryl Garratt's, *Signed, Sealed and Delivered* (Pluto) is an excellent survey of women in pop music. F. and J. Vermorel's *Starlust* (Comet) is an extraordinary document; it is a record of the fantasies of pop fans, and it undermines any simple theory about how the industry manipulates its consumers.

Official Soviet rock records are avaiable in the West. For records by the Plastic People of the Universe, contact Recommended Records, 583 Wandsworth Road, London, SW8. Recommended also distributes the Kalahari Surfers' *Own Affairs*, a bitter and discomforting attack on the South African regime. For the sounds of South African resistance, there are two excellent compilation records, *Zulu Jive* and *The Indestructible Beat of Soweto* (both from Earthworks). Hugh Masekela's *Waiting for the Rain* or *Techno Bush* (Jive Africa) are also well worth hearing. Music from Nicaragua, reflecting on a bitter past and a hope-filled future, can be heard on Guardabarranco's *Si Buscabas* (If you were searching) (Redwood). For the sound of recent British pop and politics, there are the Specials AKA, *In The Studio* (2 Tone); the Style Council's *Our Favourite Shop*; Elvis Costello's *Punch the Clock* (F Beat); Madness, *Mad Not Mad* (Zarjazz); The Redskins' 'Lean on me'/'Unionize'. (CNT). For earlier eras, there is John Lennon's *Imagine* and his chilling first solo album (both on Apple); the Clash's debut album on CBS is still exciting. For the sound of US politics, there are: Rank and File, *Sundown* (Slash/Rough Trade); the Blasters, *Hard Line* (Slash/London); any Gil Scott Heron album; Curtis Mayfield, *There's no place like America today* (Buddah); Creedence Clearwater Revival's 'Who'll Stop the Rain' and 'Fortunate Man' (Fantasy);

MC5, *Kick Out the Jams!* (Elektra). Ruben Blades' *Buscando America* (Elektra) mixes the sounds of his native Panama with many others, and draws on his experience of Latin American and North American politics. Canada's Bruce Cockburn uses deceptively gentle music to make powerful points about similar subjects; hear his 'If I had a Rocket Launcher', on *Stealing Fire* (Spindrift).

There are many more songs and singers whose politics are perhaps more oblique, but no less potent. They sit beside everybody's record player or on their cassette machine, and it does not need me to list them.

Acknowledgements

Songs

p. 6: 'Pills and Soap' by Elvis Costello © 1983 Plangent Visions Music.

p. 47: 'Every Man a King' By Huey P. Long © 1935 Bourne Company.

p. 67: 'A New England' by Billy Bragg © 1984 Chappell Music Ltd.

p. 80: 'Free Nelson Mandela' by Jerry Dammers and Rhoda Dakar © Plangent Visions Music Ltd.

p. 131: 'Street Fighting Man' by Mick Jagger and Keith Richards © 1969 Abkco Music Ltd.

p. 155: 'Masters of War' by Bob Dylan © 1963 M. Witmark & Sons/Warner Bros Music Ltd.

p. 157: 'Memphis Blues Again' by Bob Dylan © 1966 M. Witmark & Sons/ Warner Bros Music Ltd.

pp. 160–1: 'Glad to be Gay' by Tom Robinson © 1978 Albion Music.

pp. 161–2: 'The Killing of Georgie' by Rod Stewart © 1976 Warner Bros Music.

p. 162: 'Smalltown Boy' by Bronski Beat © 1984 Forbidden Fruit.

p. 164: 'Sunday Bloody Sunday', 'John Sinclair' and 'Attica State' by John Lennon and Yoko Ono © 1972 Ono Music Ltd and Maclen/Northern Songs.

p. 165: 'Imagine' by John Lennon © 1971 Ono Music Ltd/Northern Songs.

p. 167: 'Shipbuilding' by Elvis Costello and Clive Langer © 1983 Plangent Visions Music Ltd/Warner Bros Music Ltd.

p. 175: 'White Riot' by Joe Strummer and Mick Jones © 1977 copyright control.

p. 175: 'Anarchy in the UK' and 'God Save the Queen' by the Sex Pistols (Jones/Matlock/Cook/Rotten) © 1977 copyright control.

pp. 176–7: 'The Look of Love' by ABC © 1982 Virgin Music Publishing.

p. 180: 'Love Song' by Woods/Foad/Munro/Hammond © 1981 Ideal Home Noise.

p. 185: 'Please Don't Ever Change' by Gerry Goffin and Carol King © 1963 Screen Gems.

p. 185: 'Strawberry Fields' by John Lennon and Paul McCartney © Northern Songs Ltd.

p. 185: 'Karma Chameleon' by Culture Club (O'Dowd/Moss/Craig/Hay/ Pickett) © 1983 Virgin Music Publishing/Pendulum Music Ltd/ Warner Bros Music Ltd.

p. 187: 'Rednecks' by Randy Newman © 1974 Warner-Tamberlane Publishing Corp. and Randy Newman (BMI).

pp. 193–4: 'More Than This' by Bryan Ferry © 1982 EG Music Ltd.

p. 194: 'Grey Day' by Mike Barson © Nutty Sounds/Warner Bros Music Ltd.

p. 194: 'Yesterday's Men' by Graham McPherson and Chris Foreman © 1985 Nutty Sounds/Warner Bros Music Ltd.

p. 195: 'Born to Run' by Bruce Springsteen © 1975 Zomba Music Ltd.

p. 195: 'Out in the Streets' by Bruce Springsteen © 1980 Zomba Music Ltd.

p. 195: 'The River' by Bruce Springsteen © 1979 Zomba Music Ltd.

p. 200: 'Tear Stained Letter' by Richard Thompson © 1983 Island Music Ltd.

p. 200: 'Sunny Afternoon' and 'Dead End Street' by Ray Davies © 1966 Davray Music Ltd.

p. 201: 'She Never Spoke Spanish to Me' by Butch Hancock © 1977 Leeds Music Ltd.

p. 204: 'Work with me Annie' by Hank Ballard © 1954 Armo Music Co.

p. 207: 'School Days' by Chuck Berry © 1957 Jewel Music Publishing Co. Ltd.

pp. 207–8: 'Uptown' by Barry Mann and Cynthia Weil © 1962 Screen Gems EMI Music Inc.

p. 209: 'Factory' by Bruce Springsteen © 1978 Zomba Music Ltd.

p. 210: 'Somewhere' by Husker Du © 1984 Cesstone Music (BMI).

p. 212: 'King Harvest' (Has Surely Come)' by Robbie Robertson © 1969 Canaan Music/Warner Bros Music Ltd.

p. 213: 'Rank and File' by Escovedo/Kinman/Session/Miller © 1982 Black Impala Music (BMI) and Regent Music Corp. (BMI)

p. 215: 'Get Back in Line' by Ray Davies © 1970 Davray Music Ltd.

p. 217: 'Respect' by Otis Redding © 1965 East-Time-Redwall Publishing.

p. 217: 'People Get Ready' by Curtis Mayfield © 1965 United Artists Music Ltd.

p. 218: 'Love to the People' by Curtis Mayfield © 1975 Warner Bros Music Ltd.

p. 218: 'Wake Up Everybody' by Whitehead/McFadden/Carstarphen © 1975 Mighty Three Music/Blackwood Music Inc.

p. 218: 'The Message' by Grandmaster Flesh and the Furious Five (Fletcher/Glover/Robinson/Chase) © 1982 Sunbury Music Ltd.

p. 219: 'Them Belly Full (but we Hungry)' by Bob Marley © 1974 Rondor Music (London) Ltd.

p. 223: 'Do You Believe in Magic?' by John Sebastian © 1965 Hudson Bay Music Co. Ltd/Robbins Music Corp. Ltd.

p. 225: 'Midnight Train to Georgia' by Jim Weatherly © 1973 Ardmore and Beechwood (KPM).

Photos

Time Machine, Leningrad audience and illegal cassette cover, courtesy of Irena Pond.

Richard Branson, photo by Sue Singleton, © Sue Singleton.

Billy Bragg, photo by Adrian Boot © Labour Party/Union Communications.

John Lennon and Yoko Ono, photo by Barry Plummer, © Barry Plummer.

'Strike' advertisement, reproduced by permission of Rough Trade Records Ltd.

'No Sell Out' cover, reproduced by permission of Tommy Boy Music Inc.

'Unionize' cover, designed by Em and M, reproduced by permission of CNT Productions.

The Redskins, photo by Peter Anderson, © London Records.

Henry Cow, © Virgin Records.

Annie Lennox, photo by Derek Ridgers, © RCA Records.

Tammy Wynette, © CBS/Epic Records.

'Convirtiendo La Oscurana En Claridad', reproduced by permission of the Nicaraguan Ministry of Culture.

'The Indestructible Beat of Soweto' cover, reproduced by permission of Earthworks.

Woodstock, photo by Ken Regan, © Ken Regan LFI.

The Vicious White Kids, photo by Paul Cox, © LFI.

The Slits, photo by Paul Cox, © Paul Cox LFI.

Live Aid, photo Mike Cameron, © David Redfern Photography.

Every effort was made to obtain permission to use the lyrics and photographs used in this book. Some lyrics appear without acknowledgement because we received no reply from the proprietors.

Index